Views
From a Window

In Memory of Two Friends,
TOM DOYLE and JAY DE BROUX

Contents

ACKNOWLEDGMENTS   We gratefully wish to thank the following people and publications:

Lord Longford and Michael Dean, for permission to make use of their conversation with Gore Vidal, which originally appeared as "The Private Life of Public Men—Lord Longford and Gore Vidal in Conversation with Michael Dean" in *The Listener* (14 March 1974).

Malcolm Muggeridge and Michael Dean, for permission to make use of their conversation with Gore Vidal, which originally appeared as "Talking for the Camera—Muggeridge and Gore Vidal" in *The Listener* (8 August 1974).

Michael Dean, for permission to make use of selected passages reprinted from "Gore Vidal on His Latest Novel—in Conversation with Michael Dean," which originally appeared in *The Listener* (26 September 1968).

Eugene Walter, for permission to make use of selected passages reprinted from "Conversations with Gore Vidal," which originally appeared in *The Transatlantic Review* (Summer 1960).

Michael S. Lasky, for permission to make use of selected passages reprinted from "Gore Vidal: His Workings," which originally appeared in *Writer's Digest* (March 1975).

The Book-of-the-Month Club, Inc., for permission to make use of "A Conversation with Myself" (by Gore Vidal), which originally appeared in the Book-of-the-Month Club *News* (November 1973).

Harper's Magazine, for permission to make use of "Vidal to Vidal: On Misusing the Past" (by Gore Vidal), which originally appeared in *Harper's Magazine* (October 1965). Copyright © 1965 by *Harper's Magazine.*

Time, Inc., for permission to make use of selected passages reprinted from "The Rewards of Alienation" by Joseph S. Coyle, in *Money* Magazine (June 1978), by special permission. Copyright © 1978 by Time, Inc.

Gerald Clarke, for permission to make use of selected passages reprinted from "Petronius Americanus: The Ways of Gore Vidal," which originally appeared in *The Atlantic Monthly* (March 1972). Copyright © 1972 by The Atlantic Monthly Company, Boston, Mass. Reprinted with permission.

Gerald Clarke, *The Paris Review,* and Viking Penguin Inc., for their permission to make use of selected passages reprinted from "Interview with Gore Vidal," from *Writers at Work: The Paris Review Interviews,* Fifth Series.

The New Review, for permission to make use of selected passages reprinted from "The Candidates" by Jacob Epstein, which originally appeared in *The New Review* (February 1976). Copyright © 1976 by *The New Review.*

The Washington Post, for permission to make use of selected passages reprinted from "Portrait of a Man Reading: Gore Vidal" by Israel Shenker, which originally appeared in *Book World* (4 August 1968). Copyright © 1968 by *The Washington Post.*

Hollis Alpert and *American Film,* for permission to make use of selected passages reprinted from "Dialogue on Film: Gore Vidal," which originally appeared in *American Film* (April 1977). Copyright © 1977 by *American Film.*

Andy Warhol's *Interview,* for permission to make use of selected passages reprinted from "Vidal by Monique Van Vooren," which originally appeared in Andy Warhol's *Interview* (April 1976). Copyright © 1975 by Motion Olympus Inc.

Christopher Street, for permission to make use of selected passages reprinted from "Interview with Gore Vidal" by Dennis Altman, which originally appeared in *Christopher Street* (January 1978). Copyright © 1977 by That New Magazine, Inc.

Playboy Magazine, for permission to make use of selected passages reprinted from *"Playboy* Interview: Gore Vidal," which originally appeared in *Playboy* Magazine (June 1969). Copyright © 1969 by *Playboy.*

Oui Magazine, for permission to make use of selected passages reprinted from "Conversation with Gore Vidal" by Beverly Kempton, which originally appeared in *Oui* Magazine (April 1975). Copyright © 1975 by Playboy Publications, Inc.

Judy Halfpenny, for permission to make use of unpublished correspondence with Gore Vidal.

Felicia Stanton, for her suggestions and her typing of the final manuscript.

Introduction

Within these pages you will meet one of America's greatest living writers, who is also an international celebrity. During the past thirty-five years Gore Vidal has published seventeen novels, a collection of short stories, five collections of essays; he has written numerous television plays, stage plays, and films. He recently finished another novel and continues to publish controversial essays. We see him on many television shows, we know that he is active in public concerns, and we laugh nervously as he intelligently exposes stupidity and hypocrisy in American politics, religion, education, the arts, and even our lifestyles. We are delightfully astounded to learn that Vidal never attended college and doesn't regret it. We admire his independence in learning, his outstanding accomplishments with words, his genius. Yet we are surprised that he doesn't thank God for his many gifts, and we are hurt that he doesn't forgive us our sins.

As a people, Americans have *never* seemed pretty to him. And even though he vividly continues to point out our errors, to chastise the way we speak and act, to mock our pretensions, we nevertheless continue to court him year after year, to embrace him reluctantly as he quite frankly tells us that we are the descendants of barbarians, that in fact he does not love us. We allow such criticism because we, as Americans, know deep within us that Gore Vidal is telling the truth (as he sees it), that his criticism is made for our own good. He tells us that we must first look truthfully into the mirror of reality, become totally aware of ourselves, and then have the courage to make many and drastic changes. In his career, Vidal has served as a window through which we can look inward upon our past and outward upon our future. The view is clear and real. The message is obvious: we must make *changes* now if we are to survive at all.

Because Gore Vidal is a famous person (the *Information Please Almanac* says so!), he has been interviewed hundreds of times. Most of these interviews usually serve as the bases for articles about him, which frequently appear in journals and newspapers throughout a large portion of the world. I first became aware of the interviews while I was preparing a large bibliography—*Gore Vidal: A Primary and Secondary Bibliography* (Boston: G.K. Hall & Co., 1978)—on works by and about him. I wrote to Vidal and asked if I might put together a collection of interviews. He wanted to know more about my plans, and, eventually, this present volume is the result of his co-operation with me.

My first task was to select appropriate material. Keeping an English-speaking audience in mind, I chose material from American, British, and Canadian sources. I cast aside most of the published articles *based* on interviews—instead, to avoid complex adaptations, I stuck mainly with material already presented in the form of formal interviews. However, I made exceptions for Gerald Clarke's interview/article "Petronius Americanus: The Ways of Gore Vidal" (*Atlantic Monthly,* 1972); for Curtis Bill Pepper's interview/article "The Truth about Gore Vidal—Right from Gore Vidal" (*Vogue,* 1974); for Richard Grenier's interview/article "Gore Vidal: What It's Like to Be Talented, Rich, and Bisexual" (*Cosmopolitan,* 1975); and for Alvin Shuster's interview/article "Gore Vidal Loses Weight but Gains a New Novel" (*The New York Times,* 1976).

VIDAL: Well, I have no television to go on so I get a lot of writing done. That's my substitute for television.

VAN VOOREN: What time do you get up?

VIDAL: Whenever I wake up.

VAN VOOREN: Just when you wake up? You never get up before you wake up?

VIDAL: You have to have standards, Monique.

VAN VOOREN: At night, what do you do when you're in Rome?

VIDAL: Have dinner and go to bed to read.

VAN VOOREN: Do you go out to dinner with friends or do you stay home?

VIDAL: Usually I go out to the world of the trattorias which is the pleasure of Rome.

VAN VOOREN: . . . Your house in Ravello seems always to be, well, [you're] always having important people visiting you.

VIDAL: No, very seldom, and I'm a much worse guest than I am a host, and I'm not an awfully good host either. I really like being there alone.

MONEY, 1978: You have several residences, and some years back you made a handsome profit on the sale of a fine old mansion in upstate New York. Are you partial to real estate as an investment?

VIDAL: Not really, although I was raised on the rule that you never paid rent; you always bought the house. Renting was the most wasteful thing to do. So the first moment I made some money with *Visit to a Small Planet,* the play, in 1957, I bought a small apartment house on East 58th Street in New York City. But I cannot sell it because New York City saw fit to collapse during the past twenty-one years. Although the house is always rented, no one on earth would buy a brownstone with four flats in it even on a desirable street in New York. People who have the money are looking for fortresses to live in with guards and in-house television cameras studying the lobby.

MONEY: How about the house you bought two years ago in the Hollywood Hills?

VIDAL: That had to do with Italian taxes. Suddenly the Italians put in the most extraordinary set of laws, saying that any foreigner living in Italy would be treated as though he were an Italian citizen. Which meant that not only would he have to pay tax on his world income—and I make no money in Italy at all, I just bring it in—but he would also have to repatriate—a happy word—any money he held outside. Every penny I had would have to have come into Italy, be turned into lire, and then never again taken out. So I bought a house in Los Angeles. Almost a year later they changed the law in Italy. Now as long as I'm in Italy one day less than six months of the year, my foreign income is of no interest to the Italian government. I pay taxes on what I bring into the country and I own no Italian property. I rent both a villa at Ravello and an apartment in Rome.

MONEY: Do you pay U.S. federal income tax?

VIDAL: Oh, yes. I just hand over half of what I make.

MONEY: And what do you do with the rest?

VIDAL: I convert it into other currencies—principally Swiss francs and German marks. My banker in Zurich and I go over the list of bonds available in those currencies and buy whatever is the safest. I never speculate.

MONEY: Did you start doing this before or after the dollar became weak?

VIDAL: I started doing it in 1968, which makes it an extremely astute thing financially, yet I can take no credit for it. I had decided that if the Vietnam War continued much past

1968, the only moral response would be a change of nationality. I made moves in that direction but was stopped by the U.S. government, which I was afraid would seize everything in sight. I did transfer out of dollars into the only legitimate things that one could buy at that time in Deutsche marks and Swiss francs, and that was World Bank bonds. So I supported to the best of my small ability the city of Oslo and countries like Finland.

Later the law changed and one could buy anything. By that time I was quite used to living entirely in the European context financially and I began in my cautious and dull way to buy various bonds in those currencies. I didn't foresee until about 1971 that the dollar was collapsing and the American economy was—well, to put it politely—sick. From then on it has been my policy never to go into dollars at all. And all I can say is that probably the one [entirely] virtuous political gesture that I have ever made has proved that virtue is unexpectedly rewarding.

MONIQUE VAN VOOREN, 1976:   You have never made it a hidden fact that you are rich and bisexual.

VIDAL: I have never said anything about either. Other people say these things about me. [In America], what ought to be true is true, and therefore he said it.

VAN VOOREN: Do you deny it?

VIDAL: I don't deny or affirm anything. I'm not very personal.

MONEY, 1978:   What luxuries please you most?

VIDAL: Three things. One is being able to buy a book as soon as it's published and not having to wait for the paperback. The second is being able to afford to have a typist do as many drafts as I want of what I'm writing. And, finally, the major virtue of having sufficient money is that you don't have to think about money. I find that when you start to think about [money], you think about nothing else.

MONEY: These don't sound like the indulgences of a rich man.

VIDAL: I have no luxurious tastes—yachts and expensive cars and great houses, lots of servants and so forth. I have one full-time employee—my villa at Ravello is a farm, by the way, not a palace—and he's a farmer who looks after the place. I drive a little Fiat.* I would say I live rather modestly and that is probably because I wasn't born poor. I didn't have my face pressed against the window, wishing for the princess and saying, "Someday this will all be mine."

MONEY: Do you think of yourself as a rich man?

VIDAL: No. I would say as writers go I've done very well and that's about it. We writers are the most severely taxed group that I know of, with so few ways to take deductions.

MONEY: And yet you have a reputation for always picking up the check.

VIDAL: I suppose that's because I don't want to be beholden to anybody. On the other hand, when I'm out with somebody really rich my hands are frozen at my sides, and sometimes they remain frozen until all the circulation stops, because the very rich never pick up anything. So if you're worrying about whether I'm rich or not, the proof that I am not is the fact that I pick up the checks.

MONEY: What would you do if you lost it all?

VIDAL: If I lost everything, I would simply start over again. I have great belief in my own competence to do just about anything. Obviously it gets more difficult as you get older, but I would suddenly appear in the flats of Beverly

---

* Now gone. [G.V., 1979]

Hills writing whatever was the going TV series. That pays pretty well. If they didn't want me as a writer, I could probably always get a job as a librarian or book salesman. And my style is very elastic. I can live fairly comfortably on $7,000 a year, which is what I used to live on right up until I was about thirty. Mind you, that's $7,000 in terms of twenty years ago, which would be more than double that amount today.

JUDY HALFPENNY, 1978:   Of Southern California I know only what I've read, and very little more about you; but I can't easily visualize you against that imagined background. It's a gathering-place for celebrities.

VIDAL: The talk is of movies and deals and whose space was got together by est. Last night Michael Caine described in a Cockney accent (which he tended to forget at moments, the voice shifting to high RADA) what it was like to live in Windsor and incite the Queen's rejected servants to gossip about their former masters; while Jacqueline Bisset told me that her experience had been enlarged by working for French and Italian directors. I demurred and changed the subject to her recent caper impersonating Madame Onassis, which I'd not seen; but she thought it was not bad at all and then, noting that my half-sister—HER step-sister—was also in the room, she made a bee-line for her and I heard the opening question, "Did SHE see it?" My sister responded, "Of course she did," not adding that America's own Helen of Troy has a lust for publicity (good, that is ... even *tasteful*) that makes the late Jayne Mansfield seem shy. There. You have an evening in Hollywood, less the real conversation which has to do with negative costs and grosses. Celebrities, as you call them, tend to flock together largely because they have the same sort of problems. Criminals are the same.

MONEY, 1978:   As a socialist have you thought about the different way that you would have to live in a socialist society?

VIDAL: Well, it depends on which socialist society. In the Soviet Union I would live most luxuriously while serving the state and keeping quiet about my demurs about the society. That would be Soviet socialism. In the Netherlands or Denmark I would live just about the way I live now, perhaps with less large-scale travel since there would be relatively less money. But actual living would be about the same and I would have freedom in general to say pretty much what I wanted. Of those two types of socialist societies, obviously it is the second that I would prescribe for this country [i.e., America].

STANTON, 1977: James Michener stated (in 1965) that you told him you regret your not having created an image for yourself early in your career. Right now you have images of being a satirist, an iconoclast, a narcissist. What else? What image of yourself would you have liked to project strongly when younger? Is it possible that the public has a false image of you?

VIDAL: Image for myself? I don't know what I meant. I think I probably meant to say that my sort of manners is unknown to most Americans: Hemingway, Mailer, Capote tell everyone who will listen that they are Truly Great and people tend to agree or disagree but at least the clowns have rattled their bells. I make no claims and seldom discuss my work, greatness.

STANTON, 1977: Is it possible that the academic scholars and critics are repulsed by something in your image? Not by the satirist, and not by the iconoclast. But perhaps by your lack of humility, by your narcissism? By your glamor? If only you were an ugly person!

VIDAL: Perhaps you're right: I would have been more loved if I had been ugly, middle class, Jewish, academic, exclusively heterosexual. . . . Anyway, to the extent that it is possible to "win" in a career, I've won. This must cause distress.

STANTON, 1977: In a recent article appearing in the *Sunday London Times*, Peter Conrad, one of your most insightful critics, calls you a narcissist.

VIDAL: Narcissist? I don't know what the word is meant to signify. Conrad's use of it is not my reason for liking what he has written about me. The key is his apprehension of my "doubleness," "duplicity"—in the old sense. . . . I am, by the way, not at all a narcissist in the usual sense of the word— is there a *usual* sense for any word in such a sloppy age? As for lack of humility . . . well, I am not as vain, as self-serving as Hemingway, Mailer, Capote . . . so it is curious that I should be thought arrogant while they are Regular Fellows. I think politics, sex, class set me off in a way very hard for the envious Americans—are there any other kind?—to comprehend, much less admire. They want mirrors. I'm a window.

MONIQUE VAN VOOREN, 1976: You are obviously very cynical in a lot of your comments—are you really as cynical as you seem to be?

VIDAL: I don't seem to be cynical to myself but how what I say goes down with others is their problem. I'm realistic. Come to me and show me a small cancer and I'll tell you you've got a small cancer that should be cut out. That's realism but in America it's called cynicism. You're suppose to say, ah, you've got a little beauty blemish here and I have some marvelous Max Factor that will hide it. That's the American way of handling things. Anyway, I'm a diagnostician, not a cosmetician.

AMERICAN FILM, 1977: You have a well-earned reputation as an outspoken person. Are there limitations you place on yourself, areas you think it best to avoid?

VIDAL: No. The inner censor works only when I'm hired by a studio or when I was writing live television where I couldn't mention suicide and this and that—there were so many taboos. I've had to conform at times. But when I write a novel, I'm completely on my own. Occasionally, I find that I draw back from something because I think I'm not the person who can say it. I figured out that George Washington was in love with Alexander Hamilton—it's [quite] apparent—and I'm the one writer in the country who couldn't write that!

Norman Mailer could. So I'm limited, to a degree—limited, perhaps, by [the] preconceptions [of others].

MONIQUE VAN VOOREN, 1976: You've had famous feuds, one with . . .

VIDAL: I have never feuded with anyone. Others may have turned on me.

VAN VOOREN: I don't know but I recall something with Mr. Buckley which was rather interesting and created quite a stir. Does criticism bother you?

VIDAL: No. At a very early age I decided that what I thought of others was a good deal more important than what they thought of me. Somebody has to keep score and I decided I was going to do it. I'm a born scorekeeper and I realize, like an umpire, that my decisions may cause distress. I do my best to be honest and of level head. Occasionally I have to use an axe but only with regret.

OUI, 1975: Is yours a happy life?

VIDAL: Yes, since my lifework is doing what I want to do. I do notice, in talking to other people, that at a certain point most of them try to involve you in their problems. Well, I don't do that. As you may have noticed in the course of this interview, I'm not by nature very personal and rather dislike most of your questions. My instinct is to go outside myself. I'm interested in the state of the nation, the pollution of the Mediterranean, Calvino's novels. I think—as opposed to feel—more about the outside world than about myself. I don't brood much. I don't look in the mirror and say, Oh, how sad! What a time you've had!

OUI: But you do look in the mirror a good deal, as you have written.

VIDAL: True.

OUI: Why?

VIDAL: Looking for death. Seeing what inroads death has made since the last glance.

OUI: Have you always looked in mirrors?

VIDAL: All my life.

OUI: And has it always been a question of death?

VIDAL: No, that comes later. When you're young, you look hopefully—oh, dear, not "hopefully"—to see yourself growing up, to see if you're getting lines and beginning to look like a proper adult. You look for change. In one's prime, you look to see how you are faring, if you're still there. After forty, the deathwatch.

STANTON, 1977:   How does Gore Vidal want to die?

VIDAL: Death? A large subject. Age is an unexpected anodyne.

MONIQUE VAN VOOREN, 1976:   You are obviously very aware that you are a good-looking man, and in some ways you've been called almost narcissistic about your looks. Does age bother you?

VIDAL: Age bothers everybody. I was never narcissistic about my looks, but people thought that I should be so therefore I was. The whole point to American journalism is what ought to be true is true. Since I ought to be arrogant, impressed with my social position, overwhelmed by my beauty, therefore I am. Actually I was never my own type so I completely missed my beauty all through my youth. I have no social position and I stay away from what is known as society as much as possible. But people like to reinvent you, according to cliché. There are a lot of stories about me that really apply only to Capote or Mailer or somebody else. Everything is a mish-mash.

NEWSWEEK, 1974:   Some critics say that you are cold, detached, passionless; as Mailer puts it, you "lack the wound."

VIDAL: I don't accept any of that. I certainly don't accept it from Norman. I come from the wrong class to be a writer, so I had to fight that. . . . To be, like Norman, a New York Jewish boy from Harvard who had written a war novel, I cannot imagine any situation *better* for the beginning of a career. To me . . . well, *mein Kampf* has been a hell of a lot tougher than Norman's. The fact is I don't show my wounds—so I am Coriolanus—but that's something else again.

STANTON, 1979:   When I was a boy I sometimes would go into my room and withdraw into an uncaring center in my mind. That center lacked feeling, a "cold spot." It has served me well. It protects me. I can see clearly while within it. I am refreshed each time I enter and leave it.

But back to you, to your "cold spot." You seem to write while sitting within it. And I don't mean that you produce a book or two in the zero zone. Your entire work has a cold, refreshing quality. I realize that you are "not very personal" (and isn't this yet another indication of the cold center's existence?), but I think it's important to find out more about how a major quality (and attitude) in your work has originated. I imagine that the cold center developed (or was found) from some extreme experience in your youth. In my case, fear led to a clean, cool chapel. At the same time, I realized immediately that I was no longer one with my parents. I could now see them through a wall of ice. I knew that sometimes what they did to each other should be hurting me. But no, I had found a place where I just couldn't care. Do you understand of what I speak?

VIDAL: I understand what you mean about the cold center. But I don't see myself in those terms. I was brought up in the house of Atreus and so was obliged to become myself as formidable as those with whom I was obliged to contend. Electra had a more difficult time than I. The story's unfinished. The kindly ones are everywhere and the sun-god nowhere.

OUI, 1975: In the past two or three years, have you found your attitudes changing? Are you more withdrawn? Do you care less?

VIDAL: You do care considerably less about some things. And you do withdraw more and more. Whatever you are basically becomes more obvious. At heart, I just want to be alone and read. And that's what I do more and more. After a certain point, ambition stops.

OUI: But it hasn't stopped with you, has it?

VIDAL: As long as you're alive, you're going to have a certain desire to prevail, but, after a while, it's just like a tic—inadvertent.

PLAYBOY, 1969: You acted on your political concern in perhaps the most direct way possible in 1960 by running for Congress in New York's 29th Congressional District. Do you still have political ambitions, despite your defeat?

VIDAL: No. But in that election, I took some pleasure in carrying the cities of Poughkeepsie, Beacon, Hudson and Kingston, and getting the most votes of any Democrat in fifty years. Two years later, I could have had the nomination for the Senate against Javits. I was then faced with the sort of choice that seems to have haunted me all my life. If I were to be a serious politician, it was quite plain that I could not be a serious writer. Not only is there not enough energy for the two careers, they are incompatible. The writer is forever trying to say exactly what he means and the politician is forever trying to *avoid* saying what he means. In 1962, I had returned to novel writing after almost a decade's absence, and so the specific choice for me that year was between writing *Julian* and making a race for the Senate. I chose to be a novelist. In 1964, I was asked once more to run for Congress. For the last time, I said no, and with very little regret watched the man I had selected to take my place win the election in the Johnson landslide.

Also, to be practical, if one wishes to influence events, the Congress is hardly the place to do it. A writer with an audience has more power than most Congressmen. If he is also able to use television, he is in a splendid position to say what needs to be said. Best of all, in wanting nothing for himself, he is more apt to be listened to than the man who lusts for office. But no matter how I try to rationalize my situation, I *am* split between a private and public self. I was trained from childhood to be a politician, but I was born a writer. From time to time, I have tried to bring together the two selves, but it has not been easy. Example: I have a gift for being effective on television, something every politician longs to possess and few do; yet I am compelled to candor of a kind that is not permissible in a conventional politician. So I constantly undo myself, making impossible that golden age, the Vidal Administration. No doubt just as well. For me.

AMERICAN FILM, 1977:   It's been said on more than one occasion that you should be president.

VIDAL: I think you're quite right.

AMERICAN FILM: Norman Mailer, in fact, said that once.

VIDAL: That's only when Norman decided that he was aiming for Jehovah. I could have the United States [as long as] he was the Big One in the sky.

FAG RAG, 1974:   Have allegations of homosexuality ever been used to ruin anyone in politics in your lifetime as far as you know?

VIDAL: The Senator from this state [Massachusetts], David Ignatius Walsh, tried to make my father when my father was a West Point Cadet. My father and his roommate had been down [to Washington] for the inauguration of Woodrow Wilson, and Senator Walsh picked them up. They were both very innocent West Pointers. My father said it was just apalling. [Walsh] chased them around [his hotel] room. . . . When my father [joined] Roosevelt's administration, he went absolutely to pieces when he had to go before a Senate committee. . . . He regarded all Senators as potential rapists and pederasts. Walsh was caught during the war in a boy whorehouse . . . in Brooklyn. . . . Nothing ever happened to him. He was re-elected in due course. There wasn't anybody in Massachusetts . . . [including] little birds on the Common who didn't know what David Walsh was up to.

PLAYBOY, 1969: Emerson once remarked of Thoreau, "He has a military cast to him. . . . He feels himself only in opposition." You are at your liveliest on the attack. Would you say that you have an unusually aggressive nature?

VIDAL: *I* wouldn't say it, but others do. What usually sets me off is injustice. In defense of those I admire, I'm always ready—eager?—to do battle. Although I have the killer instinct altogether too well developed, I do try to deploy it in good causes. This pugnacity is inherited from my mother's family, the Gores, an Anglo-Irish clan of eloquent, bad-tempered politicians, lawyers and preachers. In me, their furious blood is only partially diluted by a more genial Latin strain.

PLAYBOY: Many men in history who have shared your moral indignation and militant iconoclasm have been bitter and lonely outsiders alienated not only from society but from the warmth of human contact. Is that true of you?

VIDAL: I think of myself as cheerful, even on the attack, and though I am not gregarious nor anxious to be loved, I have quite enough company out there on the edge of things. For me, the only danger is a tendency to drift toward the center—which means that at some point, I must make my getaway, whether it be from the White House or from literary respectability. At one time or another, I've had a number of fine conventional careers within my grasp: the popular theater, Congress, television performer. But once each of these exercises had served my purpose—or perhaps once I had got the range of it—I always found some way of getting out. I'm not a courtier; I'm a critic—something most people who consider power exciting find difficult to understand. At the time of my break with the Kennedys, Arthur Schlesinger told my sister that he feared I had a death wish. To which I answered, "I have a *life* wish—and I can't live vicariously." But most people are like Arthur. They want to belong—in his case, to *be* a Kennedy; it is a touching, even sweet, instinct—but not for me. I can only breathe outside.

PLAYBOY: Is that the way you'd like to be remembered? Outside?

VIDAL: I am outside, certainly, and by choice. As for being remembered—I have little interest in the idea of posterity. Think of the thousands of years of Egyptian literature, entirely lost. What survives and what does not is simply a matter of chance and, so, incalculable. All that matters to me is what I do this morning, and that I do it—and am here.

EVE AUCHINCLOSS & NANCY LYNCH, 1961:   Do you find much that surprises you?

VIDAL: That's temperament, isn't it? I've never been surprised by anything that I can remember—anything human. But ideas do surprise. I got one the other day reading Sartre. He was talking about how the bourgeois audience had in a sense murdered the theater in the last century. And he came up with something I hadn't thought about: he said the audience—our audience—will accept anything dark that you can say about the human condition—every sort of viciousness and violence—so long as you do not suggest that any of this can be *changed*. That was a revelatory thought, you know. It was true and it was a surprise. That is the problem we have in the theater: the second you suggest change, you have them against you. And then you have a war to fight. After that, I thought my own theater was very inadequate. On the other hand, in my novels I think I have gone to war.

MICHAEL S. LASKY, 1975:   You once said you were bored with "playing it safe" so you wrote *The City and the Pillar.* Would you say that taking chances typifies your career?

VIDAL: Well, I seem to have taken a few, yes. But my father made a very good observation. A woman was doing a piece about me for *Look* magazine ["Gore Vidal: The Elegant White Knife," by Laura Bergquist, 29 July 1969] and she said to him, "What do you think of [the way] your son [so courageously] takes on all these difficult themes, sexual and political and the like?" My father said, "There is no courage involved." "What do you mean?" the woman asked. "Well, after all," my father replied, "he doesn't care about what people think of him, so why is it courageous to offend them?" I thought it a rather wise statement.

LASKY: You don't care what people think about you?

VIDAL: No. At least not people in general. It's much more important what *I* think of them. . . .

EVE AUCHINCLOSS & NANCY LYNCH, 1961:   What kind of people do you like?

VIDAL: Those who interest me. All sorts. After a time you get so you feel, especially in New York, as if you know everybody in the world. . . . But I have found six or seven friends, and each one is in a sense living a life that I might have liked to lead under other circumstances. And so, through friendship, you extend yourself.

MONIQUE VAN VOOREN, 1976:   I've seen that you've been very kind to your dog.

VIDAL: Well, he's all right. He can't talk. He indicates an awful lot, however.

OUI, 1975:   Do people bore you?

VIDAL: Anybody's interesting if you can get him on whatever it is that interests him. But echoing Shaw, I'm comfortable only in the presence of the dead great, which means reading a book. I'd rather read Turgenev than meet someone new. But then, you see, I'm hopelessly literary, and not many people you meet are. Certainly American writers almost never are.

OUI: In one of your books [*Two Sisters*], you wrote about England's Bloomsbury group, which included Virginia Woolf, and how nice it would be to live in a house with three or four men of letters. Would that appeal to you?

VIDAL: No, no, no! That's a dream of very young people. Anyway, I was just quoting Voltaire. I do look at Bloomsbury with a certain wonder, the way they sustained one another. That's fascinating to me. I could no more go to bed with somebody whose work I admired than I could . . . well, make love to a mirror. Fame in others switches off desire.

MONEY, 1978:   If you were half your age, what would you do differently?

VIDAL: If I were twenty-five years old, I'd emigrate to Australia. It's underpopulated, it's a beautiful country, it's more and more sophisticated, and it looks upon Asia, which is fascinating. Sydney is everything San Francisco thinks it is— and far more beautiful. I think it is the only country that is going to make it through the next few decades. And beyond that, who can tell about anything?

MONIQUE VAN VOOREN, 1976:   Do you ever make love daily?

VIDAL: I used to, yes, but now I am catching up on my reading.

ISRAEL SHENKER, 1968:   Do you have any preference as to when you read?

VIDAL: When I first get up my mind is clearest, and if I'm reading anything I want to learn, I read it in the morning. And then at night I try to read two or three hours before I go to sleep. I don't read many novels, which is true of most novelists. I don't know why most novelists—myself included—keep complaining that people don't like to read novels when we don't like to read them either. But that's the sad situation. Most writers write the sort of books that they themselves would not read, which is strange. [On the other hand, I write only books that I'd like to read. If only I'd read *Burr* at twenty. . . .]

I suppose really the thing has gone now to film, the thing of telling stories. Film does it in some ways so much better. But I obviously belong to the previous establishment. For me it is print. But I can imagine the novel ceasing to exist in a hundred years, or being practiced as a formal art like writing sestinas now, an academic pursuit, and used in the classroom simply as a test of [a] student's ingenuity, like a crossword puzzle.

MONIQUE VAN VOOREN, 1976:   What other interests do you have besides reading and writing and, of course, television?

VIDAL: I like looking at buildings and I like going into them sometimes and sometimes I like to stay outside of them.

STANTON, 1978:   Are you interested in any of the nonliterary arts? For example, do you collect paintings or visit museums? Do you have any particular style of music you enjoy—classical, modern, contemporary?

VIDAL: I spend a lot of time in museums in new places . . . Rome is now just a backdrop and, sadly, I don't always see it after all these years. Piero della Francesco, Masaccio, Mantegna, Giorgione are always worth detours. I'm fascinated by architecture (the novel is essentially a work of verbal architecture and I suspect that that's why so few writers—good or bad—can master the complex largeness of it). I am an opera buff without much ear for music. I have tried to like non-representational painting and sculpture, and failed. With popular music, I stop at Alec Wilder. I was once a balletomane (*Death in the Fifth Position* is supposed to be a Broadway musical this year), but seldom go now.

JUDY HALFPENNY, 1978: You studied ballet yourself?

VIDAL: Yes, I studied ballet for a year after the war but not to become a dancer. I had arthritis in the legs, a legacy of the Aleutians, and the experience was beneficial. I had no talent at all, other than being rather strong with a good elevation. But I did learn what it was all about and that serves one well as an audience.

PARIS REVIEW, 1974: Are you interested in [any] other arts . . . ?

VIDAL: . . . I'm fascinated by the ancient Roman Empire amongst whose ruins I live. I've been in every city and town of Italy, and I suppose I've been into nearly every Roman church. I particularly like mosaics. . . . And baroque music, very loud. . . . In sculpture, well, the Medici tombs—I had a small talent for sculpture when I was young.

STANTON, 1979: Some of your works—I'm thinking of *Burr* and *1876*—contain intense relationships between fathers and daughters. Does the theme of incest interest you?

VIDAL: Yes.

EVE AUCHINCLOSS & NANCY LYNCH, 1961: What do you love?

VIDAL: What an extraordinary question. The answer could be anything from corn bread to Titian. But I suppose you mean a quality. What quality does one love? I think I might say justice. Because, though justice is relative, there is a balance, a harmony in the nature of things which I think can be struck and that, to me, is justice. Art is certainly that, or aspires to be.

PLAYBOY, 1969: You have admitted that, as a young writer, your "competitive instincts" were very intense and you deeply resented the success of other writers. Are these competitive instincts still strong—or have you mellowed over the years.?

VIDAL: Does one mellow or does one rot? The two processes are perhaps the same. Unlike most writers, my competitive instinct—though highly developed—was never personal. That is to say, I have never begrudged another writer his success, but I have sometimes deplored the taste of the moment that has made what I thought bad work successful. Happily, since injustice is the rule, one is quite as apt to be its beneficiary as its victim.

PLAYBOY: Looking back on your career, you've written, "It's sad. Sometimes I think I've misplayed it." How?

VIDAL: I was speaking ironically. I simply meant that by doing all the things I do, I have avoided being taken seriously by middlebrow academics. I don't fit any known category, so they are unable to make judgment. But, slowly, it is beginning to seep down that there may be someone quite different on the scene whose career can eventually be made a touchstone for others. Not that what I am or what I do will ever be very attractive—or easy to imitate. Mailer is more in the main tradition than I; any young man who wants to be a writer can identify more easily with him than with me. Or James Agee: a small talent who sold out in a small way and took it hard; any Princeton English major can live out *that* legend. But each of us is what he is, and the only sin is to pretend to be what one is not.

Neither Mailer nor Capote nor myself—to name three writers of very different gifts—came into his own until he found his proper voice. Mailer spent years trying to write timeless masterpieces, and the time of that time was disastrous for him. Capote was not quite so ambitious—or literary. He simply wanted to be famous through writing, and so he copied the works of writers who were currently in fashion. He plundered Carson McCullers for *Other Voices, Other Rooms,* abducted Isherwood's Sally Bowles for *Breakfast at Tiffany's:* in short, was ruthlessly unoriginal. Then he turned to reportage, the natural realm of those without creative imagination, and began to do interesting work. In other words, he'd found his own voice, and that is what writing is all about.

EVE AUCHINCLOSS & NANCY LYNCH, 1961: Where do your ideas come from?

VIDAL: Anything can set things going—an encounter, a recollection. I think writers tend to be great rememberers. I remember everything, right back to the beginning of my life. I remember myself . . . going through stage after stage, encounter after encounter. Nothing ever seems to me quite real at the moment it happens. It's part of the reason for writing, since the experience never seems quite real until I evoke it again. That's all one tries to do in writing, really, to hold something—the past, the present.

AUCHINCLOSS & LYNCH: In order to hold off death?

VIDAL: In order not to die? The point is that at every moment one is dying a bit and this action is an action against death. I'm very conscious of dying. I write a great deal about it, and I think it heightens one's pleasure in life—trying to keep those moments and perceptions you had or thought you had. Literature is really the attempt to give shape to something that has no shape. No man's life has a shape or a meaning or a point—it's a flux of sensations and experiences, coming from nothing and going to nothing.

OUI, 1975: Let's see how you fit into your social perspectives. Who, exactly, are you?

VIDAL: I was born a critic—and a tough one, I think. I always had a clear idea of who I was and what I liked and disliked. I suspect this is why I've done fairly well. In the United States, hardly anybody knows who he is.

OUI: Why do you single out the United States?

VIDAL: People in Europe tend to know who they are. When Mario gets up in the morning, he knows he's Mario, he knows who his wife is, he knows who his mother is, he knows where he lives, what he likes, dislikes.

MICHAEL S. LASKY, 1975:   Ultimately, how would you like to be remembered?

VIDAL: I suppose as the person who wrote the best sentences in his time.

LASKY: Looking back over your career, is there any one part you can cherish more than any other?

VIDAL: Looking back is not my bag.

STANTON, 1979:   It's difficult to establish a solid identity in America. A large number of people know your name, however. I find that people hold extreme opinions about you as a person. They either like you or dislike you intensely. My neighbor, for example, thinks you're quite wonderful for "telling it like it is." My mother, on the other hand, called me up the other day to warn me about you. She was watching a Dick Cavett Show. "That Gore Vidal was on. Bobby, he's an atheist!" I suspect that people react to your public personality. Important people, especially famous ones, stand out in the crowd of course. But when they say the unexpected, well, to say the least, an American will slap them on the back as often as not with a knife in his hand. Anyway, what should your future biographer emphasize about Gore Vidal the person?

VIDAL: In general, I'd prefer that the biographer refrained from theorizing about the subject. The private lives of Rousseau, Montaigne, Isherwood ... to name, haphazardly, three writers of the most subjective sort ... are relevant to a biography. But linking *Myra Breckinridge* and *Julian* through a close analysis of what a biographer thinks that their inventor's personality must be like is a hopeless task. *I* wouldn't try it. That's why if I ever do a memoir, I'll leave myself out and put in *les mots* like Sartre or *les pensees* like Herzen.

2

Floating on a Gilded Barge

STANTON, 1979:   For a long time you handled your own works, without an agent. Now Owen Laster, of the William Morris Agency, is involved. When did he begin to aid you? Does he handle all of your work?

VIDAL: I always used the Morris office for theatre, movies, telvision. That started in '54. Then Harold Franklin, my agent there, died. For a time, I had no agent at all. Finally, I went back to the Morris office because, once you've written a large number of books, there is endless trivia to deal with. I can't do it. They can.

AMERICAN FILM, 1977:   When you sit down to write, how much of the story do you have in your mind, how much do you discover as you go along?

VIDAL: You start with a shape in your head. Virginia Woolf said that *The Waves*, which was her own favorite novel, started for her this way: I saw a dark sea and the fin of a shark turning. That was her beginning image. When I wrote *Washington, D.C.*, I saw a storm and the garden of the house in Virginia where I was brought up. You start very often with an image, and I generally don't know much more than where I think [the narrative's] going, where it should end. Then I sit there roaring with laughter as the sentences appear on the page. Where is this coming from? I sometimes wonder. Oh, it is interesting, the creative process. Where was this story before I wrote it down? I don't know. It certainly wasn't in my head. You can't walk around with all that stuff on file, particularly when you've written a lot of books over the years. Arthur Schlesinger, Jr., . . . looking at his three or four volumes on Roosevelt, said, "You know, there are times when I wonder how did I ever know all those things that are in those books." Writing also acts as a kind of an eraser. I know nothing about the fourth century now, but when I wrote *Julian* I did. A kind of mental erasure takes place. That's why writing is also therapeutic. You can get rid of a lot of things.

PARIS REVIEW, 1974:   When you get up in the morning to write, do you just sit down and start out with your pen? You don't have any devices you use to . . .

VIDAL: First coffee. . . . Then the muse joins me.

PARIS REVIEW: You don't sharpen pencils or anything like that?

VIDAL: No. But I often read for an hour or two. Clearing the mind. I'm always reluctant to start work, and reluctant to stop. The most interesting thing about writing is the way it obliterates time. Three hours seem like three minutes. Then there is the business of surprise. I never know what is coming next. The phrase that sounds in the head changes when it appears on the page. Then I start probing it with a pen, finding new meanings. Sometimes I burst out laughing at what is happening as I twist and turn sentences. Strange business, all in all. One never gets to the end of it. That's why I go on, I suppose. To see what the next sentence I write will be.

MICHAEL S. LASKY, 1975:   Is it frightening when you start out with a blank page?

VIDAL: No, it's a great joy. I never believed in this agony of creation. Either you do it or you don't. Most people who go on year after year doing it continue because they like doing it. Saul Bellow had a very good line: "Genius is without strain." Something that ambitious talent never understands. . . .

LASKY: You've just crushed a lot of people [who write].

VIDAL: You have to start somewhere. You *start* when you are young. And look what you can look forward to in your middle age. *If* you haven't already become an alcoholic . . . that's *Catch-22.*

STANTON, 1977: How much of your writing come naturally, and how much do you have to work on consciously?

VIDAL: First drafts come easily. I can write two or three thousand words a day in two or three hours. I have written as much as 10,000 words in a day. But since 1954 when I began to make money I have been able to afford typists. As a result, for some odd reason, every work now requires five drafts. Some pages ten or twelve. Tone is not the problem. I generally get that right early on. Connection is difficult. Sentence to sentence. Thought to thought. This is where imagination is a great comfort; there are times when a connection is best served by not forcing but waiting. I always add the last paragraph or two to an essay some time after I have written the body of it because I seldom end up knowing what I thought I knew when I started.

PARIS REVIEW, 1974: Do you keep notebooks?

VIDAL: I make a few pages of notes for each novel. Phrases. Names. Character descriptions. Then I seldom look again at the notes. At the end of each work-day I do make notes on what the next day's work will be. I've a memory like a sieve. . . .

FAG RAG, 1974: Do you keep a diary?

VIDAL: I kept one in '48. I sealed it and gave it to the University of Wisconsin with my papers.

FAG RAG: To be opened after your death?

VIDAL: After my death or the Second Coming, whichever comes first.

PARIS REVIEW, 1974:   Have you ever had any trouble with writer's block?

VIDAL: No.

PARIS REVIEW: Do you block out a story in advance? And do characters ever run away from you?

VIDAL: When I first started writing I used to plan everything in advance, not only chapter to chapter but page to page. Terribly constricting . . . like doing a film from someone else's meticulous treatment. About the time of *The Judgment of Paris,* I started improvising. I began with a mood. A sentence. The first sentence is all important. *Washington, D.C.* began with a dream. . . . With *Julian* and with *Burr* I was held to historical facts. Still, I found places where I could breathe and make up new things. My *Burr* is not the real Burr anymore than [Dumas Malone's] *Jefferson* is the real Jefferson. By and large history tends to be rather poor fiction—except at its best. The *Peloponnesian War* is a great novel about people who actually lived.

STANTON, 1977:   In your fictional inventions how much is based on observation, how much on letting the mind take a walk for itself? How, for example, was Washington Irving created in *Burr?*

VIDAL: The blend varies from work to work. I tend to make up a great deal except when I'm doing the histories. Irving was constructed from letters, biographies, and a figure that appeared at the point of my pen, whispering.

PARIS REVIEW, 1974:   You must be enormously disciplined to turn out so much in a relatively short time. Do you find writing easy? Do you enjoy it?

VIDAL: Oh, yes, of course I enjoy it. I wouldn't do it if I didn't. Whenever I get up in the morning I write for about three hours. I write novels in longhand on yellow legal pads, exactly like the First Criminal Nixon. For some reason I write plays and essays on the typewriter. The first draft usually comes rather fast. One oddity: I never reread a text until I have finished the first draft.* Otherwise it's too discouraging. Also, when you have the whole thing in front of you for the first time, you've forgotten most of it and see it fresh. Rewriting, however, is a slow grinding business. . . . The more [drafts] the better since my style is very much one of afterthought. My line to Dwight Macdonald—"You have nothing to say, only to add"—really referred to me. Not until somebody did a parody of me, did I realize how dependent I am on the parenthetic side—the comment upon the comment, the ironic gloss upon the straight line, or the straight rendering of a comedic point. It is a style which must seem rather pointless to my contemporaries because they see no need for this kind of elaborateness. But, again, it's the only thing I find interesting to do.

Hung-over or not, I write every day for three hours after I get up until [I've] finished whatever I'm doing. Although sometimes I take a break in the middle of the book, sometimes a break of several years. I began *Julian*—I don't remember—but I think some seven years passed between the beginning of the book and when I picked it up again. The same thing occurred with *Washington, D.C.* On the other hand, *Myra* I wrote practically at one sitting—in a few weeks. It wrote itself, as they say. But then it was much rewritten.

Oui, 1975: Do you see yourself as one of the few American novelists?

Vidal: I'm certainly one of the most *persistent* American novelists. I've gone on writing novels for thirty years as though there were a public, as though it made some differ-

---

* This is not true in the case of a very long work like *Burr*. Since I keep forgetting, I must re-read. [G.V., 1979]

ence. I'm the only one who really is a novelist, at least of my generation. There are a lot of younger people who write good novels, and I'm afraid that many of them I haven't read. But of my generation? Well, there is Mailer, who is not a novelist but an autobiographer. And Capote, who wears with a certain panache the boa of the late Louella Parsons.

PARIS REVIEW, 1974:   When did you first start writing?

VIDAL: I would suppose at five or six, whenever I learned how to read. Actually, I can't remember when I was *not* writing. I was taught to read by my grandmother. Central to her method was a tale of unnatural love called "The Duck and the Kangaroo." Then, because my grandfather, Senator Gore, was blind I was required early on to read grownup books to him, mostly constitutional law and, of course, the *Congressional Record.* The later continence of my style is a miracle, considering those years of piping the Additional Remarks of Mr. Borah of Idaho.

PARIS REVIEW: When did you begin your first novel?

VIDAL: At about seven. A novel closely based on a mystery movie I had seen, something to do with *The Blue Room* or *Hotel* (not Stephen Crane's). I recall, fondly, that there was one joke. The character based on my grandmother kept interrupting everybody because "she had not been listening." Merriment in the family during the first reading. It doesn't take much to launch a wit. Then I wrote a great deal of didactic poetry, all bad. With puberty the poetry came to resemble *Invictus,* the novels *Of Human Bondage.* Between fourteen and nineteen I must have begun and abandoned six novels.

PARIS REVIEW: What were the other five about? School?

VIDAL: No. I began the first really ambitious one when I was fourteen or fifteen. I had gone to Europe in the summer of '39 and visited Rome. One night I saw Mussolini. . . . I thought him splendid! That jaw, that splendid emptiness. After all, I had been brought up with politicians. He was an exotic variation on something quite familiar to me. So I started a novel about a dictator in Rome, filled with intrigue and passion and Machiavellian *combinazione*. But that didn't get finished either despite my close study of the strategies of E. Phillips Oppenheim.

PARIS REVIEW: Finishing *Williwaw* at nineteen broke the barrier; it was published and you wrote three novels in quick succession.

VIDAL: Yes. Every five minutes it seemed. Contrary to legend, I had no money. Since I lived on publishers' advances, it was fairly urgent that I keep on publishing every year. But of course I *wanted* to publish every year. I felt no strain, though looking back over the books I can detect a strain in the writing of them. Much of the thinness of those early novels is simply the pressure that I was under. Anyway, I've gone back and re-written several of them. They are still less than marvelous but better than they were.

STANTON, 1977:   Both you and Hawthorne have gone back to the past. All of Hawthorne's short stories, and the *Scarlet Letter* do so. . .

VIDAL: Most writers tend to go at least a generation back when they set their narratives. Past time is closed time; and manageable. Also, memories of youth are intense, etc. I vary. *Myra/Myron* are now but also then; and of course outside usual time altogether . . . the way that one is at a good movie. *Kalki* and *Messiah* are near-future; and again distanced.

STANTON, 1979:   You work very hard on your writing, don't you?

VIDAL: True writing is written line by line—that's the fun of doing it and the fun of reading it. Today hardly anyone reads sentences, much less writes them. People skim pages, their TV-trained eyes looking for a word—usually sexual—to set off reverie. Best seller writers—of the better sort—write paragraph by paragraph, allowing the better reader's eyes to skip down the page, leaping from paragraph to paragraph like a gazelle. True reading requires a good deal of kinetic energy. I suppose if I were looking for a perfect reader of what I write, he'd read as slowly as I do, sounding each line in his head.

In *Burr*, for example, I was challenged by the large amount of information it had to contain. Every sentence was a great challenge to write, to make interesting. Sometimes I would emphasize the verbs: page after page, line after line, of verbs. Or I would use clauses so that any reader beginning one will not know how it is going to end but will want to read on to find out what it is—well, dangling from.

PARIS REVIEW, 1974:   What is there in writing except language?

VIDAL: In the writing of novels there is the problem of how to shape a narrative. And though the search for new ways of telling goes on—I've written about this at terrible length*—I don't think there are going to be any new discoveries. For one thing, literature is not a science. There is no new formula. Some of us write better than others; and genius is never forced. There are signs that a number of writers—University or U-writers, as I call them—are bored with the narrative, character, prose. In turn they bore the dwindling public for novels. So Beckett stammers into silence, and the rest is cinema. Why not?

PARIS REVIEW: But in the forties . . .

VIDAL: In the forties I was working in the American tradition of straight narrative, not very different from John P. Marquand or John Steinbeck or Ernest Hemingway. For me it was like trying to fence in a straitjacket. In fact, my first years as a writer were very difficult because I knew I wasn't doing what I should be doing, and I didn't know how to do what I ought to be doing. Even interestingly conceived novels like *Dark Green, Bright Red* or *A Search for the King* came out sounding like poor Jim Farrell on a bad day. Not until I was twenty-five, had moved to my house in the country, was poor but

---

* "French Letters"—From *Homage to Daniel Shays.*

content and started to write *The Judgment of Paris,* that suddenly I was all there, writing in my own voice. I had always had a tendency to rhetoric—Senator Borah, remember? But fearing its excess, I was too inhibited to write full voice. I don't know what happened. The influence of Anaïs Nin? The fact that I had stopped trying to write poetry and so the poetic line fused with the prose? Who knows? Anyway, it was a great release, that book. Then came *Messiah.* Unfortunately my reputation in '54 was rock-bottom. The book was ignored for a few years, to be revived [—underground—] in the universities. Dead broke, I had to quit writing novels for ten years— just as I was hitting my stride. I don't say that with any bitterness because I had a very interesting ten years. But it would have been nice to have gone on developing, uninterruptedly, from *Messiah.*

PARIS REVIEW: What sets you apart, do you think, from other American writers?

VIDAL: My interest in Western civilization. Except for Thornton Wilder, I can think of no contemporary American who has any interest in what happened before the long present he lives in, and records. Also, perhaps paradoxically, I value invention highly, and hardly anyone else does. I don't think I have ever met an American novelist who didn't, sooner or later, say when discussing his own work, "Well, I really knew someone exactly like that. That was the way it happened, the way I wrote it." He is terrified that you might think he actually made up a character, that what he writes might not be literally as opposed to imaginatively true. I think part of the bewilderment American bookchat writers have with me is that they realize that there's something strange going on that ought not to be going on—that *Myra Breckinridge* might just possibly be a work of the imagination. "You mean you never knew *anyone* like that? Well, if you didn't, how could you write it?"

EUGENE WALTER, 1960: You were saying you invented everything, but weren't there some characters in *In a Yellow*

Wood who were recognizably well-known New York literary and social figures?

VIDAL: Well, let's say, sometimes, I drew small caricatures in the margin . . . peripheral doodling. The thing accomplished is "made," not recorded. Odd how people—even knowing ones—think it's always one's own life. I suppose they are so accustomed to the self-obsessed Thomas Wolfe sort of thing that the whole idea of invention is both discredited and disbelieved.

STANTON, 1977:   Which of your fictional characters, if any, do you most identify yourself with?

VIDAL: Flaubert's answer. I'm in all the central figures, to a point. But I try to control the first person. That is, I will not write as "I" something I myself may or may not think. Charlie's reactions [in *Burr* and *1876*] are often like mine; often not. As analyst, Burr and I are close: Chesterfieldian; 18th-century skeptics, stoics. But when he or Julian or Myra mount their hobby horses, I am inventor not recorder.

MICHAEL S. LASKY, 1975:   Does a foreign country add any inspiration to what you write that you wouldn't get here [in America]?

VIDAL: No. . . . A certain serenity. [When one] becomes celebrated it [is] necessary to [curb one's] exhibitionism. . . .

PARIS REVIEW, 1974:   Do you find any difficulties in writing about America and Americans when you are out of the country so much?

VIDAL: Well, I think others would notice my lapses before I did. Anyway I come back quite often and my ear [is] pretty much attuned to the American . . . scream. But then I've been involved in one way or another with every election for nearly twenty years. And I spend at least two months each year lecturing across the country.

MICHAEL DEAN, 1968:   You don't seem to belong to any particular school of American literature at all. If you have a heritage, it's probably a European one. Don't you feel alone out there?

VIDAL: I have never belonged to any literary group in the United States, but it's rather nice to have a solitary passage. The early years are not particularly pleasant, but later they get used to you.

PARIS REVIEW, 1974:   Does it help a writer to be in love? To be rich?

VIDAL: Love is not my bag. I was debagged at twenty-five and turned to sex and art, perfectly acceptable substitutes. Absence of money is a bad thing because you end up writing the "Telltale Clue" on television—which I did. Luckily I was full of energy in those days. I used to write a seventy-thousand-word mystery novel in ten days. Money gives one time to rewrite books until they are "done"—or abandoned. Money also gave me the leisure to become an essayist. I spend more time on a piece for the *New York Review of Books* than I ever did on, let us say, a television play. If my essays are good it is because they are entirely voluntary. I write only what I want to . . . except of course in those money-making days at MGM—composing *Ben Hur.*

MICHAEL S. LASKY, 1975:   Your writing has run the gamut from plays to essays to novels. . . . Which genre do you enjoy the most, which comes easiest when it comes down to the actual writing?

VIDAL: Are you happier eating a potato than a bowl of rice? I don't know. It's all the same.

LASKY: Are you saying that writing *Myra Breckinridge* is the same as writing about William Buckley?

VIDAL: Sure. Writing is writing. Writing is order in sentences and order in sentences is always the same in that it is always different, which is why it is so interesting to do it. I never get bored with writing sentences. . . .

STANTON, 1979: Why did you stop writing short stories?

VIDAL: I stopped writing poetry when I realized that I was not a good poet. Although I was a good short story writer, I was more at home with the architecture of the novel. I have the vegetative temperament of the true novelist, to quote V. S. Pritchett. Finally, the audience for the short story so shrank in my lifetime that it would have taken a dedication of the sort that I lacked to keep on. There is one thing that the short story did for me back in the '40s and the early '50s when I wrote the seven that are collected in *A Thirsty Evil:* I learned how to use the first person, *how* to become someone quite unlike myself upon the page. "I am a gentle woman in middle life" . . . when I wrote those words nearly thirty years ago I achieved a negative capability of the sort that did not begin to sound in the novels until *The Judgment of Paris* and *Messiah.*

EUGENE WALTER, 1960: Which gives you greater satisfaction, your novels or your plays?

VIDAL: The novel. If only because I don't get the play deep enough or the characters rich enough for my purposes. I think this failure has to do with language. I'm not happy with naturalistic dialogue: I don't much use it, as you'll see, in those books I've written since twenty-one, and yet I haven't found an alternative to the terrible naturalistic gabble in our theatre, the racket of "Do come in," "Drink?" "Yes," "Where'd you leave it?" "Upstairs," "Well, go look, etc." I don't do it much better than the others, but what I have done, and what interests me, is to clown, to be funny, bizarre—I enjoy comedic invention, both high and low, there is almost nothing quite so satisfying as making an audience laugh while removing its insides.

PARIS REVIEW, 1974:   Do you think of your novels as *political* novels?

VIDAL: Of course not. I am a politician when I make a speech or write a piece to promote a political idea. In a novel like *Burr* I'm not composing a polemic about the founding fathers. Rather I am describing the way men who want power respond to one another, to themselves. The other books—the inventions like *Myra* are beyond politics, in the usual sense at least.

EUGENE WALTER, 1960:   Do you feel that your early interest in history and politics has done a great deal in shaping you as a novelist?

VIDAL: Yes. You know Bernard Shaw used to say that religion and politics . . . in the large sense . . . are the only things that should concern a man; they certainly fascinate me though they are currently unfashionable preoccupations. The contemporary novel has split: on the one hand there is the private University Novel; [it's] unrelated to the society around it, unrelated to the fact of death. I suppose Nathalie Sarraute has taken it quite as far as anyone in our period . . . the anti-novel (old-fashioned actually . . . the Goncourts used to write them, and very glum they were). Then there are the busy popular novels. All that concern over who divorces whom and why this marriage failed and who's to get custody of those children and finally, who cares? Even Maisie has got to know a very great deal to save that sort of novel. And love! Dear God, the horror Love has become in our culture! Mr. X doesn't write so good, but he does feel Love is the only thing which matters, and Compassion, too . . . and everyone gets a warm glow from Mr. X's stylized compassion. It is the stunning cliché of our literature, and the largest lie about man's estate. . . . A satire on the Romantic assumption is in order now. How wonderful to be the first contemporary novelist *not* to tack the ensign of Love to his mast. . . .

WALTER: Then you would deal with the grand problems?

VIDAL: Yes! The great emotions, the great crises ... anything to keep from surrendering to the idea that we are all victimized by the hugeness of society. Even if this is true, one should still attack the giant head-on; the alternative is paralysis or, worse, deliberate smallness. *We all know so much more than we write.* And why don't we write it? Because we are afraid of being thought stupid or wicked or ... unlovable.

OUI, 1975:   Do you categorize your work and see it on two levels, the popular—*Myra Breckinridge, ... Myron*—and the scholarly *Julian* and *Burr?*

VIDAL: No, it's all the same. No matter how hard I try, I am still just one person.

STANTON, 1977:   I think that *Burr* is your greatest book. It has a far greater scope than *Myra* (my second favorite), and produces several outstanding characters (whereas in *Myra* there is only one; Rusty, Mary Ann, and Buck are one-dimensional). Both books have the greatness of radical vision, but, again, I think that *Burr* is the more profound, the more complex of the two.

VIDAL: I like *Myron* as much or more than *Myra* (naturally, *Myra* was the first creation and so unique). I think the invention in *Myron* was more interesting and the jokes wilder. I put *Burr* and *Julian* on about the same level: meditations on history. I have a real fondness for *Washington, D.C.* and *The Judgment of Paris.*

PARIS REVIEW, 1974:   Do you feel ... at home with the first-person novel now? Do you think you'll continue with it?

VIDAL: Since I've done it recently in *Burr* and again in *Myron* I'll probably not do it again, but who knows?* The second person certainly holds a few charms. Perhaps no pronouns at all!

---

* We all know now. I've done it again in *Kalki.* Again in *Creation.* Will *he* ever again take the place of *me?* [G.V., 1979]

FAG RAG, 1974:   Do you enjoy the historical novel? Or is it a drudge so that you can do something mad in between?

VIDAL: No. I really like them very much.

MONIQUE VAN VOOREN, 1976:   What is your favorite book of all that you've written?

VIDAL: I think the two Breckinridges. Nobody else could have done them. I could imagine other people doing *Burr* or *1876* or *Washington, D.C.* but the Breckinridges didn't exist before me and they will never die, ever.

VAN VOOREN: They call me "the true Myra Breckinridge." I don't know why.

VIDAL: Since there is no false one you have no choice but to be the true one.

STANTON, 1978:   Have you read Nietzsche? Do you identify with his Zarathustra or with his concept of the Superman? In line with this I should like your reaction to the following quote of Dostoevsky's Raskolnikov (a failed Nietzschian superman?): "I kept asking myself all the time why I was such a damn fool, and why if others are damn fools and if I know for certain that they are fools, do I not try to be more intelligent? Then I realized, Sonia, that if I waited for everyone to be more intelligent, I'd have to wait a very long time. And later still I realized that that would never be, that people would never change, that no one would ever be able to change them, and that it was useless even to try. . . . And now I know, Sonia, that he who is firm and strong in mind and spirit will be their master. He who dares much is right—that's how they look at it. He who dismisses with contempt what men regard as sacred becomes their law-giver, and he who dares more than anyone is more right than anyone. So it has been till now and so it always will be. Only the blind can't see it."* It seems to me that you have "dared" a lot in your writ-

* From *Crime and Punishment* (Penguin Books, 1951), as translated by David Magarshack.

ing, in the novels and essays. Especially on political and religious levels. How would you characterize your writings by how much you have dared to do? What is your most daring novel? Your most daring essay? I think you are very daring in not exposing your personal wounds, or is this because you lack them?

VIDAL: I have read about Nietzsche. But I've never read him. I like your quote. It has brutal truth. . . . The Vidals came from the Engadine where Nietzsche had a house. With that the connection ends. I suppose *Myra/Myron* is the most daring of the novels. Of the essays . . . *West Point?* It's hard to tell because an essay (with a polemical intent) must be seductive; it's advocacy, and so. . . . Well, Shaw said it to Granville-Barker: the comedy of my plays is the sugar I use to disguise the bitter socialist pill. Granville-Barker replied: how clever of the audience to lick off the sugar and leave the pill unswallowed. As for personal wounds, I draw no strength from them. Or weakness. After all, Philoctetes was a superb archer *before* the accident. And after. His wound was distressing to others, not to him.

PARIS REVIEW, 1974:   What do you feel about going back and rewriting? Don't you think in a way that you're changing what another person, the younger Vidal, did?

VIDAL: No. You are stuck with your early self for good or ill, and you can't do anything about it even if you want to—short of total suppression. For me revising is mostly a matter of language and selection. I don't try to change the narrative or the point of view, except perhaps toward the end of *The City and the Pillar.* I felt obligated to try a new kind of ending.* But something like *Dark Green, Bright Red* needed a paring away of irrelevancies, the fault of all American naturalistic writing from Hawthorne to, well, name almost any

---

* I think that the last paragraph in the revised edition of *The City and the Pillar* is inferior to the original. But I stand by the rest of the revision. [G.V., 1979]

American writer today. I noticed recently the same random accretion of details in William Dean Howells—a very good writer yet since he is unable to select the *one* detail that will best express his meaning, he gives us everything that occurs to him and the result is often a shapeless daydream. Twain, too, rambles and rambles, hoping that something will turn up. In his best work it does rather often. In the rest—painful logorrhea.

PARIS REVIEW: What is the procedure once a book is revised? Do publishers accept this with grace? Are the old books recalled from libraries?

VIDAL: *Williwaw* and *Messiah* were only slightly altered, *The City and the Pillar* was much revised. *The Judgment of Paris* was somewhat cut but otherwise not much altered. *Dark Green, Bright Red* was entirely rewritten. Except for *The City and the Pillar,* the new versions first appeared in paperback. Later the revised *Messiah* and *The Judgment of Paris* were also reissued in hard cover. I have no idea what the publishers thought of all this. It is not wise to solicit the opinions of publishers—they become proud if you do. As lovers of the environment, I suspect they were pleased that the new versions were so much shorter than the old, thus saving trees. The original editions can also be found in libraries, margins filled with lewd commentaries, and the worms busy in the bindings.

PARIS REVIEW: One of the comments sometimes made is that your real position—your greatest talent—is as an essayist. How would you answer that?

VIDAL: My novels are quite as good as my essays. Unfortunately, to find out if a novel is good or bad you must first read it and that is not an easy thing to do nowadays. Essays, on the other hand, are short and people do read them.

OUI, 1975:   . . . Where do you see yourself drifting?

VIDAL: . . . Drifting toward death like everyone else. As a writer, I am highly critical of society, and I think I have been at various times in my life capable of viewing, if not the whole, at least a large part of it. So I continue to be a constant critic, motivated by an overdeveloped sense of justice, as opposed to that awful word of the 40's, compassion. I lack compassion, but I do have a sense of justice and I do believe that words mean what they mean—that in the Army you kill somebody with a gun at My Lai, you do not "waste a fire area with an anti-personnel weapon."

STANTON, 1978:   You made some interesting, unsentimental comments about love in your essay "Love Love Love." The only other writer I know of who has expressed similar opinions is the poet Rainer Maria Rilke, especially in his *Letters to a Young Poet.* Even his attitude towards criticism comes very close to your own. Have you read him?

VIDAL: I have read perhaps five poems in translation by Rilke. In my work (if not life) Anaïs Nin's love thesis promptly created Vidal's antithesis.

HOLLIS ALPERT, 1977:   Your essays often draw on your own life. Are you thinking about your memoirs yet?

VIDAL: Oh, I'm not into memoir-time. That's what you do when you're broke. Or the waters of the mind have gone dry. I am in the glorious summer—well, early September—of my days.

PARIS REVIEW, 1974:   Has your writing been influenced by films?

VIDAL: Every writer of my generation has been influenced by films. I think I've written that somewhere. Find out the movies a man saw between ten and fifteen, which ones he liked, disliked, and you would have a pretty good idea of what sort of mind and temperament he has. If he happened to be a writer, you would be able to find a good many influences though not perhaps as many as Professor Bernard F. Dick comes up with in his . . . study of me [*The Apostate Angel: A Critical Study of Gore Vidal,* 1974]—a brilliant job, all in all. Myra would've liked it.

AMERICAN FILM, 1977:   What sort of literature is most adaptable to the movies?

VIDAL: The best movie adaptations have not come from high literature. A great novel like *Madame Bovary* always fails. *From Here to Eternity,* a so-so novel, was a marvelous movie. It seems to be a kind of rule that secondary works often make extremely good films. A first-rate work is hard to adapt because you can't capture in a movie the writer's personal tone. At one point I was asked to write the screenplay for *The Great Gatsby.* I thought and thought about it and decided not to because the tone of Fitzgerald's prose is what makes the book work, a lyric tone that cannot be filmed. Also, you don't get an English director like Jack Clayton to direct something so peculiarly American. The whole tone was wrong.* I did some adaptations for television and the movies. But obviously I preferred my own original work. *Visit to a Small Planet* started on television. Then it went to the theater. Someone else made a lousy movie of it. *The Death of Billy the Kid* was also done on television, and another lousy movie called *The Left Handed Gun,* which began the career of [the director] Arthur Penn, for which we're all grateful.

STANTON, 1977:   Did you adapt the play *Rabelais?*

VIDAL: Yes, for a film. But it wasn't really an adaptation. I prepared a treatment for Barrault to direct in English, but the project was not "commercial," and came to nothing.

STANTON, 1977:   What are the titles of the six TV plays you wrote for "The Devil's Theatre" in 1955?

VIDAL: I don't think I wrote any plays. I merely devised a title and an idea for the series.

FAG RAG, 1974:   You do a lot of projects. It was mentioned in the *Atlantic* that you were doing a screenplay entitled *Plaza.* I looked for this and never saw it.

---

* This is not quite true. I said, provisionally, yes to the film . . . and never heard from them again! [G.V., 1979]

VIDAL: That was [for] Robert Aldrich. [But] he blew the financing. It never got made.

AMERICAN FILM, 1977:   When you sell the rights to a novel or a play to the movies, do you keep any proprietary interest in it?

VIDAL: No. You assume that the [studios] will do what they want with it and that it's pointless to complain. I would complain about something like *Caligula,* which I wrote directly for the screen, or about a play, which is pretty close to a movie. *Visit to a Small Planet* was originally done with Cyril Ritchard. Then the movies bought it and gave it to Jerry Lewis. . . . Well, it's never in my contract that I have to see the results. I have never seen *Myra Breckinridge, Visit to a Small Planet,* or *The Left Handed Gun.* They do crop up on television, and sometimes I'll hear something familiar and realize, "Oh, my God, it's that!" And the blood pressure starts to go up, and I switch to another channel, to the commercials, where all the genius goes.

STANTON, 1977:   Do you use the writings of others for more than literary purposes? What is the primary aim of sometimes writing like James, sometimes like Henry Adams, sometimes like Hemingway?

VIDAL: I write in different styles because I hear different voices in my head. It would be boring to have always the same voice, point of view.

STANTON, 1977:   Certainly I will not disagree with your statement, "It would be boring to have always the same voice, point of view." But in having this attitude you, as an artist, don't allow yourself much room for the exploration of a theme. So you produce single works, a separate *tour de force* each time you finish a work. I wonder if there is a connecting link between your individual works?

VIDAL: Do I create, as you put it, separate *tours de force* rather than confine myself to the endless exploration of the same theme or themes? Probably not. There is more likeness between *Myra* and *Williwaw* than might at first be apparent though the language of each is a world apart from the other. One uses different voices in order to avoid monotony. I enjoy Graham Greene's novels but how can *he* enjoy that same narrator? If I were stuck with such a voice, I would abandon prose and devote myself to psephology or sestinas.

STANTON, 1977:   Shakespeare created a particular, certain voice. And so did Donne, Swift, Hawthorne, Melville, Yeats, Eliot, Dostoevsky, Kafka, and a few others. I don't want to imply that the creation of an outstanding, imitable VOICE is the only criterion of greatness in literature, but I will go so far as to say that the creation of such is found in all great writers. Does any one of the writers I've named talk in two or more voices? Faulkner writes like Faulkner, not like John Knowles. But has Knowles established the voice of Knowles? No one can not know the vocal sound of Capote, but is his writing voice as well known? And Vidal? The VOICE of the essays is clear, can be imitated because unique. But does Vidal have a clearly defined VOICE in his novels? How can you, when you sound like something different in almost every one of them? I think you have gone out of your way not to provide one.

VIDAL: Two academics at Columbia [Susan P. Lee and Leonard Ross] in the local mag [*Columbia Forum*, NS 3 (Spring 1974), 39–40] did a parody of *Burr*. It was pretty inept. I still don't think that a predictability of tone and subject is a good thing despite the writers you admire who manage always to sound the same. By the way, the writers you mention as possessing this desirable wholeness (or monotony) don't always support your case. Obvious example: early vs. late Yeats. Anyway, leave poets out. Our greatest novelist, after all, was known to have at least three manners: James I, James II and the Old Pretender. A great and rare gift is that of mimesis. Few writers have it. Most writers are barely able to get one voice right and that one voice must serve them for all sorts of stories. Think what a great novel Hawthorne might have written in *The Blithedale Romance* if he had ever mastered an ironic style or a comic style or anything but that strange romantic but moving sort of clumsy twadddle.... But then he was a Puritan and Puritanism is the enemy of art (life, too; as opposed to paradise or hell predestined). So we must always make allowance for the clumsiness of so many of our Great American Writers because it is wonderful that they could write at all.

STANTON, 1977:   Yeats uses several different forms but his voice is unmistakable. I recently read three novels by Kerouac and found the same unique voice in all of them. Maybe I, as reader, am somehow comforted by the fact that I can trust to find "Kerouac" when I turn to Kerouac the writer. Christ, I don't want to open my next Graham Greene and not find that sad, compassionate VOICE. What a horror if he should sound anything like a screaming chicken. And after having read those twelve novels in Anthony Powell's famous sequence, I only wish he were young enough to do another twelve, and of course without changing that wonderful voice of his.

VIDAL: Kerouac does sound all alike. The works of Powell I am saving for my old age. Recently, we got on splendidly in Bulgaria. He had prepared two elaborate numbers for me (on Harold Acton and L. P. Hartley); and splendid they were. He walks like Groucho Marx.

STANTON, 1977:   Many Americans like novelty. Every day they want a new stunt to be performed. Well . . . perhaps your many different voices keep them amused and as a result you are a popular writer. I wonder if you could retain their attention if you suddenly developed the same voice in your novels?

VIDAL: If you think that the variousness of my manners as a writer (or "novelty") is what publishers want, you have had little experience of them or of the marketplace. The commercialites want you to do what will make the most money for them in exactly the same way as long as you can bear it. In my case, historical novels (years ago I might have cornered the far-out sex genre but that is a more hazardous game). Variety is hateful to the commercialites because it is not predictable—or bankable. Mr. Maugham's *The Mixture As Before* title is a nicely ironic shaft at his publisher, his public, himself. Since I am as interested in surprising myself as in delighting what small public there is for novels, I will always try to make a new form or, failing that (and one usually falls short), to make a different sound. Anyway, you will find, if you don't seek, as you read the books, sufficient repetitions, monotonies, themes, to put me smack in the middle of the stream of Great American Literature. I float on my gilded barge like a Doge; and marry if not the sea then the Mississippi with a ring.

STANTON, 1978:   Are you under the influence of Jonathan Swift? You don't employ his famous style, but your aims are similar and the methods used to obtain them are also parallel. He, too, spoke in several voices, wrote through the use of many personas, revealed the truth by distorting, posing, fabricating, and mimicking. He also was a great social reformer who kicked abstractions, speculations, equivocations, and complacencies in the ass—excuse me, *asses.* Like you, he was a master of the contemporary scene and yet was himself strange, unpredictable, and solitary. He, too, was a man of the world who attacked hypocrisy, banality, the fleeting and trivial. Each of you is the great destroyer of Puritanism, and literary pretentiousness, and political ineptness. Most of all, each makes great fun of things.

VIDAL: I haven't read a line of Swift in thirty years but if you can make a connection, why not? Certain types of mind recur from time to time and that seems to me to be an interesting critical task . . . to spot the sudden return of Sarah Orne Jewett, say, in the rich pages of Brautigan. Anyway, like Swift, I see the Yahoos at the door, at the window, coming down the chimney. It's all their game now.

EUGENE WALTER, 1960:   Have you consciously designed the different pitch, or tone, of each of the books?

VIDAL: It comes out of the subject and out of oneself at the time. I am a dry clown who has often miscast himself in the drama; when I've gone wrong in novels it has usually been that my view was not, simply, the useful one for the subject. . . . It seems to me, when I am playwriting seriously, that I'm not writing. Yet the emotional concentration is the same. Final relief is more gratifying, yet it's like doing charades. Cousin germane to prose yet not prose.

MICHAEL S. LASKY, 1975: On a different track, you talked about how you had trouble with *Julian.* I would think you would have had unusual problems in the way you styled it, as you did with letters and diaries?

VIDAL: Actually, it was kind of a relief to do it that way. It would have been much more difficult as a third-person narrative. They are the most difficult to write. First-person books are the easiest to write and the hardest to do well.

LASKY: Why is that?

VIDAL: Because any writer can do it and appear to have achieved a plus. And you [are able to] slough over what you can't handle. The most difficult thing in writing is to describe something—whether it be an emotion or, quite literally, a table. Very few writers are good enough to do this. The first person removes the need for description. In fact this is what the New Journalism does. You go on and on to excessive length: it's all cheated and has a kind of immediacy, the same way that [the gossip columnist] Earl Wilson has. But to really make something of it you have to create a character outside yourself. The last third-person novel I wrote was *Washington, D.C.* and that gave me an awful lot of trouble—the business of playing the omniscient author and yet not intruding in the best Jamesian tradition. I found that very difficult.

I've gotten into the habit now of using first person. I ought to start using something else. I have even used [simultaneously] several first persons . . . to make contrapuntal effects, to comment on my text. There are no original statements—only additions that matter. . . . That is why revising is so interesting. The more you go over a text the more you find that you have to add or subtract. . . . Most of our writers just give you their first wild rush and assume that because it comes from *them* it is valuable. This is the romantic fallacy of the bad writer.

STANTON, 1979:   Do you have any opinion about the work of editors?

VIDAL: I have had no experience at all with the Max Perkins kind of editor. I write the books. Give them to the publisher. The text is copy read carefully (if not by the publisher by a copyeditor that I pay myself). The historical novels are gone over by historians—the advantage of Random House as a publisher is that they publish so many history text books and know to whom to give what to read.

STANTON, 1979:   What narrative point of view did you choose for your new novel about the Golden Age of Greece? Why?

VIDAL: Since my protagonist is, in effect, answering Herodotus, the form is not unlike Herodotus's own first person narrative . . . he tells us this and that, more or less at random. But since my character is a Persian who wants to give the Persian view of what he calls the *Greek* wars, the tone is somewhat acid. . . . Also, as the grandson of Zoroaster, when he meets in his travels Confucius and the Buddha and any number of other religious figures as well as every sort of philosopher, he is somewhat cool—to say the least. The ultimate irony is that he is interested not in religion but in trade, and serving his close friend and exact contemporary Xerxes the Great King.

STANTON, 1978:   Because you have been writing more than thirty years, and have been very successful, you have had time to reflect on your importance as an artist. What "rank" do you belong to? Who are your artistic peers?

VIDAL: I'm now so un-American that I don't think in terms of the Great American Novel or this year's rating of Important Novelists and am I one, two, three or off the list? Of contemporaries I feel . . . *enforced* by Burgess, Calvino, Nabokov, Golding . . . perhaps Fowles, Isherwood, Bowles. I've just finished reading *Henry Esmond* for the first time and as much as I like the unfashionable Thackeray I couldn't help but think how much better I do that sort of book than he does. *Burr, Julian, 1876* are better than *Esmond* and quite as good, in somewhat different ways, as *Vanity Fair*. This recent reading is the first time that I have ever consciously compared a dead master to myself. I don't think much about the living because I'm not that attentive. I deeply dislike the writers of Romances (Melville, Hawthorne, Faulkner), despite their great gifts. The windy obscurity of so much American literature derives from the windy obscurities of so much of the beautiful but often opaque King James version of the Bible. Our Serious Solemn Writers are the result of a religious tradition whose central dogmas (the trinity, for instance) make no sense at all. Therefore, in order to make sense of the nonsensical, a vague windy periphrastic style is all to the good. Serious Solemn Folk (most Americans) feel positively sanctified by rolling, roiling sentences that contain perfect confusions posing as mysteries. Just like a good sermon. Currently, the University-novel is the embodiment of the quack religio-style. Written in what I call Near-English, these books can only be understood by diagrams on blackboards, helped out by commentaries as clumsy as the texts examined. But then clarity has never been admired in the great republic, possibly because everyone has always been so busy conning everyone else—usually in the style of the evangelicals (rabbis, too—and their spin-offs the mental therapists), who peddle the incredible in a language that will only yield its meaning if you have Faith—or tenure.

STANTON, 1977: Hawthorne wrote to an Ideal Reader, and he described that reader. What is your Reader like? Is he the same as your TV viewer? By the way, when do you plan to be on TV again?

VIDAL: My ideal reader would doubtless resemble Mrs. Woolf's Common Reader. But in the age of TV such concepts as reader begin to fade. I have no plans to be on TV soon. I've pretty much decided not to make any appearances when *Kalki* is published in March [1978]; the press will be a bit worse than usual; and I don't like talking about books . . . something I can avoid when the subject is history/politics like *1876* but not when entirely invented like *Kalki.* *

STANTON, 1977:   Virginia Woolf's *Common Reader*. Are you referring to her essay "How Should One Read a Book?" Your ideal reader, then, is one who loves to read, who can bring great sympathy as well as great severity to the task of reading? One who can banish all preconceptions before the act of reading takes place? The ideal reader is one "capable not only of great fineness of perception, but of great boldness of imagination"?

VIDAL: Yes, I like Mrs. Woolf's essay; and concept. But anyone publishing in the U.S. has not a clue as to who reads what or why or at what level. The tone of voice of my essays is close to the tone of my own conversation and that, I suppose, is what an essay should try to do . . . a talking on the page, an argument with a text, or an idea. As for novels. . . . well, my popularity is a marvelous mistake. Admittedly, only ten percent of the population reads novels and of the ten per cent only three, four (I am now guessing) can bring to bear upon a text much knowledge of anything—especially of words. The simplest (to me) words are no longer familiar to most readers. Finally, to be popular, you must share the same prejudices and superstitions of your readers. Either I share more of those prejudices and superstitions than I suspect or the two or three per cent of the population that read me are as opposed to the views of the majority as I am. Anyway, this is not a problem for me but for critics—or sociologists.

---

* As it proved, the press was "a bit worse than usual" and I made very few television appearances. [G.V., 1979]

STANTON, 1977:   C. P. Snow said that he is happy to be an English writer rather than an American one because an English writer knows his audience whereas an American is never quite sure. Do you have a clear idea of your audience?

VIDAL: No, I don't have an idea of an audience in America; I do in England. That's why, if I had to, I would be English rather than American. Fortunately, I don't have to choose; and live in Italy.

MICHAEL S. LASKY, 1975:   What type of feedback do you get from your readers? Do you get a lot of mail?

VIDAL: Not as much as you might think. Not as much as I used to, anyway. I don't think anybody is reading any more. Sales [are] large but mail from paperbacks is very little—I have never understood why.

LASKY: How about hardcovers?

VIDAL: Twice as much. [On] a hardcover that sells 20,000, you can expect a couple of hundred letters, but with a paperback that sells a million you'll get fifty.

STANTON, 1979:   I doubt that you care much for the opinion of others, especially when they attempt to challenge your unpopular beliefs. Do people still try to convince you to change your ways?

VIDAL: Those who love Jesus spend a lot of time writing me hate letters. In fact, the most mail that I ever got was the result of a Phil Donahue television program. I said that I was an atheist. A spasm of hatred went through the Bible belt . . . I think a metaphor is beginning to mix. The next largest response was when, *pro bono publico,* on the Tonight Show, bored with the usual chat about oneself and this and that, I demonstrated—or rather revealed—the workings of a waterless toilet invented in Sweden. People were really interested. Jesus and toilets. Well.

STANTON, 1979:   How many letters do you get after the

publication of an "invention" novel? A historical "medita-
tion" novel? A book of essays?

VIDAL: *Myra Breckinridge* occasioned a flood of letters—including several from trans-sexualists. One sent me a
series of photographs of the various stages of the operation
that had freed her from the masculine principle. Mine is a
strong stomach. Historical novels almost always bring forth
what I call "the relatives": Adamses, Harrisons, Burrs all write
to me. These letters are often very interesting.

MICHAEL S. LASKY, 1975:   Do you sense that your intel-
lectualizing sometimes goes above your readers so that it loses
its intrinsic value?

VIDAL: Well a book exists on many different levels.
Half the work of a book is done by the reader—the more he
can bring to [the text] the better the book will be for him, the
better it will be in its own terms.

LASKY: How do you make people care what you
think?

VIDAL: I have no idea how I do it. I'm often surprised
that I *do* do it. . . . It's been a mystery to me why they read
me. I provide them with no comfort. I also note that I am not
the least bit popular with the young which I think is correct.
What I do is really disturbing to them and often very off-put-
ting. Whether it's sexual matters or intellectual matters, they
[tend to be] romantic and slightly soupy and they want their
self-pity, which is enormous, to be . . . cherished. So they
withdraw to the softsweet writers like Hesse or to the lazy,
fun-writers like Vonnegut. My kind of shock is, I think, really
kind of horrifying to them.

STANTON, 1979:   Do students read your works?

VIDAL: At the universities there are now Vidal cells.
They must keep out of sight, of course. This is the Age of
Barthing. But, I *think* they begin to proliferate.

MICHAEL S. LASKY, 1975:   Are you surprised that people are interested in reading what you have to say?

VIDAL: Astonished! It's [also] more mystifying than pleasurable. Since [most of our readers are now] page-readers, not line-readers, I can't help but think that there is something I am doing that's very wrong.

3

Inventions and Meditations

EUGENE WALTER, 1960:   . . . When did you first publish?

VIDAL: In the *Exeter Review,* of which I was an editor. I published three stories before I graduated in June 1943; went into the Army, July, 1943, was sent to Army [Special] Training [Program] at V.M.I. for one term, where I wrote part of . . . [a] novel. The writer I had read and studied and chosen for my model was—this may surprise you, but then I was an unworldly seventeen!—Somerset Maugham. I had also met, in the bridge-playing world of my mother, Michael Arlen who knew Maugham, so the novel I was trying to write was really *Cakes and Ale* all over again, with Maugham instead of Hardy, Arlen instead of Hugh Walpole, and myself as Maugham writing it. It was a beautifully weary book, in what is now the grand tradition of adolescent novel-writing.

WALTER: You must have started *Williwaw* about then . . .

VIDAL: Well, let's see: when I left V.M.I. I was dumped into the infantry, and then got into the Air Force, then into crash boats, then passed an examination as a First Mate, knowing nothing of navigation save what I learned from memorizing a book on the subject. Finally I was sent to the Aleutian Islands as First Mate of the F.S. 35. Fortunately, it was so foggy that no one ever discovered I couldn't set a course. We relied on point-to-point navigation: a symbol? Anyway, up there making a regular run between Chernowski Bay and Dutch Harbor, in December, 1944, I wrote half of *Williwaw* in pencil in a grey ledger marked *Accounts*. . . . Meanwhile, I had slyly contracted arthritis, was hospitalized in [Van Nuys, California]. After, I was sent to Florida to train 18-year-olds. One night alone in headquarters—I was officer of the day—there was [a] hurricane warning, and everything was shuttered against the coming storm—I had just seen Boris Karloff in the *Isle of the Dead*—that night I finished *Williwaw*.

WALTER: How did *Williwaw* come to be published?

VIDAL: I first took the novel and a bunch of poems to Roger Linscott at Random House who liked the poems but wouldn't read the novel because it was in longhand. He seemed to lack dedication. But I had the book typed. There was a woman doing a life of Amelia Earhart, and when she came to interview my father, who had known the flyer, I showed her the manuscript. She suggested I take it to Nicholas Wreden of Dutton's. I did and we got on well; he said he'd publish it, and offered me a job when I got out of the Army. I worked at Dutton six months, until *Williwaw* came out in [June], 1946, and I quit on the strength of the notices. Couldn't stand going to an office. I have never gone to an office since. . . . [Movie studios don't count.]

STANTON, 1979:   Do you know that the first edition of *Williwaw* is now a collector's item which currently sells for $40?

VIDAL: Often—if in mint condition—a good deal more.

PARIS REVIEW, 1974:   You once said that the test of a good work, or a perfect work, is whether the author can reread it without embarrassment. How did you feel when you reread your early books?

VIDAL: . . . Rereading *Williwaw*, I was struck by the coolness of the prose. There is nothing in excess. I am still impressed by the young writer's control of this very small material. When I prepared the last edition, I don't suppose I cut away more than a dozen sentences. The next book, on the other hand, *In a Yellow Wood,* is in limbo forever. I can't rewrite it because it's so bad that I can't reread it. The effect, I fear, of meeting and being "ensorcelled" by Anaïs Nin. Or Jack London meets Elinor Glynn. Wow!

PARIS REVIEW: What about your first "successful" novel, *The City and the Pillar?*

VIDAL: A strange book because it was, as they say, "the first of its kind," without going into any great detail as to what its kind is. To tell such a story then was an act of considerable moral courage. Unfortunately, it was not an act of very great artistic courage since I chose deliberately to write in the flat, gray, naturalistic style of James T. Farrell. Tactically if not aesthetically, this was for a good reason. Up until then homosexuality in literature was always exotic: Firbank, on the one hand; green carnations, on the other. I wanted to deal with an absolutely ordinary, all-American, lower-middle-class young man and his world. To show the dead-on "normality" of the homosexual experience. Unfortunately, I didn't know too many lower-middle-class, all-American young men—except for those years in the Army when I spent a good deal of time blocking out my fellow soldiers. So I made it all up. But the result must have had a certain authenticity. Tennessee Williams read it in 1948 and said of the family scenes, "Our fathers were very much alike." He was surprised when I told him that Jim Willard and his family were all invented. Tennessee also said, "I don't like the ending. I don't think you realized what a good book you had written." At the time, of course, I thought the ending "powerful."

PARIS REVIEW: Now you've changed the ending to have the young man—Bob—not killed by Jim as he was originally.

VIDAL: Yes. Twenty years ago it was thought that I had written a tragic ending because the publishers felt that the public would not accept a happy resolution for my tale of Sodom, my Romeo and his Mercutio. But this wasn't true. The theme of the book which, as far as I know, no critic has ever noticed, is revealed in the title. . . . Essentially, I was writing about the romantic temperament. Jim Willard is so overwhelmed by a first love affair that he finds all other lovers wanting. He can only live in the past, as he imagined the past; or in the future as he hopes it will be when he finds Bob again. He has no present. So whether the first love object is a boy or a girl is not really all that important. The novel was not about the City so much as about the Pillar of Salt, the looking back that destroys. Nabokov handled this same theme [with infinitely greater elegance] in *Lolita.* But I was only twenty when I made my attempt while he was half as old as Time. Anyway, my story could only have had a disastrous ending. Obviously, killing Bob was a bit much even though the original narrative was carefully vague on that point. Did he or didn't he kill him? Actually, what was being killed was the idea of perfect love that had existed only in the romantic's mind. The other person—the beloved object—had forgotten all about it.

JUDY HALFPENNY, 1976: I still find it funny that *The City and the Pillar* should have been taken as autobiography. There must be more fantasy invented on the subject of sex than on any three other subjects combined; but whenever someone sits down to write about it he's assumed to have no other resource than his own experience. People are very odd.

VIDAL: I think no one has ever made enough (or anything) of the fact that I was brought up a Southerner. In Washington D.C. and "neighboring nearby Virginia," boys mature early, slip with the greatest of ease (most of them) into bisexuality, which ends (for most of them) with Manhood and Marriage. I told Jules Feiffer that the beginning of *Carnal Knowledge* would have been truer to life if, when after we hear the two roommates in college discussing tits, et al., in the dark, the lights were to come on and show them making love. Jules was horrified. No. Never. Apparently Jews never do this sort of thing unless they are going to be queens. It's also a class thing, he added nervously. Maybe so. Unfortunately between school-teaching and book-chat—and psychiatry—the homophobes have pretty well poisoned the atmosphere in the land of the free.

Oui, 1975:   Certainly some of the reviews of . . . *The City and the Pillar* were less than generous, to say the least.

Vidal: I took the attacks as a compliment. After all, the two books prior to *The City and the Pillar* were extremely well reviewed. I was the first of the war novelists and much overpraised. Then came *The City and the Pillar* in 1948, when I was twenty-three. With an axe, I took on the heterosexual dictatorship of the country. The panic and the rage and the resentment that this caused still reverberate. . . . The book-chat world doesn't mind a faggot who comes on like a cripple. When Tennessee moans and groans about how decadent he is and how he's going to die tomorrow anyway because he's been spitting blood all morning, well, how can you hit this poor gallant old thing? Or Truman, who comes on like Cousin Hetty from Kansas. But for the "tough" war novelist to say I'm here to challenge the heterosexual dictatorship and before I'm finished with you, you're going to accept the homosexual act as being equal to the hetero—well, that challenge to the sexual mores of the uptight American male was and is unforgivable. If you don't honor him for the desperate battle he's fought to be a heterosexual, you might just as well cut his powells off, as Myra would say. After all, the only thing a great many American men have to be proud of is being heterosexual.

Judy Halfpenny, 1979:   You are represented in Roger Austen's depressing catalogue, *Playing the Game*, only by *The City and the Pillar*—if you hadn't written that book someone would have had to invent it.

Vidal: Austen is dull; I think he's not had much of a life and the fag ghetto is a grim place to spend a life. I have an allergy to fag-novels; most of the books he mentions are unknown to me or known by reputation like *Giovanni's Room* which I couldn't get through. After the meeting in the coach house between Lucien de Rubempré and Vautrin,* it's been down hill.

MICHAEL S. LASKY, 1975:   Were you trying to affect some sort of sexual revolution with *The City and the Pillar?*

VIDAL: I don't think that was exactly in my mind at the time but I did want to establish very firmly the parity between hetero and homosexual acts.... [In] 1948 [this] was just about as stunning as anything you could have proposed to people. But I knew what the response would be. And as a matter of fact, the "sexual revolution" did begin around then, and I certainly did my bit. Actually, a book that came out six months later did far more than I did—it was the *Kinsey Report.*

LASKY: I'm surprised that the publisher took on this book of yours at all.

VIDAL: Well, I was a pretty important writer then—of the young ones.... They didn't like it, and they told me so. But [the book] ended up a considerable bestseller for those days.

EUGENE WALTER, 1960:   What effect did the publication of the book have on your life, literary and personal?

VIDAL: Let me take a deep breath and tell you. First, I was at the time the author of two books embarrassingly admired—embarrassingly because I was under twenty-one and newspaper praise is a false thing at best, though, I suspect now, preferable to blame. I was the Huck Finn of the younger novelists, photographed against ships for *Life Magazine,* boyishly scowling. I seemed as safe as . . . who? Herman Wouk? I was in the running. Then came the bomb: *The City and the Pillar.* I remember I read it through once before it was sent to the printer, and I thought that if I ever read it again I'd never publish it . . . so I sent back a hardly-corrected proof. Then the re-

---

* Vidal refers to two characters from Balzac's *Comédie Humaine.*

views, what few there were, began and I discovered what happens in America if you tamper with the fragile—people avert their eyes, and go on talking. Half my former admirers did not review it at all. *The New York Times* refused to advertise it—and when the publishers took the matter directly to Mr. Sulzberger, he decided to uphold his censor. Of the reviews received, a few were thoughtful and lengthy, most quite bad. Two words popped up to haunt that book, and all my writing ever since: "clinical" and "sterile." "Clinical" is used whenever one writes of relationships which are not familiar—I dare say that if the story had dealt with a boy and a girl instead of two boys the book would have been characterized as "lyrical." "Sterile" is an even deadlier curse upon the house, and comes from a dark syllogism in the American *zeitgeist:* the homosexual act does not produce children and therefore is sterile; Mr. X's book is concerned with the homosexual act and therefore the book is sterile. (This syllogism was first proposed by the Russians when they turned on André Gide and it used to be a standard Stalinist line). . . . Aesthetically, the book was very youthful, very naïve, hasty but "felt," and I suppose in a way that the rudeness of its execution was part of its strength and the reason why it goes on year after year being read. . . .

WALTER: Interesting, . . . how *The City and the Pillar* was considered scandalous in America, and considered a moral work in Europe.

VIDAL: I am . . . a moralistic writer in a very American way. I seem always to be writing about a moral choice and . . . well, that's for the critics to worry about.

MICHAEL S. LASKY, 1975: You wrote it in Guatemala. What the hell were you doing there?

VIDAL: The war ended and I wanted to get out of America to think. This was 1946 and Europe hadn't opened up yet so I started south. I got as far as Guatemala where I found an old monastery, a beautiful 16th-century ruin which I fixed up and lived in off and on for three years. . . .

JUDY HALFPENNY, 1978:   Your novel *Dark Green, Bright Red* (1950) seems like an episode rather than a complete-in-itself story.

VIDAL: *Dark Green, Bright Red* has a mystery at its center and I never defined it, which is always a mistake. I was working with a notion of history as being nothing more than a random chain of irrelevancies, but somehow I forgot to bring into focus the theme.

EUGENE WALTER, 1960:   The historical romance, *A Search for the King,* how did that pop up in the list of your books?

VIDAL: A *jeu d'esprit.* I like the fabulous, the invented, and I dislike repeating myself. I am not captive to one region nor to one unflinching attitude toward life. I am always conscious that we live, in Sir Thomas Browne's phrase—"in divided and distinguished worlds," and I should never be so presumptuous as to say finally, "That is it!"

PARIS REVIEW, 1974:   You have said that *The Judgment of Paris* is your favorite of the early books.

VIDAL: It was the first book I wrote when I settled in on the banks of the Hudson River for what proved to be twenty years of writing, my Croisset.... Certainly *The Judgment of Paris* was the novel in which I found my own voice. Up until then I was very much in the American realistic tradition, unadventurous, monochromatic, haphazard in my effects. My subjects were always considerably more interesting than what I was able to do with them. This is somewhat the reverse of most young writers, particularly young writers today.

JUDY HALFPENNY, 1976:   In the final part of *The Judgment of Paris* you tell the story of a character named Jim. Is this the story of what happens to Jim Willard, the main character found in *The City and the Pillar?* I wish you would confirm this, as it makes a difference to my view of *The City and the Pillar.*

VIDAL: Yes, that was Jim Willard from *The City and the Pillar.* High romantics who fall from the heights make very good drug addicts. I suppose, unconsciously, I was grafting onto him . . . some characteristics of a marvelous Southern whore named Denham Foutts, whom I describe in "Pages From an Abandoned Journal" and Isherwood describes in "Down There on a Visit" and Capote, our literature's Suzy, makes a hash of in the current *Esquire* [in an excerpt from *Answered Prayers*].

STANTON, 1977:   Have you written anything anonymously?

VIDAL: Not that I can think of.

MICHAEL S. LASKY, 1975:   Can you tell me something about your Edgar Box mysteries? I mean how did you come to write them in the first place—they seem so out of league with the rest of your work . . .

VIDAL: I was broke, the usual reason for writing mysteries. Unless you regard them as a high art form as do the creators of a recent Who's Who in detective fiction. . . . I wrote all three mysteries [*Death in the Fifth Position* (1952), *Death Before Bedtime* (1953), and *Death Likes It Hot* (1954)] in 1951 and 1952. I was actually at a very low ebb in my life then.

LASKY: Do you regret having written them now?

VIDAL: Oh no, I think they are very funny. I pick one up in an airport every now and then and read it and see I've completely forgotten it. They were the idea of New American Library (Signet) which was the big paperback publisher then. And although they wouldn't do much for *my* books because by then I was thought of as much too outrageous or high brow, they said what we really need is a sort of elegant, witty version—and yet totally unlike—Mickey Spillane, then the popular writer. I wrote each of them in about seven days. That was 10,000 words a day. I rather enjoyed it until the last one in which something came up [his house was burning down] and when I went back to [the story] I couldn't remember who was supposed to have done the murder, couldn't detect any of the clues. They are not what you call beautifully-made mysteries—they are full of loose ends. Stylistically though, I think they are very funny.

STANTON, 1977: Did you write any articles for your newspaper, *The Hyde Park Townsman?*

VIDAL: None.

MICHAEL LASKY, 1975: In looking over your biography, I see that you wrote lyrics for one of the great Broadway composers, Vincent Youmans.

VIDAL: Where did you find *that?* Yeah, I did lyrics for two songs of his. I started out thinking I was a poet as do most prose writers. And the best prose writers turn out to be the worst poets and I was no exception. . . . My mother was living at the Beverly Hills Hotel [where Youmans was dying]. Youmans was lonely and one day he asked me if I would write lyrics. So I tried. [I've forgotten the result.]

STANTON, 1977: Do you recall their titles?

VIDAL: No, they were never published. My copies were lost during the war—my foot-locker vanished between Dutch Harbor and Van Nuys, California.

PARIS REVIEW, 1974: In your novel *Messiah* . . .

VIDAL: I didn't know the end of the book when I started writing. Yet when I got to the last page I suddenly wrote "I was he whom the world awaited" and it was all at once clear to me that the hidden meaning of the story was the true identity of the narrator which had been hidden from him, too. *He* was the messiah who might have been. When I saw this coming out upon the page, I shuddered . . . knew awe, for I had knocked both Huxley and Orwell out of the ring. Incidentally, ninety per cent of your readers will not detect the irony in my boxing metaphor. And there is nothing to be done about it.

PARIS REVIEW: Except for me to interject that you are

playing off the likes of Hemingway and Mailer in the use of them. Shall I go on?

VIDAL: [No].

STANTON, 1978:   The "critical" reaction to *Messiah* was lukewarm, at best. Would you be willing to urge people to re-read it again? What's the most interesting thing about it to you?

VIDAL: *Messiah*'s history as a book is astonishing. The reviews were not only bad but very few—in the U.S. Several good ones from England: *Sunday Times,* a letter from Edith Sit-well, *Tatler* review by Elizabeth Bowen. One translation, I think, into Danish. But the paperback edition by Ballantine sold and sold year after year. The book was a favorite with the likes of Alice Cooper, I think. I suppose the fact that Ballantine made the book look like science-fiction helped. Few people can be got to read A Novel. After *Hair,* Michael Butler Productions bought the film rights; prepared a couple of bad scripts; the rights then reverted to me; just sold them again this week [in June, 1978]. In the last year the book has appeared or has been contracted for in French, Italian, Spanish, German, Swedish and Hebrew. I have no idea why. It's not in print at the moment in the U.S., but jogs along in the United Kingdom Panther edition. Something is going on but I don't fathom it. I've not reread the book since whenever it was [in 1965] I revised the early books . . . I don't think I much altered *Messiah.* . . .

STANTON, 1978:   Have you read Theodore Ziolkowski's *Fictional Transfigurations of Jesus* (Princeton University Press, 1972)? He presents an interesting view of your *Messiah*. It is seen as a "Fifth Gospel," a rich parody of the Jesus story; "in fact, it is an analogue to the entire New Testament, including specifically the Acts of the Apostles and Paul's Epistles. In all of this parody, however, . . . there is little sense that Chris-tianity itself is being attacked or ridiculed. . . . Filtered through the moral neutralism of Gore Vidal, the fictional transfiguration has become aesthetic play." Any response?

VIDAL: Never heard of Ziolkowski's work. He's right that I was making a parody of the Jesus Christ story. My dislike of Christianity is well known but, perhaps, he is right about my "moral neutralism." I don't take overt moral stands in the novels. Characters evolve; they are shown in this light, that shadow. Perhaps the reason that bookchatterers are so uneasy with my "unreal" characters is that I don't take obvious moralizing positions, don't work in crude American crayon (call me Melville).

STANTON, 1978:   What about *Julian?*

VIDAL: I have my own self-interview on it.

STANTON, 1978:   Go ahead.

VIDAL, 1965:   So, Mr. Vidal, when did you first become interested in the Emperor Julian?

VIDAL: Reading Gibbon twenty years ago. Julian was a hero to Gibbon and the idea of writing about Julian occurred to me as long ago as 1952. . . . While preparing a new edition of . . . *Messiah,* I was startled to find that one of the characters in the book had contemplated writing a biography of Julian the Apostate. But he gave it up because "the human attractive part of Julian was undone for me by those bleak errors in deed and in judgment which depressed me even though they derived most logically from the man and his time: that fatal wedding which finally walls off figures of earlier ages from the present, keeping them strange despite the most intense and imaginative recreation. They are not we. We are not they. And I refuse to resort to the low trick of fashioning Julian in my own image of him. I respected his integrity in time and deplored the division of the centuries."

I nearly imitated my own creation and abandoned the project, but for different reasons. In 1954 I began to write plays for television, films, theatre. I also became active in politics. Now we all know that a serious and important writer in America is one who seriously and importantly tills the same ground year after year until, weather permitting, there is a splendid harvest which nourishes us all. From William Faulkner to Saul Bellow, this is a most respectable way of being a writer. But there are other ways of getting the thing done. Some of us are driven to use many means to attain ends quite as obsessive and singular as those achieved by the writers who stayed home and wrote, as Flaubert used to say of himself, quoting Horace. Where a writer like [Faulkner] is an hereditary farmer, I am more a Johnny Appleseed, moving restlessly about the world, planting trees wherever I think they are needed ... which rather exhausts that bucolic metaphor.

VIDAL, 1965:   While you were busy as a dramatist, did you continue to think about Julian?

VIDAL: Yes, I made notes for years. There is a good deal of source material about Julian. Three volumes of his own writing exist, and there are half a dozen contemporary accounts of his life. In the course of a decade of reading, I became more at home in the fourth century, and to do a man's life it is necessary to know the time perhaps better than the man, because the character you finally create will be a work of your own imagination, and that is why, paradoxically, one must not be free with facts. By remaining absolutely accurate in detail, one can invent a good deal in spirit. By 1959, I thought I was ready to write the book. I composed the first two chapters. Then I got the idea for a play called *The Best Man* and that gave me the idea of running for Congress, and otherwise contributing to the merriment of the nation. Once more, the novel was postponed, although on a visit to Athens in 1961 I wrote the Athenian chapter, as part of my delighted first response to Greece. Finally, suspecting that I might never finish the novel, I moved to Rome in 1962 and the book was written.

VIDAL, 1965:   Why did you write an historical novel?

VIDAL: I've noticed that question usually means: Why write about the past since most people dislike reading about the past? We are the most self-regarding of generations.

We lust to read about ourselves and our neighbors and what happened last summer. John O'Hara outsells Robert Graves two thousand to one. So why bore readers with the unfamiliar and the old? The obvious answer is that one writes novels largely to please oneself. Also, in my case, I'm interested in history for its own sake, though it is usual to pretend that in reading history we will find lessons from which we can profit today. For instance, the American conservative firmly believes that Rome fell because of a Decline in Moral Values.... History, of course, is not all that easy.

Rome fell for a variety of reasons. The best and most cogent was, simply, a flaw in their political system. They were never able to devise a means of orderly succession. Whenever an emperor died, there was apt to be a struggle for his place. By the time Julian became Augustus, the Roman Empire had been dangerously weakened by a series of wars of succession. The barbarians took advantage of this state of affairs and slowly engulfed civilization. Incidentally, we should never forget that we are the descendants of the barbarians, *not* of the civilized. Today there is a similar situation in the Soviet Union, though we cannot say that it will work itself out in precisely the same manner. Yet it is true that the Soviet Union has not achieved a viable method of succession, and it is possible that in time this flaw in its system will bring it down.

In reading history, fictionalized or not, there is a certain value in seeing a period of time at a great distance as a story that is entirely told ... and familiar. After all, a desire for power is the same at any time, and so are most human responses. André Malraux once remarked that if Napoleon Bonaparte and Rameses the Second were to meet, in limbo, though they were separated in time by several thousand years, they would have more to say to one another than either would have had to say to a contemporary who kept a shop. As emperors, they would have discussed the police, agriculture, bureaucracy, and their points of view would be much the same.

Julian himself would feel quite at home in the White House or the Kremlin, though I am not so sure that the present occupants would feel very easy with him. After all, Julian was a reformer, and reformers don't often become chiefs of state.

As for the Age of Julian, it is perfectly fascinating. In fact, without some understanding of what happened then, it is impossible to have a clear idea of what Christianity is and how it came into being. And if we do not understand Christianity, then we cannot make much sense of the world we live in, because our society, morally and intellectually, for good and ill, is the result of that great force. At a series of Ecumenical Councils during Julian's lifetime, the Trinity was invented as well as the Doctrine of the Holy Ghost and the beginning of the Cult of Mary. All these things were hammered out in a series of stormy conventions, and there was much violence. In fact, the murderous instincts of Christian absolutism first emerged in the fourth century. And I do not think it an exaggeration to say that over the centuries, Christianity has been responsible for more bloodshed than any other force in Western life. It was a fourth-century man who remarked with a certain awe that "not even the wild beasts of the field are as savage to one another as the Christians."

VIDAL, 1965:   What is the point of revealing all this now?

VIDAL: Because if one does not understand how Christian absolutists behaved with—say—the Incas, Aztecs, and Mayas in this hemisphere, with the Jews everywhere, with Africans and Asians, as both conquerors and missionaries, then one will find mystifying the fact that we are so much hated in so many parts of the world, or that the Jews in America tend to be politically liberal, or that Pius XII is being examined so suspiciously by so many observers. To understand what is happening now, one must recall that for centuries Christianity maintained that it was the only true religion and that those who resisted it must be converted or destroyed. Julian, an eager young intellectual, was among the first to counter-attack and though he died at thirty-three, his arguments against the Church are a permanent contribution to a dialogue which still continues. He opposed the Christians because they refused to tolerate the religious views of others. But he did them no violence—for which he was denounced. "You will not even allow us to become martyrs," shouted one furious bishop.

I find Julian an engaging and a good man, even though his own religious views were very peculiar, to say the least. He loved magic, believed in omens, tried to organize every superstition and rite into one grand Hellenic Church, and of course he failed. But had he lived, there is no doubt that Christianity would have been but one of several religions in the West. And this diversity might have saved the world considerable anguish. For one must again make the point that until the Christians appeared, no one was ever persecuted simply because of his religious beliefs. Whenever Rome conquered a new territory, the Roman Emperors immediately paid homage to the local gods and set up temples to them at Rome. It never occurred to anyone that, because a man chose to worship a bull or a ram or a star or the sun, he was wrong and must immediately be converted to something else, even if he had to be killed in the process.

PLAYBOY, 1969:   . . . In writing it, did you discover any similarities between Rome's decline and fall and contemporary American society?

VIDAL: No. But some of the problems the book poses are relevant to both times. For instance, Christianity, with its hatred of the flesh, was repulsive to the civilized man of the Second and Third Centuries, perhaps the most brilliant of Western centuries. But then the Christians, those intellectual barbarians, conquered the civilized and called them pagan and decadent. Our problem today is that we are the children of the barbarians, not of the civilized, and we have only just begun to realize that there are other values than those preached by the savage Saint Paul.

VIDAL, 1965:   How was . . . *Julian* received?

VIDAL: Mysteriously. A number of scholars found the book to be accurate and said so. Unfortunately, the publishers did not get these affidavits to the American reviewers, many of whom could not believe that the facts were right, particularly my account of the religious controversies. Fortunately, by the time the book was published in England, its scholarship had been attested to. . . . My only bad moment occurred on the BBC with a classics don who announced that there were several grave errors in the book. My heart sank.

What, I asked, was the worst error?

"Your reference to the Petulantes as a legion. They were not a legion but an auxiliary to the Palatine legion, as *everyone knows.*"

I promised to make the change in the next edition.

VIDAL, 1965: Is it inhibiting to write a novel while having to bear in mind a thousand facts?

VIDAL: Yes, but one gets used to it. Christopher Isherwood, when he read the book, said, "My God, Gore, how could you write anything without wondering if it was true? I mean there you'd be describing a bird in a garden and suddenly there would be that awful question in your mind, did they have birds in the fourth century?"

But after ten years of reading, I found myself reasonably at home in that strange period, and of course, there were birds in those gardens. The trick was to see them plain through the footnotes. As the writing of the book finally came to an end, I must say I felt not the usual relief at having completed a difficult task, but a certain melancholy that the thing was done. Yet the result exists, and I can now echo the words of a Renaissance historian when someone asked him why he bothered to write about old things. "To make the past live," he said. "That is, to my mind, a congenial occupation."

MONIQUE VAN VOOREN, 1976: If you were making a movie of *Julian* who would you pick as Julian?

VIDAL: Albert Finney. And I think he'd like to do it, too. He likes the book and I've talked to him about it.

STANTON, 1977: Was *Julian* ever produced as a film?

VIDAL: *Julian* has been bought or optioned several times as a film; once for Peter O'Toole; but never made.

PARIS REVIEW, 1974: What about writing in the third person?

VIDAL: I wonder if it is still possible—in the sense that Henry James used it. *Washington, D.C.* was my last attempt to write a book like that—and I rather admire *Washington, D.C.* [But] the third person imposed a great strain on me, the constant maneuvering of so many consciousnesses through the various scenes while trying to keep the focus right. It was like directing a film on location with a huge cast in bad weather.

STANTON, 1978: What makes you so fond of *Washington, D.C.* and *The Judgment of Paris?*

VIDAL: *Washington, D.C.* seems to me to have a certain magic, as does *Judgment.* There is a sense of devoured time recalled in reverie. The houses in *Washington, D.C.* are my grandfather's place in Rock Creek Park (Burden Day's house) and Merrywood in Virginia (Blaise's house). I do the houses well. The characters *could* be my family but I don't work that closely from actual people. The atmosphere is authentic; those summer days when we wore white suits. The moral dilemma is exquisite and no reviewer (including John Kenneth Galbraith) got it. Burden Day's sell-out for a higher good: the saving of the republic from FDR. Recently, Joseph Kraft did a piece in the *New Yorker;* he thought mine the best of Washington novels in this century. I think he's right. I also prefer it to *Democracy* [by Henry Adams] which, in some ways, inspired my efforts. To show things the way they really are confounds the American. *Judgment* I like because it is now "historical" though it was a contemporary novel in the late '40s when I wrote it. The prose came to life for the first time in any of my novels. Voice was found.

JUDY HALFPENNY, 1976: I like *Washington, D.C.* because it's so exotic.

VIDAL: I can see how it would be exotic to you. What astonished me is that it should be exotic to the few American critics/book-chatterers who read it. They thought it had to be fantasy because they have never met the country's rulers and cannot believe that anyone but a Harold Robbins or Drury would want to even guess at the way they are. Clay was—is—somewhat close to JFK. Camelot thought what I had done was Bad Taste (their favorite pejorative phrase—as it was Myra's). Jack's war exploits were somewhat invented and totally inflated (Dunkirk as victory sort of thing). Burden Day's dilemma is the most interesting problem I have ever posed; no solution.

FAG RAG, 1974:   One of the delightful things about rereading your work is finding clues for one book in another. For example, the boy Peter, in *Washington, D.C.,* mentions that there was a statue of Burr either in his house or in Senator Day's office. Do you remember that?

VIDAL: It was Cicero and they thought it was William Jennings Bryan [at bottom of p. 149].

FAG RAG: No. What Peter wanted to do: it had been suggested to Peter that he do graduate work while continuing to study the life of Aaron Burr.

VIDAL: Did I [write] that?

FAG RAG: Yes [near the top of p. 128].

VIDAL: I was thinking about it then. That was written in 1966. I didn't realize I was thinking about it [*Burr* was published in 1973] that long ago.

JUDY HALFPENNY, 1977:   Will you revise *Washington, D.C.* now that it has two big brothers [i.e., *Burr* and *1876*] to live up to?

VIDAL: Yes, I should revise *WDC* to conform with the other two. At present the only connections are the reference at the beginning to Sanford's death at St. Cloud, I think. Also, the protagonist's (what's his name?) fascination with the career of Burr and desire to write about him; and of course the bullet that goes through the portrait of Burr. Clues to the unconscious mind, I suppose. Burr was obviously in my head for a long time but when I wrote WDC I never thought that I'd write about him. But things do come together. *Burr* was written. Then I saw that I could connect epochs and families by doing a center piece. It was a toss of the coin between Tilden-Hayes and the impeachment of Andrew Johnson. Since the impeachment of Richard Nixon was in the air I backed into the centennial year. I was also fond of Charlie, a loyal witness and cicerone, as Gibbon said of Ammianus Marcellinus.

STANTON, 1977:   Which book has given you the most satisfaction to write?

VIDAL: Probably *Myra.* I have never laughed so much in my life . . . with surprise, too. I've never had the slightest interest in drag queens, trans-sexualists, whatever. Metamorphosis was the name of that game. The moon was new when I started the book. New when it ended.

OUI, 1975:   *Myra* . . . you wrote quickly—*Myron,* also. And then there is *Burr,* a very long study.

VIDAL: Yes, but of the two, *Myra* is not only the better book but also, I think, a part of the history of literature. A lot of people could have written *Burr* or *Julian,* but I am the only American who could have written *Myra.*

OUI: Why?

VIDAL: Because it isn't like any other book that's ever been published in America or anywhere else—as the British critics have noticed. The locals, on the other hand, still think it's a dirty book. I'm afraid it will be years before our bookchat writers figure out that *Myra* is a serious work of art. Fortunately, their opinion matters to no one.

PARIS REVIEW, 1974:   Is it true that you were thinking of putting out *Myra Breckinridge* under a pseudonym?

VIDAL: No. Oh, well, yes. I wanted to make an experiment. To publish a book without reviews or advertising or a well-known author's name. I wanted to prove that a book could do well simply because it was interesting—without the support of bookchat writers. Up to a point, the experiment worked. The book was widely read long before the first reviews appeared. But for the experiment to have been perfect my name shouldn't have been on the book. I didn't think of that till later. Curious. Twenty years ago, after *Messiah* was published, Harvey Breit of *The New York Times* said, "You know, Gore, anything you write will get a bad press in America. Use another name. Or do something else." So for ten years I did something else.

PARIS REVIEW: What do you start with? A character, a plot?

VIDAL: *Myra* began with a first sentence. I was so intrigued by that sentence that I had to go on. Who was she? What did she have to say? A lot, as it turned out. The unconscious mind certainly shaped that book.

PARIS REVIEW: Well, you seem to have had an enormous knowledge of movies for *Myra.* Did you have to go back and research any of that?

VIDAL: I saw all those movies of the forties—in the forties. At school and in the Army. They're seared on my memory. There wasn't anything in the book that I did not see first time around. Also—to help the Ph.D. thesis writers—almost every picture I mentioned can be found in Parker Tyler's *Magic and Myth in the Movies.* A work which has to be read to be believed.

STANTON, 1977:   That style in *Myra Breckinridge,* is it totally yours? Or are you mimicking someone?

VIDAL: I don't know anyone like Myra. That was original if anything can be called original.

MICHAEL DEAN, 1968:   Myra is a figure of fantasy, a sort of glamorous hermaphrodite avenger, who sets out to slay some of the norms and conventions of American life.

VIDAL: I'd be very disturbed by any reader whose libido was disturbed by this book: anybody who really finds this erotic has so many problems that literature should probably not intervene. There is no desire to titillate at all. It's rather graphic sexually, but I don't find it in the least stimulating. I'd much rather that people got the point of my use of old films. Myra believes that between 1939 and 1946 no bad movie was made in Hollywood. Hollywood's been very important. After all, my generation, which is now pleasingly middle-aged, was brought up on the talkies, which were just coming in, and we all think of ourselves, I'd say, in terms of film characters. Though some of us had very nice educations and spent our youth translating Flaubert, it was really Humphrey Bogart we were modelling ourselves on. So Myra's a reflection of the great period of the movies. Hollywood is still with us in every sense. Take the unreality of people nowadays, particularly in the United States, where I see it amongst the young almost everywhere. The desire to dress up, well, what's that, what's it all about? It's a) boredom and b) who am I? what shall I be? Myra says: be everything, change everything. She changes her sex two or three times. She's a sort of Hollywood Bowl Tiresias.

DEAN: André Malraux said the other night on BBC Television that since men have killed God, having first invented him, they're now looking round for human heroes to worship.

VIDAL: And Malraux proposed himself? There's always been this thing of finding in one's own life a certain amount of dullness, a certain amount of redundancy: it doesn't take an extremely brilliant child to walk down a street and realize there are plenty more where he came from. I think that a character like Myra in her strange, mad way goes out to confront this, and decides to save the human race, decides she's the messiah. She comes a cropper.

DEAN: Are you perhaps suggesting through *Myra* that there aren't, or shouldn't be, absolute sexual categories?

VIDAL: Oh I think that's obvious. I think we *start* knowing that, that the categories are imposed by society, that everybody is everything—polymorphic perverse, as Norman O. Brown would say—that this is indeed the common human state. Where you take it from there . . . after all, Myra's very serious about birth control—she believes in any activity which does not lead to the making of redundant personalities.

DEAN: Do you think it might be healthy for us if more of us in fact recognized that we had characteristics of the other sex in us?

VIDAL: Anybody who doesn't recognize that has totally blocked off his or her unconscious. Of course, everybody is everything. But Myra has left that long behind and she's moving into quite another area, quite another arena. She says, in a sense: invent yourself.

PLAYBOY, 1969:   What new horizons do you foresee for that . . . great tribal pleasure, sex? . . . Do you believe the trend would be toward the type of polymorphous transsexuality you exalted in *Myra Breckinridge?*

VIDAL: I exalted neither Myra nor her views. But I do think that if we survive long enough to evolve a rational society, there will be a trend toward bisexuality. For one thing, bisexuality is, quite simply, more interesting than monosexuality. And we are bisexual by nature. The tribe, however, has done its best to legislate our behavior, and this has done an enormous amount of damage. Homosexual behavior is as natural as heterosexual behavior. That it is not the norm is irrelevant. Blue eyes are not the norm in Mexico. If we really insisted that everyone try to conform to that sexual activity that is most practiced at any given moment, then we should have to admit that the statistical norm is neither hetero nor homosexual but onanistic. Myra found group sexuality intriguing, and so do I. It was something our pre-Christian ancestors recognized as a part of man's religious life, as well as a means of pleasure.

PLAYBOY: Your late father reportedly told you that with *Myra Breckinridge* you had gone "too far." How did you answer him?

VIDAL: My father did wonder if perhaps I had gone too far, to which I replied that only by constant skirmishing on the frontier are new territories opened up. Being an inventor and an aviation pioneer, he saw the point to that. Twenty-one years ago, *The City and the Pillar* created a much larger scandal than *Myra.* Now it is wistfully alluded to as a delicate, sensitive book. The scandal of 1948 has become the worthy book of 1969. But the judgments of those who write for newspapers are generally worthless, because journalists are paid to anticipate and exploit the moral prejudices of their readers. If you want to know what the stupider members of the tribe are thinking, read the *Chicago Tribune* or the New York *Daily News.* Their attitudes reflect every sort of ancient superstition and bear no relevance to the world we live in. That's why I enjoy the various underground newspapers. They are dizzy and often dull-witted, but they reflect the living aspects of our civilization as opposed to our tribalism, which is decadent and [let's hope] dying.

PLAYBOY: *Newsweek* charges that *Myra Breckinridge* "becomes in the end, a kind of erotic propaganda" for homosexuality. Is this true—and, if so, is it intentional?

VIDAL: Myra favors *anything* that would limit population, but there is considerable evidence that she dislikes homosexuality. Why else would she have become a woman and fallen in love with Mary Ann? Certainly her depressing reports on the activities of Myron, her alter id, can hardly be called erotic propaganda. Despite her temporary view of herself as a messiah, Myra was never strict; anything goes, she maintained, as long as it doesn't further crowd the world.

MICHAEL DEAN, 1968:   You've written screenplays for Hollywood films that in ideal circumstances you wouldn't have written: you were making money out of them because books weren't enough to live on. Could *Myra* perhaps change this: will you now be able to write what you want, when you want?

VIDAL: Oh but *Myra* is very much what I want to write. I've been in that happy position for the last ten years, so I shall just go right on doing whatever it is that I do. I daresay that as my talents decline, my popularity will soar.

PLAYBOY, 1969:   So far, you've earned more than one million dollars from *Myra*—almost as much as Jacqueline Susann and Harold Robbins have made from the sexy soap operas you satirize in your book. Some critics have charged that you have emulated and exploited that which you purport to condemn. Is there any validity to that?

VIDAL: It is quite true that *Myra* has earned me a great deal of money. If I were to say that I had written it *in order* to make money, I would be immediately understood and absolved of every sin. But at the risk of shocking everyone, I must point out that if I wanted to use writing to make money, I would have settled in Hollywood long ago and bought a chain of Encino supermarkets. I write to make art and change society. That I do either is certainly arguable, but money is not an interest.

MONEY, 1978:   Does sex sell books?

VIDAL: No. Quite the contrary. The most successful books have nothing to do with sex at all. Mind you, there is a kind of ongoing pruriency at the Harold Robbins level, but there is no real sex. It's all just stylized—hinting and snickering. Any novel with a profoundly strong sexual component is immediately unpopular. Just forget about it for the large audience. No book club will touch it. Many bookstores will refuse to stock it. You write instead something like a James Michener book or Irving Stone's *The Agony and the Ecstasy*. You put together a lot of little facts about Michelangelo and it's somewhere between popular biography and run-of-the-mill novel. That is where the main line of popular fiction runs.

MONEY: Why, then, was *Myra Breckinridge* so successful?

VIDAL: What sold *Myra Breckinridge* was that it was one of the oddest, most unusual novels ever written—and for those with a sense of humor, which I would put at about one-tenth of one per cent of the American population, it was a wildly funny book. People who might have bought it thinking they were getting a pornographic novel were not pleased. And this is one of the reasons why the movie was such a failure. The producers thought they had a sexy novel and everybody would go to see Raquel Welch rape some young actor with a dildo. But people had been buying the book for a lot of other reasons.

FAG RAG, 1974:   . . . I read in *Life* that you were doing a novel called *Dreams*. Then I never read anything else about this.

VIDAL: I wrote part of it. I never finished it. I think it's mostly going into *Myron*.

MICHAEL S. LASKY, 1975:   Why did you wait so long to write a sequel to *Myra?*

VIDAL: Mark Twain waited ten years, I think, before he followed up *Tom Sawyer* with the so-called sequel, *Huckleberry Finn*. I regard Myra as America's Tom Sawyer and Myron as America's Huck.

OUI, 1975:   Does . . . [*Myron*] have a unique and American voice?

VIDAL: Anything I write I regard as being very American, since I am very American. So, obviously, whatever comes out of my consciousness will always be the same. I can't judge *Myron.* I prefer it to *Myra,* but I don't think others will.

JUDY HALFPENNY, 1976:   I feel that any novel that's so much fun to read should also have been fun to write.

VIDAL: *Myron* was a great effort to write (not that the writer's ease or difficulties with a subject are of any moment). The book staggered along for a year. I couldn't figure out the time sequence. My publisher thought the beginning unclear, and I kept bringing Myra closer and closer to page one when her original delayed entrance was, to me, gorgeous.

MICHAEL S. LASKY, 1975:   For someone who can't be concerned with trivia, your books *Myra* and *Myron* are certainly loaded with it and seem to revolve around the very recitation of it. How did you do your research?

VIDAL: I never underestimate trivia. I think it was Mary McCarthy who said [that] the novel is nothing but gossip—it's just what you do with it that matters. And I *saw* all those movies. During World War II, contrary to what legends you may have heard, nobody did any fighting. There were eleven million in the service of which maybe one million saw any action. The other ten million of us sat and saw movies. That's all we did on these Army posts. So I saw every movie made in the '40s. And everybody else my age who was in the service saw those movies. I did have to double check my facts, though; I did spell Margaret Sullavan's name wrong and got letters about that. Horrified letters. *Crushed* letters.

OUI, 1975:   Your idea in *Myron* of substituting the Supreme Court Justices' names for dirty words is a marvelous joke. How did you come up with it?

VIDAL: How did man discover fire? Or, not to be a sexist, how did woman discover the wheel? It was just there. I laugh when I think about it. I only hope that the Justices will now take the hint and Rehnquist will change his name to cock, Whizzer White to cunt, and so on.

MICHAEL S. LASKY, 1975:   Did you think there was any risk in using the names of Supreme Court Justices in place of expletives in *Myron*?

VIDAL: That was an afterthought. I had to go through the book changing all the words. I wish there had been some risk—I'd love to take them on. . . .

LASKY: How did you decide which Justices would replace each particular word?

VIDAL: Onomatopoeia.

STANTON, 1978:   You have a self-interview on *Burr*?

VIDAL: Yes.

STANTON: We're waiting.

VIDAL, 1973:   Why a novel about Burr instead of a biography?

VIDAL: Because in the novel one has the right—the duty—to speculate on motives, while the biographer is honor-bound to deal only with facts.

VIDAL, 1973:   Then you don't feel yourself honor-bound to respect facts?

VIDAL: None of that! I've spent several years trying to avoid what Jefferson so nicely called "false facts." Two or three times I have rearranged chronology, but I never ascribe to any actual figure views he did not hold.

VIDAL, 1973:   Why did you pick Burr as a subject?

VIDAL: When I was ten years old my mother married a man called Auchincloss whose mother was a descendant of the Burr family. In fact, the ladies on that side of the family were so proud of the connection that Burr was always part of the names they were know by. Annie Burr, Emma Burr. . . . My half sister has now burdened one of her sons with the name Burr Gore Steers. Not only does the lurid light of us Gores and of those Burrs flicker about his innocent head, but his name sounds like the national food. Fortunately, he is not yet old enought to hate her for what she has done to him. In any case, I was Burr-conscious at an early age; recall a family portrait of Burr's daughter Theodosia; knew that he had been a great gentleman (a species valued in the years before the Second War but now impossible to describe in less than seven hundred pages).

VIDAL, 1973:   How did you research your subject?

VIDAL: Three years ago an Aaron Burr collection came on the market, and I bought several hundred items, the basic texts. On visits to New York I haunted the New York Historical Society Library. Finally my publisher nicely (nervously?) put two historical researchers onto the book and they triple-checked my true as well as my false facts.

VIDAL, 1973:   Is there a lesson for today?

VIDAL: There is always a lesson for today in the past. Whether it's painted on the walls at Lascaux or buried in last week's *Congressional Record.* If we don't know where we've been, we cannot determine where we are and so cannot chart a future course.

VIDAL, 1973:   Doubtless you regard those early days of the republic as more virtuous than the Age of Watergate?

VIDAL: No. I am not romantic. The founders were vain, irritable, tricky, and by no means devoted to the system of government they had contrived. Yet unlike today's politicos, Hamilton and Jefferson were, first, men of extraordinary brilliance and, second, they believed passionately in their own theory of government. I cannot for the life of me determine what Nixon or Humphrey, Agnew or Kennedy believe in except winning elections. The collision between Jefferson and Hamilton struck real sparks. Each was a sort of monster driven by vanity, but each was also an intellectual philosopher of government, and each thought he was creating a perfect or perfectable system of government. Our politicians have not thought about such matters for half a century.

VIDAL, 1973:   Why were these men so different from
the politicians of today?

VIDAL: Jack Kennedy asked himself the same question in the spring of 1961 at Hyannis Port. "You know," he
said, "in this . . . uh, job I get to meet most of the important
people in the country, the best minds, and I'm struck by how
mediocre they are." Modestly he included himself amongst
the reigning mediocrity. He had read so little, had mastered
no foreign language, no art. Then he asked, "How did the
original United States, a colonial society of three million people, produce so much intellectual genius?" More leisure, I proposed. Slow travel. Short sessions of Congress. Long months
at home in the country reading and writing and thinking
thoughts. Kennedy was not convinced. He thought there was
something in the air that was different then. I suppose—
now—there was: the sense of human comity, that a good life
makes contribution to a good society. Now we live entirely in
the age of the little foxes, and what grapes are not spoiled are
soured for all.

VIDAL, 1973:   Obviously you like Burr, but he certainly
cannot be regarded as a good man or a philosopher of government. In fact he was one of the first professional politicians,
representing only himself.

VIDAL: That is not quite true. Burr's mind was as
good as Jefferson's or Hamilton's but he was not a zealot. Yet,
to the extent he was the man on the make—to that extent—he
is interesting to us now. Also, don't forget that the idol of his
generation was not Washington the Dull but Bonaparte. Every ambitious man of the period saw himself conquering the
earth, like Bonaparte. Both Hamilton and Burr wanted to conquer Mexico, Cuba, South America—and simply for the fun
of conquest and the delights of a crown.

MICHAEL S. LASKY, 1975:   You portrayed Aaron Burr as
a real women's libber—and that it was then as now an un-
American thing. Aren't you equating this un-American way
with being unmanly?

VIDAL: Well, American men don't *like* women—regard them as inferior. Therefore, any American man who tends to like the company of women is suspect. Burr was indeed the way I described him. . . .

VIDAL, 1973:   In doing your research what most surprised you?

VIDAL: Jefferson's hypocrisy.

VIDAL, 1973:   What surprised you most about Burr?

VIDAL: The journal he wrote in Europe for his daughter to read. He described in great detail every sexual encounter.

VIDAL, 1973:   What was their relationship?

VIDAL: Perfect, I should think. "Women have souls," Burr used to say, to the consternation of those whose minds had been shaped by his Calvinist grandfather Jonathan Edwards. Burr had no son, so he brought up his daughter the way he would have brought up a son. He made her a prodigy of learning and of charm. Burr was a devoted women's libber and despite his lechery, he really liked women, preferred their company to that of men. . . .

VIDAL, 1973:   What about Jefferson?

VIDAL: Jefferson never forgave Burr for having behaved well when they both tried for President in 1800. Jefferson was also eager to have a Virginian succeed him. To accomplish this Vice President Burr must be railroaded.

VIDAL, 1973:   Yet Jefferson was a great man.

VIDAL: Certainly an interesting one. I like him better than Burr does. But in action he was not unlike the late Joe McCarthy. For decades he used to smear his enemies as "monarchists"—the equivalent at the time to yelling "Commie" in the 1950s. He tried on two occasions to break the Supreme Court. With Nixonian zeal, he went after editors who disapproved of him. Kurt Vonnegut to the contrary, he did *not* free his slaves. He allowed some to buy their freedom. He had a penchant for other men's wives.

VIDAL, 1973:   But he wrote the Declaration of Independence.

VIDAL: He was a bit like Jack Kennedy. Sooner or later Kennedy said something very wise and luminous on almost every subject, then did nothing about it. After battling Hamilton's ideas of government, Jefferson ended up the sort of President Hamilton would have been, deliberately subverting the Constitution in order to buy Louisiana in order to create what he called with satisfaction "our empire."

VIDAL, 1973:   You have been called a cynic.

VIDAL: I have always resented the word! "Realist" is more fitting.

VIDAL, 1973:   Whatever. Lately critics have been saying that your dark view of America since the Second War might be justified in the light of Watergate.

VIDAL: Yes. Watergate has been revelation to a good many inattentive people. To me it is simply a confirmation of what I have known for some time was wrong.

VIDAL, 1973:   But when—how—did it go wrong?

VIDAL: When Adam ate the apple. In our case the apple was empire. It is not possible to have a just and democratic society and also be an empire. Pericles knew this, and Jefferson knew this. But Jefferson coldbloodedly launched us upon empire. Jackson (whom I really dislike; Burr loves him) continued the process by the savage removal of the Indians to the West. We've been on the march ever since. . . .

VIDAL, 1973:   But whom do you like among the early figures?

VIDAL: George Mason, who was responsible for the Bill of Rights. James Madison was a good man, with a first-rate mind—like Jefferson but without Jefferson's vanity and strain of madness. John Adams gives pleasure for his sublime tactlessness. Washington commands awe. He was one of the worst generals we have so far produced, but as a politician he was without equal until Eisenhower. People thought Hamilton used the dimwitted old general to create the Federal Government. Nonsense. Washington, the shrewd land speculator and millionaire, used the brilliant but unstable Hamilton to put together a government which would protect the rights of property. I found Hamilton, all in all, enchanting, and usually "right." It is interesting for someone like me who has often been identified with the American Left to find most appealing in our history the figures of the Right. I suppose it's because they knew what they wanted and were practical. Certainly the Left as represented by Jefferson and Jackson was simply dizzy—*laissez-nous faire.*

VIDAL, 1973:   Is your character named Charles Schuyler real?

VIDAL: No. Charlie evolved. One of Burr's wards was called Charlie and turned into a novelist. That was the germ, but I did not mean for Charlie to become a writer. However, his character got stronger and stronger as the story proceeded.

VIDAL, 1973:   Was there really such an establishment on Thomas Street as Mrs. Townsend's bordello?

VIDAL: Yes. And Helen Jewett was also real. I got the story from Philip Hone's diaries. Invaluable for a picture of the 1830s. When I say there was a red moon over the Battery on such and such a night, I have taken it from his diaries.

VIDAL, 1973:   What effect do you think your novel will have?

VIDAL: Do books have effect now? I only know that readers can learn in a few hours just about everything it took me twenty years to discover about the first half-century of the American republic. And I am slightly resentful. They won't have to work (I assume!) as hard as I did. *Burr's* reader might be heartened to know that things were always pretty bad but that, from time to time, a few devoted figures were thrown up by history to save us from ourselves.

VIDAL, 1973: It has been said that Americans don't like history.

VIDAL: History is the least popular of fifty subjects listed in a recent national high school poll. But what kid could enjoy the endless Mount Rushmores carved in soft soap our schools present them with?

VIDAL, 1973: Then why do you write about things that most Americans are not interested in?

VIDAL: To try to make these things interesting. To teach myself. After all, to make the past live is a lovely task. Without undue self-congratulation, I wish that at twenty I had had *Burr* to read. Instead I had to write it, and that was the hardest work I have ever done.

MICHAEL S. LASKY, 1975: What were you trying to get across in *Burr?* That is, what would you like the reader to come away with after reading it?

VIDAL: A sense of what the world of power is like, the psychology of men who aim to be the first in the state—what these people are like. It's not often done by American writers. I don't believe in all this relevancy business; history is interesting for its own sake. . . . Today is neither more nor less interesting than yesterday. A book is as interesting as the book is. If people want to sit there and figure out "is this really Richard Nixon?"—well, they are wasting their time.

LASKY: What are you doing now—what's in the works?

VIDAL: I'm working on a historical novel about 1876. I would like to re-do Mark Twain's *The Gilded Age.* He made an absolute mess of it. And yet there are marvelous passages in it. Very, very funny. I would think of my book as a variation on a theme of Twain's.

ALVIN SHUSTER, 1976:   It was in Miami, Mr. Vidal recalled here [in Rome] recently, where he kept himself to 800
calories a day, saw no friends, made no lunch appointments
and spent much of his time in the Miami Public Library where
he browsed through old *Harper's Monthlies,* took notes for his
. . . book [*1876*] and posed, unwillingly, for a young photographer who turned up every day to take Vidal's picture at his library desk, as if he were changing day by day. . . .

VIDAL: I must have been in Miami for three or four
weeks. . . . I can tell because my weight dropped from 200 to
181 pounds. Little did [that] 19-year-old author of a war novel [think] that thirty years later [he] would be one of the
greatest living authorities on William Cullen Bryant.

MONIQUE VAN VOOREN, 1976:   Do you think that people
are more interested in historical events than they were previ-
ously or is it an awareness in the American public that wasn't
there before?

VIDAL: I think since Watergate they're interested in
what the past of this country was really like. Therefore
they've turned to me because, at least in . . . *1876* and *Burr,* I'm
telling them the history of the country in a way they've never
heard it told before and, presumably, they find what I have
found interesting.

ALVIN SHUSTER, 1976:   [How do you go about your research?]

VIDAL: The only way to look up facts for books is to
do it yourself. . . . I do not look with a kindly eye upon some
of our most celebrated academic historians whose works on
our founding fathers represent the result of vast teams of
graduate students doing everything for them.
   In writing, I am not very systematic. . . . I was not trained
as a historian and everything probably takes me twice as long
as it should. But I got into the habit of research when I wrote
Julian, after I came to Rome in 1961 following my defeat in the

House race in New York. All that was valuable experience. After that came the novel *Burr,* helped along by a stroke of luck in Los Angeles where I read about the sale of an Aaron Burr collection, bought [two] hundred volumes and moved most of them to my place in Ravello.

MONIQUE VAN VOOREN, 1976:   Do you have many people to help you in your research?

VIDAL: Nobody. But once I am finished Random House hires graduate students or, in the case of *1876,* Professor Eric McKitrick of Columbia, who is perhaps the best authority on post-Reconstruction American history, to read every line to make sure there are no errors.

ALVIN SHUSTER, 1976:   Unlike *Burr,* which took ... [you] ten years, including three years of solid work, *1876* was researched and written in a year and a half.

VIDAL: My only fear about *1876* is that it will serve as a marvelous weapon for those right-wing jingoes who will say, see, Nixon and Agnew were just like everybody else in the United States.... The Grant Administration, of course, was corrupt and there will be those who say that American politicians have been on the take from the beginning, which isn't quite true. But I am afraid I may be giving ammunition to the bad guys. But that's the way it was then.

In my novels, [when] I [introduce] an actual figure [from] history, whatever he says and does is what he actually said and did. The real thing is usually much more interesting than any gloss. You can do whatever you like with the fictional characters.

All novels are historical since they all deal in some way with time passing—whether it is autobiographical (adultery last summer at the writers' workshop) or about Roman Emperor Julian or about President Grant. Every novel is essentially history [to the extent that it deals with time's passage].

JUDY HALFPENNY, 1977:   I don't know what relative importance you yourself attach to the political plot and Charlie and Emma's private affairs in *1876,* but everyone I've read or spoken to has concentrated on the former, as they did with *Burr.*

VIDAL: Yes, I've been somewhat put out by the emphasis on the political aspects of *1876.* My story is that of Emma, and survival. The political background was just counterpoint, a bright Darwinian jungle in which to set her story.

HALFPENNY: No one I know of has speculated as to whether Emma deliberately sacrificed her friend in order to gain a husband. Did she?

VIDAL: Did Emma kill her friend deliberately? Yes. Just as Grant and Co. killed Tilden and Co. I work close to life.

HALFPENNY: Your "borrowings from Flaubert" in *1876* went serenely over my head.

VIDAL: I can't imagine what I borrowed from Flaubert for *1876.* Are you sure I didn't write Proust? I took the name d'Agrigente from him. Flaubert was in my head only when I contemplated Charlie's off-stage life, particularly at the time of that book he wrote (whose title no one ever got straight), for that was the period of my "favorite" novel *L'Education Sentimentale.* On the other hand, I raided Wharton's *Age of Innocence* and New York tales.

MONIQUE VAN VOOREN, 1976:   Of all the books that you've written, which one has been the most financially successful and why?

VIDAL: *1876,* because more people have bought it in hardcover than they have bought any of the others.

ALVIN SHUSTER, 1976:   What would ... [you] write about the year 2076?

VIDAL: I would say there was once a country called [USA] that occupied part of the Northern Hemisphere. We mainly remember [USA] for its artifacts, its curious bottles labeled Coca-Cola. They were natural artists but unfortunately they did not make it. The downfall began with those nuclear reactor stations around the country and . . .

PARIS REVIEW, 1974:   *Two Sisters* is hard to categorize and put in any tradition. You call it a memoir in the form of a novel, or a novel in the form of a memoir. What led you to write in that form?

VIDAL: It created its own form as I went along. I didn't feel that a straightforward memoir would be interesting to do. On the other hand, I don't like *romans à clef.* They're usually a bit of a cheat. You notice I keep talking not about the effect my writing is going to have on others but the effect it has on me. I don't really care whether I find a form that enchants others as much as I care about finding something that can delight me from day to day as I work it out. I was constantly fascinated and perplexed while writing that book. It's done with mirrors. One thing reflects another thing. Each of the three sections is exactly the same story . . . but each section *seems* to be different. Each section contains exactly the same characters, though not always in the same guise.

PARIS REVIEW: It's typical of your newer novels that you make such use of interjected letters, tape recordings, and diaries. Do you find that technique easier, or better, or preferable to a straight narrative?

VIDAL: It makes for immediacy. I know how difficult it is for the average American to read anything. And I'm speaking of the average "educated" person. It is not easy for him to cope with too dense a text on the page. I think the eye tires easily. After all, everyone under thirty-five was brought up not reading books but staring at television. So I am forced to be ingenious, to hold the reader's attention. I think I probably made an error using the screenplay form for part of *Two Sisters.*

PARIS REVIEW: Why?

VIDAL: I'm told it was hard to read. Poor Anthony Burgess, following me, has just made the same mistake with

Clockwork Testament. Also, I kept saying all through the book what a bad screenplay it was. Predictably, the reaction was, well if *he* says it's a bad screenplay, why, it really must be a bad screenplay and so we better not read the bad screenplay. One must never attempt irony this side of the water.

PARIS REVIEW: But you do in your work, on television . . .

VIDAL: Yes. And it has done me no good. In America the race goes to the loud, the solemn, the hustler. . . . Speak of yourself with the slightest irony, self-deprecation, and you will be thought frivolous—perhaps even a bad person. Anyway, the playing around with letters and tapes and so on is just . . . I keep coming back to the only thing that matters: interesting [to] myself.

PARIS REVIEW: *Two Sisters* . . . does invite that intense search for clues you abhor. You meant for it to, didn't you? You wonder who is who and what's what.

VIDAL: It would be unnatural if people didn't. After all, it is a memoir as well as a novel. But mainly it is a study in vanity and our attempts to conquer death through construction or through destruction. Herostratus does it in one way, and I do it in another—at least, the self that I use in the book. Eric does it in yet another way. Those girls, each has her own view of how she's going to evade death and achieve immortality. And it's all a comedy from the point of view of a stoic writer like myself.

JUDY HALFPENNY, 1976:   Early on in *Two Sisters* [page 12], you write: "Most people—and all women—are eager to read other people's mail, eavesdrop upon other people's conversations, to find out just what it is that others say of them." It's not exactly a secret that women are not Real People, but why make things worse by saying so?

VIDAL: Although I have not known all women, every woman I ever knew read other people's mail and listened in on extensions. Many men I know also do this. I don't. There is no virtue in this omission. It could be argued that the captive race is intensely eager to know what their masters are up to and so. . . .

HALFPENNY: I was actually complaining about your phraseology rather than your 'facts'—if you'd only written, "Most people—*including* all women. . . . " you'd have got clean away with it—though I don't mind giving you an argument on the 'facts' too. I maintain you're talking about a general human weakness rather than a sex-linked characteristic. I can quite believe it's a weakness you don't share, but then how could you look me in the eye and deny that you're exceptional?

VIDAL: Women and eavesdropping. My observation was political not hormonal. Slaves are always eager to know what their masters have in store for them. Some masters are paranoid and equally curious for news of the serfs but, by and large, masters tend not to want to be distressed by mutinous mutterings. Most women in the present arrangement are in a slave situation vis-à-vis men and so are naturally curious to know what is being said, written, whispered. Men behave the same way when they are in that situation . . . i.e., listening in on the conversations of their masters as recorded (inaccurately) in the press.

STANTON, 1979:   Does Anaïs Nin play an important role in your literary development?

VIDAL: Yes. She was the first to point out to me the terrible inadequacy of my Crane-Hemingway style. What sense of language that I had went into bad poetry. So I stopped the poetry. When this happened, the prose was considerably enriched. First, short stories. Particularly, "A Moment of Green Laurel" and "The Ladies at the Library." Then came *The Judgment of Paris.* So Anaïs was the spur. Her ideas. . . . Well, *Two Sisters* and my piece about her put them . . . in perspective.

STANTON, 1979:   You recently said that most of the commentary on your relation to Anaïs Nin is wrong. Have you seen Bernard F. Dick's "Anaïs Nin and Gore Vidal: A Study in Literary Incompatibility" in the Winter, 1978 issue of *Mosaic?* If so, do you have any reaction to it?

VIDAL: No. I'd like to read it. I saw that God-awful piece in the *Village Voice.*

STANTON, 1978:   How was *Kalki* born? How was it made? What did you discover in writing it? What's the most interesting thing about it to you? Do you have any reaction to its critical response?

VIDAL: *Kalki* seems to me to be very lively; and the last part is as strange and effective as anything I've done. The style is also a *forceful tower;* but that sort of thing is wasted on our countrymen whose tin ears are forever deaf to grace notes, and the music of our language. I found it fascinating to write as a woman and was pleased that women seemed to like the result . . . there is and there is not a difference between male and female sensibilities; and that's not easy to capture, to say the most.

JUDY HALFPENNY, 1978:   Kalki seems like a paranoid acting out his fantasies, but your presentation of him never supports this reading. I give up. Tell me.

VIDAL: I think that Kalki is perfectly sane. So was Hitler. So was Stalin. He is just more ambitious than anyone who has ever lived. This uniqueness was not noted in book-chat land, largely because reviewers seldom finish the books they review, no matter how short. (*The New York Times* had him shot at Madison Square.) I can imagine—indeed have—the straightforward desire to end the 4-billion and start over again. I can also imagine that Something Would Go Wrong. Robespierre did not give France Liberty/Equality/Fraternity, but Bonaparte.

STANTON, 1978:   You're working on a new novel set in the 5th Century B.C. In Greece? With Socrates and the boys?

VIDAL: Well, no. My hero . . . I mean protagonist is an elderly Persian, grandson of Zoroaster; he takes a dark view of

Greek "atheism" in general, and pederasty in particular. At the moment I am sinking beneath the weight of four cultures: Greek, Persian, Hindu, proto-Confucian. But these large tasks do keep the mind from eating itself up.

STANTON, 1979:   Do you have a title for your upcoming novel?

VIDAL: Random House likes *Creation.* It reminds me of Michener. Maybe that's why they like it. The title's not inapposite but. . . . I haven't thought of anything better. They are very nervous. For once, I may be too "highbrow" . . . their word.

JUDY HALFPENNY, 1978:   I thought you might call it *Voyage.*

VIDAL: *Voyage* is not a bad title. I want *O* but the publishers do not. *Creation* seems all right. It is apt, certainly. But one does not quite like the Michenerian ring. Confucius starts as Master Kung . . . but we slip into Confucius rather quickly. He is the only one of my Great Figures done in the round. Most likeable. I haven't got to Socrates but I suspect he'll be a minor irritant. He sets on edge the teeth of my Persian narrator. Anaxagoras comes out well. Gosala is chilling in one scene. The Buddha is the Cheshire cat . . . but then he is *not.*

DANIEL HALPERN, 1969:   Would you say that you are happy with your novels now, as you finish them?

VIDAL: Well, as Valéry said, you don't finish them, you abandon them. I do them as well as I can. I think the later ones are certainly better than the early ones. I take some pride in that fact, since it is exactly the reverse with most American writers: their early ones are the best, and then they either repeat themselves or try to become something they're not.

HALPERN: How do you think your novels compare with what's being written today by other novelists?

VIDAL: I think I'm a hell of a lot funnier than most of them. I like humor. Actually, I don't seem to me like an

American writer at all. Perhaps that's why I no longer live in that country. All the assumptions, culturally, socially, aesthetically, that most American writers have are not mine and have nothing to do with me. I mean Jimmy Jones is a very nice guy. I see him in Paris. Yet his idea of what it is to be a *man,* with capital *M,* and to be *an American,* and so on, is as foreign to me as the native sagas of the bushmen. This even goes for Norman Mailer, who's far more intelligent and talented than Jimmy. I don't really know what they're all about. I mean, I think I know, and what I know I don't much admire. But I'm willing to give them the benefit of the doubt. Perhaps I'm just dense, and there's something that I can't seem to get a line on, but I think my portrait of Buck Loner in *Myra Breckinridge* comes closest to my view of the average American man at this time and place.

MICHAEL S. LASKY, 1975:   Are you particularly concerned with the way your books look—the typography and design?

VIDAL: I am very interested in the typeface and I go over that very carefully with the publisher.

LASKY: Have you ever seen a rejection slip in your career?

VIDAL: Sure. *Williwaw* . . . was turned down by Random House. . . . Some of my essays were turned down. The *New York Review of Books* turned down some pieces they commissioned from me and they were eventually picked up by *Esquire* and *Encounter.*

EUGENE WALTER, 1960:   Tell me about your televison adaptations, about dealing with Faulkner, James, etc.?

VIDAL: I did them for money of course—but I always tried to pick a writer I respected—or at least that I thought I could do something respectable with. I was most successful with Faulkner and James. I have a considerable affection for James, but not much for Faulkner. I failed entirely with Hemingway, and so has nearly everyone else, which makes one wonder about the original . . . or at least about its viability in *our* time.

EVE AUCHINCLOSS & NANCY LYNCH, 1961:   Do you think you've paid any price for the years you deliberately gave to writing TV scripts in order to make enough money to live on comfortably the rest of your life?

VIDAL: I don't think I have. Of course, one doesn't know, the game isn't over. But it always interested me, trying to write well, and I would say I was one of the few American writers, in my generation, who cared about writing well. To me, there is such a thing as a good sentence and a bad sentence, and I don't think you can be a good writer unless you do care. In that sense (TV or not), I think I am a better writer now. My sentences are better.

AUCHINCLOSS & LYNCH: What is a good sentence?

VIDAL: Appositeness, I suppose, is the main thing. To say a thing as precisely and clearly as you can, and if you can make it happen, say it unexpectedly. That's the secret of dialogue. It must always surprise. You see, it is simply a matter of craft—a word no longer used, now that everyone's an artist with a remarkable, beautiful person to impart. But there is a craft to this thing, though it's a pedestrian word that embarrasses us. But it has to be learned. No one's born knowing it. And no one can be taught it. But it can be learned—by reading, by thinking, and by writing.

EUGENE WALTER, 1960:   Do you think writing for movies, television and so forth is corroding to a writer's more serious work?

VIDAL: . . . For me it was less compromising to write for films than to teach, or review other people's books. Or journalism. Yet there is a destructive element in writing for hire and it is, simply, indifference: a man's defense when he believes or is made to believe that he is misusing his talent (and the world which was indifferent to the talent itself is usually eager to point out its misuse). The sullen response—and especially if he is successful in a worldly way—is indifference. And it must be fought against in the dark hours for indifference is death to the artist. Somewhere in that is a peculiarly American tragedy.

JUDY HALFPENNY, 1977: If you remember *Weekend,* how would you rate it?

VIDAL: *Weekend* is a very odd and effective play. The relations within the candidate's family are not like anything else (American school that is) by me or by anyone. The failure was (a) the ongoing dislike of me in New York City which can kill a play in a night but affects a book's career not at all and (b) the politics which were too realistic to be popular and (c) the fact that show-biz reviewers are interested in New Forms. Since they had just heard of Ionesco and Brecht and I had written what I called a drawing room comedy, didn't the author know that that sort of theatre was dead . . . ? Unable to listen to the dialogue for any sustained length of time, they look at the set, the costumes, the form (as they guess) of the piece. Alan Pryce-Jones, bless him, was the only reviewer to get the fact that the play's content was too novel for them to absorb while the calculated irony of the old-fashioned rendering missed them completely. But then there are no ironists (along with second acts) in American life.

AMERICAN FILM, 1977: You are writing novels and screenplays. Does writing for television still appeal to you?

VIDAL: There's nothing to do. It's all hour-long adventure-gangster things. We used to do plays for television which were performed live. But that's all ended. I have been asked to narrate about four, ninety-minute shows on the American presidents, and I might do that. . . . Done the right way, it would be interesting.

AMERICAN FILM: What would be the right way?

VIDAL: Objectively. Not disguising what the country was like, what its past really was. The interesting thing about the United States has been its unremitting imperialism, from the very first moment we killed our first Indian right up to Vietnam. We have been almost continually at war and on the march. To show all this, as reflected in the Presidents and their rhetoric, would be very interesting to do. But I'm not sure that Xerox would pick up the tab.

AMERICAN FILM: But television otherwise doesn't interest you—no specials or movies of the week?

VIDAL: No, thank you. I'm not what they want. They have enough trouble with me as a talking head on television, without having me write things that offend. About every few years they try to bring back the golden age of television. People like Mike Dann call me in for lunch. He has lunch with Paddy Chayefsky on Monday, me on Tuesday, Reggie Rose on Wednesday, and then announces we're going to do something, and it never gets done. I've stopped having those lunches.

AMERICAN FILM: There are people who regard the fifties as indeed television's golden age. How golden was it?

VIDAL: Most of our stuff was terrible in the golden age. We did so much, too much. There were seven live hour shows a week out of New York. I don't know how we did it. Someone would ring up suddenly and say, "Tad Mosel's script hasn't come in. We've got the sets built: we've got a bar, a bedroom, and there's a kind of ballroom. We've got Kim Stanley, we've got Paul Newman, and Vinnie Donehue is going to direct. Can you think of a play?" In three or four days you'd write something to fit the sets and the cast. That really is Lope de Vega time. I don't know how we did it. Most of the time it was pretty bad, but every now and then it was very exciting. It was also wonderful for actors—you would be up there live, knowing one mistake and twenty million people will see it. I remember the night that the girl vomited in Albert Salmi's lap because she was so nervous. They were in a two-shot. Albert was talking, and she just—very quietly— vomited in his lap. You didn't see much because they were cutting in very tight. But there was a strange look on Albert's face. Then the camera cut to her face, and there was a little saliva. God, it was wild. There was the night Cloris Leachman went up. [One of the cameras exploded.] She was playing a Southern belle with long hair. She was sitting beside a pond and she said, "I'm just going to sit here and trail my fingers in the water trail my fingers in the water," and she did. She kept on trailing those fingers until they cut away from her.

FAG RAG, 1974:   Did you make money out of your television plays?

VIDAL: For me it was a hell of a . . . As a writer I never seemed to be able to make more than $7000 a year, year in and year out.

FAG RAG: But you were published before you went and they [the other television writers] were not.

VIDAL: Oh yes.

FAG RAG: They were just sort of Kitchen Writers from Brooklyn.

VIDAL: Radio men. Radio joke writers.

AMERICAN FILM, 1977:   Do you ever wonder if society is creating television or if television is creating society?

VIDAL: If I could answer that, I could walk on water. It's a good question. I think society and television are totally interrelated now. I remember seeing one of Andy Warhol's early movies, *Chelsea Girls,* and I told him, "It's kind of dull." He said, "Oh, yes, that's the point." I said, "What do you mean, that's the point?" He said, "Well, you know, people will always watch something rather than nothing." There's a great deal of wisdom in that. There is the screen with these rippling colors and bang-bang and a decibel level that keeps you moderately interested. To think that an average American sits there six hours a day looking at that junk. . . . What sort of society is going to evolve I don't know. But I'm glad I won't be around writing books. Nobody will be able to read them.

HOLLIS ALPERT, 1977:   Have any of the movies made from your screenplays satisfied you?

VIDAL: I think *The Best Man* was the least awful, but I really don't like any of them much, as opposed to what I had in mind.

ALPERT: And if you had directed?

VIDAL: They would have been more satisfactory to me. They might still be bad, but I would be making my own mistakes. The tiring part of movies is having to explain yourself all the time. I had to explain jokes to the director of *The Best Man,* which was based on a play of mine that had run two years, so I knew where the laughs were.

MICHAEL S. LASKY, 1975:   You . . . worked with Tennessee Williams at one point?

VIDAL: I never worked with him. I did the screenplay for the film *Suddenly Last Summer.* Tennessee had nothing to do with it but at the last minute Sam Spiegel decided that he wanted Tennessee's name on the screenplay—which was illegal. But Tennessee, my old friend, conned me into it because he thought this would be his chance to get an Academy Award for adapting a screenplay. I did not forgive Spiegel—I know Tennessee is weak—but the screenplay is entirely mine. In fact, I had to add another sixty minutes to his forty-minute play.

STANTON, 1979:   Do you have any response to comments made by Tennessee Williams about you in his *Memoirs* (1975) and in *Tennessee Williams' Letters to Donald Windham 1940– 1965* (1977)? He seems to have started off with you on good terms but eventually finds you a nuisance.

Vidal: Whatever I have to say about Tennessee I said in the review of his memoirs. As for the letters to Windham. . . . Well, like all good letter writers, Tennessee accommodates himself to the moods and prejudices of the person to whom he is writing. Windham was—is, I suppose—an uncommonly bitter failed writer who tends to take the success of anyone else personally. This is a fairly common American characteristic. So Tennessee would be bound to satirize me to Windham since I was something of a black beast to the author of *The Dog Star*. Also, there is Tennessee's extraordinary paranoia. I was astonished to read that he thought that I had used influence at the *New York Times* to kill or alter or whatever his piece about Paul Bowles, as if I had any influence at the *Times* then or now—or would have used it to suppress him. I suspect that this might have been due to guilty conscience. He began the piece with a swipe at today's highly touted young writers (Capote and me) and how good it was to read a mature artist like Bowles, etc. I ran into Windham on the street shortly after I read the book of letters. He was not un-nervous. I was bland. I did ask him why he thought that the Bird had felt it necessary to attack his two Young Friends. "Because," said Windham, "even then he hated being old, hated anyone younger. He never forgave *me* for being younger." I then chided—I chide nicely—Windham for what he'd said about me. After Tenn had told Windham that I had plagiarized one of Windham's books (!), Windham says he was then obliged to read all my early novels . . . a task he found painful, or some such word. "Well," he said, eyes not meeting mine, "you never read *my* work." "I don't think," I said, "that that is the same thing." Actually, I'd read and praised some of Windham's work. But he had forgotten.

American Film, 1977: Back in the early sixties you formed a company to produce films, Edgewater Productions, with Robert Alan Aurthur and Reginald Rose. Whatever happened to it?

Vidal: I'm glad you brought that up because I've never known what happened to that company. We were the three hot television writers of that day. Well, Robert Alan Aurthur was a bit cooler than Reggie and I. Anyway, Columbia wanted to have a writers' company; Edgewater was the name of my house up the Hudson River. We had a marvelous press conference—I remember that part—very nice and agreeable. It was a very *warm* feeling, and then I never heard another word from Columbia or anybody. I think Bob Aurthur inherited the company, which was nothing but a name. I'm glad you asked that question. I must find out why we didn't make any movies.

STANTON, 1978: Why didn't Edgewater Productions make any movies?

VIDAL: I don't know. . . . I remember I never had any project that seemed suitable. I have a hunch that Rose and I were doing Aurthur a favor. He got a large salary as company president for a year or two, and that was that. I was a bit annoyed when he ended up with the company itself, named for my house.

AMERICAN FILM, 1977: Did you write *Myra Breckinridge* at the Chateau Marmont with that awful, revolving figure outside?

VIDAL: No, I didn't write it there, but when I was at Metro I lived at the Chateau Marmont. Oh, God, to wake up in the morning with a hangover and look out and see that figure turning, turning, holding the sombrero—you knew what death would be like.

MONIQUE VAN VOOREN, 1976: Why didn't you see the movie *Myra Breckinridge?*

VIDAL: Because I read the script.

VAN VOOREN: Do you think this film will come back?

VIDAL: If it comes back I go away.

VAN VOOREN: It's actually a movie that could be done over again.

VIDAL: It was never done. I'd always hoped that we might do *Myron* with our friend Mick Jagger. Not only would he play Myra Breckinridge and Myron but also Maria Montez.

AMERICAN FILM, 1977:   You once mentioned Woody Allen for *Myron.*

VIDAL: Oh, I think Woody Allen would be great playing Myron. Or Paula Prentiss.

HOLLIS ALPERT, 1977:   You've been involved in your own Italian movie, *Gore Vidal's Caligula.* I read . . . that production has finished.

VIDAL: In every sense. One of the interesting things I have discovered as I proceed along the great road of life is that you make the same goddamned mistakes over and over and over again. I can tell you right now that every mistake you've made so far in your life you will continue to make. There's not a chance of getting out from under. Now I know quite a lot about movies. I know how they're put together. Yet I go from disaster to disaster. Obviously, I'm getting stupider. This time I have to get my name out of the title. I fear that Hugh Briss was back in town, as W.C. Fields would say. I'll probably have to sue to change the title of a movie.
Penthouse Films picked an Italian director, Tinto Brass. I said, "All right, if we can use him as a pencil, take him." I mean, he's a competent cameraman and editor. He's made about ten pictures, each failed. Failure is a habit people seldom break. That's another thing to remember when you're picking a director. Peter O'Toole, who played Tiberius in *Caligula,* referred to Tinto Brass as "Tinto Zinc." O'Toole has a nice sense of the way the world should be ordered. "In a well-run world," he said, "this man should be cleaning windows in Venice. Instead, here he is spending $8 million and destroying a script." Bob Guccione of *Penthouse*—the mag for the gynecological set—is actually quite visual-minded and not entirely stupid; I thought that if the two of us had control of the picture, it would work. The script was strong, which is why we

got O'Toole and John Gielgud and Malcolm McDowell and so on. Well, another disaster.

In any case, I should never have accepted an Italian director. The film was supposed to be made in English with direct sound—something Italians hate. The Italians make silent movies, then they add a lot of noise they take to be dialogue. As a result, few Italian directors know anything about dialogue or how to tell a story—in *Italian,* much less in English. This is true even of the master, Fellini. When it comes time to make the English version, he calls in [the nearest] *au pair* girl from Finland who is supposed to know English very well. "Yez," she says, "I know verry well the Eenglish." Then ten bad actors in Rome do the dubbing.

ALPERT: I take it you're more than dissatisfied with the way *Caligula* has turned out.

VIDAL: It's not just another bad movie. It's a joke movie like *Myra Breckinridge,* which was not just a bad movie, it was an awful joke. And I have you, Mr. Alpert, to thank for that. You once reviewed a film called *Joanna,* made by an English pop singer named Michael Sarne. This film was like fifty-two Salem commercials run back-to-back—people running in slow motion through Green Park, girls with long hair, and lots of plummy dialogue. Anyway, you must have suffered a sudden lapse, because your judgments are usually impeccable.* Richard Zanuck and David Brown, who were then running Twentieth Century-Fox, suddenly asked me to see *Joanna,* and I knew something was up. I looked at what I thought was one of the ten worst films. The next thing I knew they said, "Well, he's directing *Myra Breckinridge,* and he will also write the script." I said, "What has he done to justify giving him a major film to direct, a movie about Hollywood, a town he had yet to visit?" They said, "*Joanna* is a great flick." I said, "It's a terrible picture." They said, "Just look what the critics say." And there was the Hollis Alpert review. I said, "What about the other reviewers?" They said, "What differ-

* This is an example of irony. [G.V., 1979]

ence do they make? He's the best." Anyway, Michael Sarne never worked in films after *Myra Breckinridge.* I believe he is working as a waiter in a pub in London where they put on shows in the afternoon. This is proof that there is a God and, in nature, perfect symmetry.

MONIQUE VAN VOOREN, 1976:   What was your reason for calling *Caligula* "Gore Vidal's Caligula"?

VIDAL: A number of reasons aside from perfectly normal megalomania. For one thing, I didn't want anybody to think it was Albert Camus' *Caligula.* He seems now to be somewhat forgotten but you can never tell, he might have a revival. The dreaded Lina Wertmüller threatened to do her *Caligula* when she discovered that we would not take her as the director for my *Caligula,* so there's the chance that she might do one. So I thought it better to put my name in the title; something I learned from Fellini. When he began to make *Satyricon* four other Italian directors announced that they were making *Satyricon,* too. So he put his name in the title, which was something they couldn't do or hadn't thought to do. Can't you see *Rossi's Fellini's Satyricon?*

AMERICAN FILM, 1977:   What would you like to direct?

VIDAL: Looking back on it, I think I probably should have tried to direct *Caligula.*

AMERICAN FILM: Would you have changed anything?

VIDAL: As soon as you hire John Gielgud, which we did, you start thinking. You have for two weeks one of the most beautiful voices in the world. It's like being given a marvelous oboe. You want to give it some more notes—to write for the actor. I think I might like to direct my novel *Myron,* but it's complicated. It all takes place inside a Westinghouse television set. I don't completely visualize that.

MONIQUE VAN VOOREN, 1976:   By the fact that you wrote the script for *Caligula* you were obviously well versed in that period of history since you have already done *Julian.* Did you have to do more research for *Caligula?*

VIDAL: No, there are only two texts. There's Tacitus and Suetonius and once you've absorbed them then you've got everything anybody knows about the character.

VAN VOOREN: Where do you think the film is going to be made—entirely in Italy?

VIDAL: No. I think location stuff will be in Romania, Yugoslavia. We're going to need a lot of people and it's very expensive in Italy now, the crowds.

STANTON, 1979:   Whatever happened to *Caligula?*

VIDAL: It is to be released *without* my name in the title somewhere somehow on the porno circuit. It could have been. . . .

STANTON, 1979:   Does anyone plan to make *Kalki* into a film?

VIDAL: Everyone was interested and then no one was interested.

※

CURTIS BILL PEPPER, 1974:   What is the purpose of your lecture tours?

VIDAL: [To] make waves. [To] drop pebbles into the black heart of the nation. I'm essentially a teacher, as was Aaron Burr, whom I resemble in temperament. What else is being an adult? Nature programs us more or less well to train children. But we live in decadent times. Families break up, generations turn against one another. The adult loses faith in the worth of his own experience. But for the artist, the purveyor of ideas—well, he acts out his maturity by sharing what he knows with others. At the least, he tells you the hole in the road needs fixing.

PEPPER: So this is a biological as well as a civic duty?

VIDAL: I'm sure it is. It's certainly no great joy to have to get up at four in the morning to get to Boise, Idaho. And then to make three more stops in the day, when you don't need the money. In fact, it costs me money by the time I've finished.

PEPPER: So what do you get out of it?

VIDAL: The response of the audience. Two or three thousand people in a movie house in Yakima, Washington . . . with a great deal of interplay between me and the audience. . . . That's very exciting. And I learn a good deal. Or, when I hit a town like Phoenix, I'm able to get attention for the liberal minority. Last year I met most of the young Democratic candidates for Governor, Congress, the Senate, and they're marvelous . . . really full of beans. They're out to crack the Goldwater machine, its attitude. So I think if I can rustle up a couple thousand people for them in an auditorium and make some money . . . and go on television and discuss their enemies, I do some good in a small way.

FAG RAG, 1974:   What do you think of the talk show circuit?

VIDAL: There's a whole technique to it. You just have to study how to do it. Use it to your own purposes.

MONEY, 1978:   How much do personal appearances and interviews help sell a book?

VIDAL: My view is that they do not sell one single copy.

FAG RAG, 1974:   How do you get through mass media with what is essentially an anti-mass message?

VIDAL: You have to become an explainer. You have to make up your mind before you go on that you are going to make the following points. Don't make too many points because they can't remember them. You are going to say: If I want to get the sex laws changed, I will then have thought it out in my head how I'll lead the conversation. It doesn't make any difference what *they* ask; you just go right on. "Yes, that's interesting," and go right on to the point you were going to make. It's like any other kind of skill. You have to learn how to do it. It's very useful.

FAG RAG: But the medium itself. It's sort of a reverse from McLuhan. The medium itself has such a powerful . . .

VIDAL: It's better than nothing. People don't listen. All day yesterday and the day before in Chicago, little old ladies, cabdrivers who I know hate my guts, all came up and wanted to talk about the exchange with the priest [on a Dick Cavett show]. They were all very pleased by it.

FAG RAG: Did you talk with the Jesuit [John McLaughlin, a speech writer and Deputy Special Assistant to Nixon] after the show?

VIDAL: He told me that Walter Cronkite is a notorious left-winger.

FAG RAG: The nature of the bourgeois press, the very fact that they teamed you with someone like that, does this make you feel compromised having to deal with slime? That you're on a par with slime?

VIDAL: No! I'm the detergent!

FAG RAG: I think you did an "Inouye." You said: "Lies. Lies. Priest." You weren't on camera then.

VIDAL: No, no. I said "You are lying, priest. Think to your immortal soul." The Brother gulped on that.

PARIS REVIEW, 1974:   Have you ever thought of acting, as Norman Mailer does?

VIDAL: Is *that* what he does? I have always been curious. Well, I appeared briefly in my own *The Best Man.* I also appeared in *Fellini Roma,* as myself. I made no sense, due to the cutting, but the movie was splendid anyway. I have been offered the lead in Ustinov's new play for New York. To play an

American president. What else? I said no. For one thing, I cannot learn dialogue.

AMERICAN FILM, 1977:   You appeared on "Mary Hartman, Mary Hartman" recently. Had you acted before?

VIDAL: No, I hadn't. But I had always said acting was very easy for most people to do, except for certain professional actors. The Europeans discovered a long time ago that if somebody was physically right for a part and if he was reasonably at ease with himself, acting was easy. I wound up coldly upstaging Louise Lasser in our farewell scene—I must say the grips wept. We were sitting in the loony bin at Fernwood, and Louise, who has normally quite a loud voice, turned to me and said, "Gore, I've got to tell you—I'm in love with you." I said, "Are you?" "Yes," she said softly, "I am." "Oh, really," I said more softly. I wasn't going to let her outtender me, so every time she dropped her voice I dropped mine under hers. Well, by the time we finished all you could see were lips moving. I believe we were totally lovable.

AMERICAN FILM: What attracted you to "Mary Hartman"?

VIDAL: I like Norman Lear. I think he's trying to do something a little different. He said, "We'll write you in." I said, fine. I thought I was going to come for one show. Instead I did eight of the damn things. I got interested in the technical end. After fifty you have to keep thinking of new things to do, to keep yourself interested. Obviously, being a soap-opera star is new for me. I now sit by the phone waiting for job offers. On "Welcome Back, Kotter" there's a chance I might play a friendly psychiatrist, if one of the kids goes really off the rails.

The difficult thing was learning the lines, because soap operas have no action. You just sit at the kitchen table with the coffee in front of you, and talk. There's never any reason for you to get up except when you run out of pages. Sometimes the camera shows you going to the door; sometimes you are discovered halfway to the door. I finally worked it out so that

I kept the dialogue on my lap. While Louise was on camera doing one of her arias—her speeches would run six to eight pages, mine about five or six—I would be reading my next speech. As a result my dialogue sounded very fresh because it was quite new to me. But there's that awful moment when you know you're going to forget it. This happens to me on television. Whenever I say, "Now there are three things that you've got to remember," I've already lost "three," "two" is beginning to fade, and "one" is crumbling.

AMERICAN FILM: You're referring to your talk show appearances?

VIDAL: Yes, but it's interesting talking on television. I do it quite cold-bloodedly, to propagandize. I pick a general direction I want to go in. Now you can't get on the tube unless you're hustling something, so I have to pretend to be selling a book or play. I get that over as quickly as possible. I've even stopped Johnny Carson in the middle of a conversation about the book to get on to the attorney general's crimes. In a funny way, television is the only way you can get to people. Certainly, you can't trust a journalist; you end up as his invention, for good or ill. But on television your voice is actually heard without an intermediary. I was told that when I go on the Carson show, the ratings go up in all the cities, and the entire Midwest and South turn off. The show has to sort of work it out—when they feel they need the cities and don't really need Tulsa.

MONIQUE VAN VOOREN, 1976:   What would you consider . . . the perfect day . . . including everything possible that you could have or do from the time you rise to the time you fall asleep?

VIDAL: Well, I would go on the Today Show, that's how I would begin, and have a half hour with Barbara Walters and then I'd be driven down to Philadelphia to do the Mike Douglas Show; then I'd come back and do my state of the union with David Susskind, ninety minutes taping just the two of us; then I would somehow magically get out to

California in time to tape Merv Griffin in the afternoon back to back with Johnny Carson. Then there come the late night shows in Chicago—a really good day, a well-spent day.

AMERICAN FILM, 1977: What do you think of the talk shows?

VIDAL: Each show has a different feel to it. Merv Griffin has got terribly good. He used to be about the worst, and he's almost the best now. I don't know what happened. He became a conglomerate. I think that's it. I think enormous wealth has relaxed him. He's also got a very interesting studio audience out there to play off. I don't know where they get the audience on Carson's show. I find them slow. But Carson is still the best of the lot when he's interested. But I think he must go crazy, being on night after night. On "The David Susskind Show" I do my state of the union once a year. We do an hour or two together. I suppose we lose all the [cities] before the end.

AMERICAN FILM: Is there any attempt by network powers to keep you off?

VIDAL: They don't like me, and Dick Cavett told me that the blacklist still goes on. He said that, periodically, [at ABC] he would be given a list of people not to have on, and sometimes I would be on that list. Then, for no reason at all, I'd be off it. Nobody ever figured out the rationale for it. But there is indeed a blacklist, and it does continue.

STANTON, 1978: You told me last year that you had made up your mind not to appear on television after the publication of *Kalki*. Yet you did. Why?

VIDAL: The pressure from the publisher was fairly strong when *Kalki* appeared. Aside from the usual bad press, the book was one of my "inventions" (which the public in its lust for Facts is supposed to dislike) and it was, also, "The off-year book," as they think of *Two Sisters, Myron,* and *Kalki* at Random. So I made the TV rounds and I think my boredom came through. I had nothing at all useful to say . . . at least, in the seven in-depth minutes one is allowed. I would like to see the Federal Republic dissolved and rearranged on Swiss cantonal lines. This takes more time and thought than mere TV chat can suggest. One day I may try to work out in detail a political alternative, not that our corrupt masters are about to dissolve themselves.

STANTON, 1978:   I have seen you appear on many talk shows recently. You sometimes button your jacket, unnecessarily. Are you ever nervous about your public appearances? At the same time, you come across very well—nervous or not. But *why* do you bother? Apparently, you don't have enough time to develop ideas. Are you looking to plant a vivid line or two in people's heads, and hoping that it (they) will grow into questions?

VIDAL: No, I'm not particularly nervous about TV or any kind of public appearance. That was the family trade and I learned it early. The buttoning of the jacket depends on how much weight I've picked up on tour and how best to disguise it. At its best, TV is enormously useful and I've done some good work over the years. You plant often a good deal more than a vivid line or two. Before a program where I know that I'll have thirty or forty minutes, I determine a line that I want to develop (elimination of victimless crimes, say, from the statute books) and what I then say, though perfectly ordinary and sensible, comes through like revelation to an audience that has never heard anyone on television not lie—whether about the product being sold or the self being promoted. My last go-round was dull because I was neither selling nor explaining; every now and then I mentioned our actual situation (no problem now facing us can be solved, e.g., energy); this caused a chill. The best TV that I do are the State of Unions with Susskind . . . sixty to ninety minutes. Ratings actually go up in the cities (from the miniscule to the small).

4

Artists and Barbarians

PARIS REVIEW, 1974: What [movies] did you see between ten and fifteen?

VIDAL: I saw everything. But I was most affected by George Arliss. Particularly his Disraeli. I liked all those historical fictions that were done in the thirties. Recently I saw my favorite *Cardinal Richelieu* for the first time in thirty years on the Late Show. Absolute chloroform.

MONIQUE VAN VOOREN, 1976: What is your favorite movie?

VIDAL: *Marriage Is a Private Affair* with Lana Turner, written by Tennessee Williams from the forties. Myra Breckinridge admired it tremendously.

VAN VOOREN: What is the best play you have ever seen, outside of *The Best Man,* of course?

VIDAL: Well you're narrowing the field. I don't much like plays.

PARIS REVIEW, 1974: Why do you prefer movies to the theater?

VIDAL: I'm embarrassed by live actors. They're always having a much better time than I am. Also, few plays are very interesting while almost any movie is interesting—if just to watch the pictures. But then I'm typically American. We weren't brought up with theater like the English or the Germans. On the other hand, I saw every movie I could in my youth. I once saw four movies in one day when I was fourteen. That was the happiest day of my life.

HOLLIS ALPERT, 1977:   Gore, you're first and foremost a novelist, but you've mysteriously managed to function with enormous success in a variety of fields. . . . Lately, you've been turning out some provocative essays on Hollywood and the movies for the *New York Review of Books.* Let me quote the last few lines of a recent one—your definition of the director: "that hustler-plagiarist who has for twenty years dominated and exploited and (occasionally) enhanced an art form still in search of its true authors." Would you explain that?

VIDAL: My characteristic understatement has obviously led to ambiguity. I wrote a very long piece, and my thesis is that ever since the movies started to talk—that dread moment when Al Jolson said, "You ain't heard nothin' yet," certainly the most sinister line in all of world drama—it's been a writer's medium. But nobody ever knew this, except the writers—and the directors. I saw an interview with Henry Wilcoxon about Cecil B. De Mille, that gorgeous egomaniac, and he said, "You know, it's all in the script." Akira Kurosawa said, "It's the script." I think even Delmer Daves would say it's the script. The script is all-important. But the director is obliged to get the script away from the writer in order to become an *auteur du cinéma.* My piece in the *New York Review* is really an attack on the French theory of the auteur—that the director alone creates the film.

I call the directors plagiarists because they, literally, steal the script. Now this is done in a very sly fashion. First, they go to a writer for a script, because very few of them can write themselves—very few of them can direct, either. Once the script is acquired, they bring in a second writer in order to confuse authorship, so, just to make it tidy, they say, "Well, I guess I'll take the credit." In my piece I described how the noble Jean Renoir did that with *The Southerner,* one of the few good movies that Renoir was associated with in the United States. Renoir was a man who had great trouble speaking English, much less writing it, and the script was written by William Faulkner. According to Zachary Scott, who acted in it, Faulkner really liked the script and would have been pleased to have had the credit. But Renoir so muddled the business that the credit finally read: "Screenplay by Jean Renoir." That was a great heist.

Somebody recently asked me, "What about René Clair?" Everybody is trying to save their favorite directors from my axe. I said, "All right, what about René Clair?" I got a collection of his screenplays, each introduced with an elegant, pretentious preface. He sounds like Marcel Proust on a very good day as he discusses his own greatness. There was a film he did called *The Grand Maneuver,* and he said, more or less, "This film began when I was a small boy in the Bois de Boulogne. As the cavalry would go by I would hear their trumpets sound. . . . " I was in tears by the time I got through the preface. Then I looked at the credits: "From a story by Courteline, screenplay by Jerome Géronimi and Jean Marson." So who the hell heard that trumpet in the Bois de Boulogne? Was it the man who wrote the play? Was it the two other writers? What did Clair contribute? We will never know. What we will know is that he took credit for everything. . . .

AMERICAN FILM, 1977:   You've written that once production starts the director might as well go home. In your view, what is it the director does?

VIDAL: It varies. Some do more than others. I give credit where it is due. Ingmar Bergman writes his own script, knows the actors well—he is, in every sense, the creator of his own films. But, in the old days, they used to say that the director was the brother-in-law. The producer was the important person. He put the thing together. Then he picked the stars, who were usually under contract; he picked the cameraman, who was very important, and the editor, who was more important still. And at the last minute, he'd call in one of the studio's staff directors, give him the script, and say, "Do you

want to do it or not? If you don't want to do it, you go on sus-
pension." That's what it was like in the fifties at MGM when
I was under contract, and the forties and the thirties.

Nobody bright or ambitious wanted to be down there on
the set all day. It was boring. If the director changed the
script—if I had written "Medium-close shot" in the script and
he decided suddenly to do a long shot—all hell would break
loose upstairs in the executive dining room. Each day, Bennie
Thau would watch the rushes, and he would say, "What happened here? You changed the shot. Why?" So [a large horse-
laugh] went through this town when the French, who are always wrong, suddenly decided that all these hacks were truly
great creators. Whenever the French invent a theory, *méfiez-
vous.* France is a nation devoted to the false hypothesis on
which it then builds marvelously logical structures. The idea
that Nicholas Ray—a dear friend of mine—is a great director
is something that never would have occurred to those of us
who lived in the Chateau Marmont at the time he was down
there in the bungalow "prepping," as *Variety* would say, *Rebel
Without a Cause,* a pretty good movie but nothing more. Orson
Welles, a very funny man, once said to me, "You know, the
French ruin everything. They come up to you and say, 'You
are one of the three great directors of the cinema.' " Orson
said, "I nod, I nod." " 'There is D. W. Griffith. There is Orson
Welles. And there is Nicholas Ray.' " He said, "There is always that third name that crushes you."

HOLLIS ALPERT, 1977:   When you call movies "an art
form still in search of its true authors," you're looking to writers to take over the function of directors?

VIDAL: Yes. What the French were saying was, essentially, you must get rid of the screenwriter. Then the director
would make the movie himself—with his own script, or perhaps without a script, or improvising. In my piece ["Who
Makes Movies?" in the *New York Review of Books,* 25 November
1976] I turned their theory around. I said, let's get rid of the
director. We don't need him. We do need the cameraman, the
editor. But above all we need the script. Movies are stories;

only writers can tell stories. So the wrong people are making the movies.

You see, I don't think there is much of anything to directing. I've worked on about fifteen movies, I suppose. I've done perhaps a hundred live television plays. I've done five plays on Broadway. I've never seen a director yet who contributed much of anything. Some are better than others; some are nicer than others; some are brighter than others. It's very good to have a director to play off—to say, "You're too long," or "You're repeating yourself." As editors, they can be quite useful. When I got to Cannes for *The Best Man*—I got the critics' award for the best script—there was a banner with the title in French and "Un film de Franklin Schaffner." Well, I hit the ceiling. This was *my* play, *my* movie. I had helped put the thing together—we had hired Frank. "Un film de Franklin Schaffner." I said, "There's something going wrong here." Anyway, that's when I first confronted the auteur theory—in 1964.

AMERICAN FILM, 1977:   Do you believe you could look after the directing chores?

VIDAL: I had a chance to direct in the fifties, and I turned it down. In those days, nobody who was a serious novelist would have dreamt of directing. And a great many successful screenwriters felt the same. Directing was for the hustlers. Then along came the Europeans with their theories, and suddenly directors were ennobled. We novelists who had been central to the culture began to float out to the far perimeter where the poets live, and I now think that, perhaps, I missed a chance. The other night I asked Peter Falk how much those little movies he does with John Cassavetes cost. He said about $500,000. They don't take salaries up front, so the actual cost of making the picture is not a great deal. Well, a William Faulkner—at the peak of his powers, as indeed he was when he was out here—could have directed as well as written the script of *The Southerner* for his friend, Zachary Scott.

So you don't need the director. You can go right through him. The cameraman, after all, does a great deal for you. Unfortunately, most directors are sometimes slaves of their cameramen. In Italy you should see one of the cringing little directors at work, say, with a huge Giuseppe Rotunno. The Italian movie is a photographer's medium, which explains why most of them are so bad. Movies are stories. . . . I spent most of my time as a movie writer trying to explain to directors what a story is: where you start it, where it goes, how to keep the audience interested for a hundred minutes. I never worked with one who had a clue [as to] the mystery of narrative. They think about shots—usually of two cars racing. As for working with actors, forget it. Never ask a movie director about actors. You'll get an extremely dark stare. Actors are on their own. If the director remembers their names, they're lucky. They're moved around like furniture. That is why type is all-important. That is what [the actor is] cast for.

Fellini has solved the problem by not using actors at all. He likes types. He tends to use people from restaurants. He loves eating. That marvelous man who played Trimalchio in *Satyricon* was the owner of Il Moro restaurant in Rome. Fellini had had so many good dinners there that when it came time to cast Trimalchio, the man who gives the great banquet, he said, "Ees good. Ees nice man. Makes me hungry. I take him." It was an effective performance, too. All the man had to do was *be* there, and occasionally count. Fellini literally has his performers count: "One, two, three, four, five, six." "I like what you do around thirty-two," he once said to a "performer."

AMERICAN FILM: Do you regard the director as useless for the theater, too?

VIDAL: The director is even more useless in the theater than in the movies. The American theater is, thank God, controlled by the writer. The Dramatists Guild contract makes it possible for us to get rid of the director, to shut the play the night before it opens, to do almost anything [we want]. The writer hires the director to manage the traffic. Obviously, some contribute more than others. They also serve a more human function than in the movies, where the work is largely mechanical, technical. Directors in the theater must be good with actors. For some reason, I've never known a writer who was ever much use to an actor in a play. I don't know why. I certainly can't do it. Whatever it is that an actor needs to build a performance writers don't seem able to supply, other than the play itself. You need to be a sort of lay analyst, and most of the best theater directors—like Elia Kazan—are gurus. They make the actor fall in love with them, and then they [extract] the performance. . . . Yes, that is a very useful function.

AMERICAN FILM: Is there a director you think would *add* to your work, who would challenge and reinforce your contribution?

VIDAL: I'm sure such a person exists. I just never worked with him. Anyway, a truly creative director is one who does his own movies—script and all—like Ingmar Bergman or Jean Cocteau, and they have no need of me.

AMERICAN FILM: Would someone like Francis Ford Coppola come close? The novel *The Godfather* is a gangster story, but he turned it into a study of power.

VIDAL: Yes, it was a junky novel that provided the basis for a good movie. Francis was my assistant writer on *Is Paris Burning?* which has got to be one of the most awful movies ever made. He used to write a script in about three days for his employer, Ray Stark. Stark would, let us say, pay Carson McCullers twenty-five dollars for a three-month option on *Reflections in a Golden Eye.* Then he would go to Francis in the back room, and say, "I want a script by Friday." This would be Monday, and on Friday there would be a 210-page screenplay. Then Ray would gallop across town and say to Elizabeth Taylor, "Here's a fine property. So the script is lousy. Forget the script. I'll get you Harold Pinter for the rewrite." And she'd say, "Well, I kind of like it, but what about the director?" Ray would then go to John Huston and say, "Forget the script, John. You can write it yourself. Have we got a deal?"

And that's how a certain kind of movie got made, because Francis spent five days typing in a back room without credit. But he learned a lot about the movies working for Ray Stark.

AMERICAN FILM: Are there any directors you like?

VIDAL: Well, I like Fellini. I think he's becoming terribly—I won't say repetitive, but he's got so proud now that he won't have actors, he won't have scripts, he won't have a narrative. But I think people don't approach his films in the right way. You must think of him as the last of the great painters. He is painting on celluloid. He's doing the Sistine Chapel over and over again. You look at him, but you don't listen to him. God knows he has no narrative gift at all. When he did have good writers like Ennio Flaiano, his pictures were very different. *La Strada* was totally different from these fantasies he is now painting for us.

I seem to be running out of directors. I liked the first half of *Zabriskie Point* of Michelangelo Antonioni. I thought what he did was amazing—the first time an Italian had a clue as to how anybody outside of Italy sounds. The New Left meeting with Kathleen Cleaver was marvelous stuff, but then at the end of the picture he started to paint that Sistine Chapel all over again, with that interminable explosion, like a Joan Miró painting. They're so pretty, the Italians. *Last Tango in Paris*, you know, might have been a good movie had it not been so idiotically pretty. Paris, when autumn leaves are falling! There's not one cliché that Bernardo Bertolucci missed. He should have shot it in Stuttgart or Duluth, and taken Marlon Brando's pants off. One look—and you could have eliminated a lot of dialogue.

AMERICAN FILM: What about some of the directors who have claimed to be storytellers, like Alfred Hitchcock and John Ford?

VIDAL: Hitchcock I exempt in my piece. He was always his own moviemaker; he creates his own pictures. He is a true auteur—of very amusing junk. I suppose John Ford ['s pictures] but I don't remember liking them either. I'll tell you a young director I do like, Marco Bellocchio. I think he's one of the most interesting to come along in years. He writes his own scripts—very exceptional in Italy.

To watch an Italian director putting a film together is wildly funny. Usually, he has a brother-in-law in one part of town who writes a bit. Then he's got a newspaperman who's moonlighting. Perhaps an *au pair* from Finland to do the English version. He runs around town, getting a scene here, a scene there. Then he puts it all together and announces that he is the sole creator. In a sense, I suppose he is. The result is almost always terrible.

AMERICAN FILM: As long as we're on the Italians, what about Lina Wertmüller?

VIDAL: She's a very likable woman. I have seen only two of her movies. I didn't much like them. She is a peculiarly New York phenomenon. She is not well regarded in Italy. She's unknown in France and England. She is really the invention of one John Simon. Beware of anybody he likes because he is consistent in his judgment. I didn't see *Seven Beauties.* I saw *Swept Away* and *Love and Anarchy.* But the two pictures I saw just seemed to me awfully cutesy-pie and very much what people think Italians are. You know, lots of fun, life-enhancing, kind of dumb but lovable. Actually, Italians are not like that at all. They tend to be gloomy, nervous, hypochondriacal. They bite their fingernails. Their hands sweat. They're very nervous people. She doesn't get any of that. She just shows a bunch of Italian waiters being bravura.

MONIQUE VAN VOOREN, 1976:   I think *Seven Beauties* you should see. I would like your opinion of it.

VIDAL: . . . I don't think I could take Giannini's eyes in one more movie. He looks to the right. He looks straight ahead. He looks to the left. Then they get glassy, then he blinks them, then they get brighter.

HOLLIS ALPERT, 1977:   Norman Mailer has made a couple of movies that can hardly be called total successes. They were even worse than *Myra Breckinridge.*

VIDAL: Norman is an odd person. But somebody like Graham Greene, who writes the sort of novel that translates beautifully to film, could direct with the greatest of ease. But, as I said, in those days we didn't want to be bothered with directing, and now it's too late. . . . Those who have the gift [of writing] should go straight into the movies. Write your own scripts. Become your own director.

AMERICAN FILM, 1977:   If even you have had difficulties with directors, how can an obscure writer assert himself?

VIDAL: You're going to have a rough time. But it's not impossible. And if you go into directing, you can then write directly onto the celluloid. I see quite a few directors around town, and what are they looking for? A script. They're busy hustling. For any writer with any success at all, it's very pleasant to have every director at a party come over to you, looking for a script or, as they say, property. Warren Beatty came to me about doing a movie—the actors are now getting into the act. I told him how much I liked *McCabe and Mrs. Miller*, and he said, yes, he liked it too. "Did Robert Altman write it?" I asked. He said, "Well, actually, . . . I did most of it." So I said, "Warren, if you can write that well you don't need me." And he said, "Oh, well. . . . " If you can create a story, you are way ahead of anybody else in the business. In the fifties we got rid of the producers—they became extinct. As the last memo fell from the hand of D. O. Selznick, that was the end. Now we've got to get rid of the directors. This can be done by becoming a director if you are a writer, a storyteller. If you're not, then become a director and hustle.

AMERICAN FILM: When you emphasize the writer, are you also emphasizing more dialogue instead of more of what's called visuals?

VIDAL: I like a talky movie. I believe that an audience will sit still for a great deal of dialogue, if it's good. A director told me the other day that you couldn't have any scene that lasted more than three minutes. The audience wouldn't sit still for anything longer, which is nonsense. If the scene is interesting, the audience will listen for as long as necessary. But you have to be interesting. Most directors seem to have given up on dialogue in favor of moving the images very quickly in order to create a spurious sense of motion, which is not the same thing as narrative. The director who gave me the advice had just finished creating *The Cassandra Crossing*.

Dialogue is not prose. I think that's the first thing to learn. I once adapted *A Farewell to Arms* for television, and it was awful because I was trying to be faithful to Hemingway. I used his dialogue, his famous dialogue, and though it looks all right on the page, it does not play. We were not helped by Guy Madison's performance.

AMERICAN FILM: How do you feel about movie actors?

VIDAL: Oh, I love actors. Movie actors are a very special breed. Gregory Peck and I were once talking about Ronald Reagan, and I said, "I wouldn't want a professional screen actor to be President of the United States, no matter how nice or bright he is because he's spent his entire life being moved about like a piece of furniture. He's used to being used." That's why all the male actors, almost without exception, become alcoholics. Traditionally, it is not in the male nature— this is a sexist remark—to be totally passive. The actor feels unmanly. He gets drunk. The women take up needlepoint, and survive. A major female movie star will have created ten miles of tapestry by the time her career is over. I couldn't imagine an actor as president. I could imagine a director. After all, he's a hustler, a liar, a cheat—plainly presidential.

MONIQUE VAN VOOREN, 1976:   You have known friendships with a number of beautiful ladies and in particular with Claire Bloom. What do you think of her?

VIDAL: I think she's a marvelous actress. She was the best Blanche Du Bois I ever saw and I've seen them all since Jessica Tandy played it originally. She's very intelligent with a rather literary mind and I hope she plays the lead in *1876* should anyone dramatize it.

VAN VOOREN: What do you think of Richard Burton and Elizabeth Taylor?

VIDAL: You're just making me tired, Monique. I've had a rough day. To have those two vials of chloroform broken beneath my nose just before a party. I never want to hear their names again.

VAN VOOREN: Are you interested in her jewels and her luxurious life?

VIDAL: No.

VAN VOOREN: Do you think she deserves it?

VIDAL: I'm sure she deserves it, I just don't want to hear about it anymore. I liked the trichotomy, that's the only thing I ever liked.

FAG RAG, 1974:   I suppose literary criticism is one of the penalties for being prolific when you're young. By middle age, you have to start dealing with critical biographies.

VIDAL: [It now happens to] writers younger than I am like Updike and Harold Pinter. There are more books about Harold Pinter than there are about Chekhov. Most extraordinary thing.

FAG RAG: It's Sputnik again. It's all the college-educated *Time* subscribers who buy books now and belong to book clubs.

VIDAL: Nobody reads these books. It is make-work so you can get tenure in the universities. Who's not being done from the 1940s? Ah, there's Vidal. Willingham. Let's do Willingham.

EUGENE WALTER, 1960:   Have you noted any critical ideas of any importance in America?

VIDAL: I wouldn't know! I read a good deal of criticism, but only as a vice, not so good as reading science fiction, rather better than reading mystery stories. But I do admire the confidence of our nobler critics. They've got it made, and they know it!

DIANE JOHNSON, 1977:   No doubt to be a critic one must be a well-educated moralist with an experiencing nature, but one thing is troubling: Is it also necessary to be good? You mention in your essay on Louis Auchincloss [in *Matters of Fact and of Fiction,* 1977] that it is an article of faith with Americans that only a good person can write a good book. But you do not exactly say whether you agree.

VIDAL: That's an abiding question, and I've often thought about it. But in a way it's like saying that you can't be a good writer and bad in bed.

JOHNSON: Well, I don't see that it's *quite* the same. Anyway, some of our most famous writers—Hemingway and Mailer, among others—have seemed, by their works, to believe just that. Despite what people may hear of them privately.

VIDAL: Well, almost all American male writers are alcoholic, and as a result of the alcohol they become less capable sexually as they get older. They also become confused about which is their penis, which is their pen. Think of all those clones of Hemingway, drinking and worrying—fortunately they write very little.

But human goodness—to return to the question—may be beside the point. Mailer said he would be a better writer if his contemporaries had been better writers and, pitiful statement that it is, one knows what he means. If there were a half dozen good literary critics around, all writing would be better. As it is, an act of publication is almost for its own sake—there are so few critics writing whose opinions one would care to read. It's better to publish in England because the level of criticism is a bit higher. At least they know how to *describe* books. And there is some continuity. Critics themselves have careers, develop, change and modify their views. Having careers themselves, they feel obliged to deal with the careers of the writers they discuss. Here it's hit and run. There's no accountability. A critic whom no one knows strikes out at a writer whose other work he doesn't know.

JOHNSON: Like playing literary Battleship. Yet in your book [*Matters of Fact and of Fiction*] you deplore the panegyric as much as the unillumined attack.

VIDAL: Yes. With us the ability to detect mediocrity or anything else is rare. Evaluation descends, through ignorance, to mere opinion, and opinion is a matter of fashion. And fashion is based on middle-class, middlebrow values, despite the mock defiance of an occasional licensed fool, like Vonnegut.

Where are the critics with commitment to study and reflection? Is there any other critic who would do today what I did in *Matters of Fact and of Fiction* for Italo Calvino? I read him, thought about him, and presented my findings. I wait for a critic to do this for my work. Oh, academics do it, and their works are useful in helping you keep track of when you wrote what—you can always look in their appendices. But in academe the tone is wrong. The object overwhelms the subject. One does not know who the scholar is; therefore it does not much matter what he thinks. The opposite case is the mad egotism of a writer like Mailer, whose subjectivity becomes the topic, whatever the occasion. What's wanted is the essay, in Montaigne's sense—the attempt. The critical act must ultimately be the examination of one's own life.

JOHNSON: Matthew Arnold held disinterestedness, with curiosity, to be the properties with which the critic would save culture, by which he meant much more than just literature. From the wide range of subjects in your new volume, I gather that you too are concerned with this connection.

VIDAL: The relation of literature to culture is evident, though it seems widely to have escaped notice. Culture is in the hands of schoolteachers who enter literature in much the same way that the Victorians went into the Church, and once safely inside the academy, increase their own kind, spawned by misreadings of Joyce. They are insulated from most of the public novels, by writers like Saul Bellow and me, who expect their work to be read by people. Academics particularly delight in novels that mistake the university for the universe, of the sort Professor John Barth writes. But to paraphrase my own essay, it seems not to matter to American culture whether any given book is good or bad, for who, after all, would know the difference?

STANTON, 1979:   In 1975 you told an interviewer from *Oui* that you were "born a critic—and a tough one...." In what ways are you a tough critic?

VIDAL: I mean critic in the large sense. One who casts a clear eye upon the prospect about him. Henry James and Edith Wharton are critics in this sense and so, to my mind, they are the only two American novelists that might be called great. The others tend to impose some moral view upon what they see at the expense of what is there. James and Wharton also work from a moral sense but we are shown Maggie Verver absolutely in the round unlike what's-her-name in *The Marble Faun.* Most American writers are romantics and they write Romances. Melville, Hawthorne, Faulkner. I suppose these writers are good in their way but their way is not the true critic's way, the novel's way . . . as I see the novel, as I see the critic's function.

STANTON, 1977:   I recently read a letter written by Hawthorne to a magazine editor. In it, he said, "In all my stories, I think, there is one idea running through them like an iron rod, and to which all other ideas are referred and subordinate...." I found an idea running through the work of Africa's greatest poet, Christopher Okigbo—an idea which made him into a martyr. Most recently, I found, I think, an idea full of life in the work of the British poet Charles Tomlinson.

VIDAL: You have your own methods as a critic. You look for that "iron rod." I don't. I set out on a voyage (as in the case of Calvino). I read the books in the order that they were published. I get impressions, points. No doubt miss as much as I get. At the end I have *some*thing. I make a description of what I have read. If there is One Theme it will be there. If not, not. I don't look for it. I take the works as they are. Relate them to one another; to other works by other writers that come to mind. Ultimately, the imagination must do the work of synthesis. To my mind, you are working backwards (I have sworn not to mention Procrustes but there he is). Why not just weave a text (from the Latin *textum* meaning net) and throw it upon the waters and haul in your catch (the works) and see what you get? The American vice is explaining, I recently explained in the *New York Review of Books.*

DIANE JOHNSON, 1977: Mr. Vidal, you recently wrote in the *New York Review of Books,* "when it comes to matters of prose and of fiction at this time and in this place, I am authority." Is this authority conferred by fiat? By whom? Or is it seized? Or revealed?

VIDAL: It is earned, mostly, but it is also a matter of temperament. The critic must know more than either writer or academic. He must also value experience and have a truth-telling nature. I think I have that. In their youth most people worry whether or not other people will like them. Not me. I had the choice of going under or surviving, and I survived by understanding (after the iron—if not the silver—had entered my soul) that it is I who am keeping score. What matters is what I think, not what others think of me; and I am willing to say what I think. That is the critical temperament. Edmund Wilson had it, but almost no one else now does, except for a few elderly Englishmen.

JOHNSON: Oscar Wilde said that criticism is the record of one's own soul, the only civilized form of autobiography, with which, I take it, you would agree. And you mention another great critic, Montaigne. Have you been influenced by these men? Or by whom?

VIDAL: I must read more Wilde. I read and reread Montaigne. But what really started me writing critical essays was my reading of George Saintsbury. When I was twenty-five I bought a house up on the Hudson, and for ten years I read, and supported myself by writing for TV. Saintsbury was a terrible Tory, but good on the French.

JOHNSON: And good on style. Do you give him credit for your brilliant style, or do you reserve credit for that to yourself? I don't remember that Saintsbury was ever funny.

VIDAL: He was good on the text. It was through Saintsbury I came to read the French, especially Sainte-Beuve, and another critical line that interested me was Peacock/Meredith/Huxley.

JOHNSON: Peacock, Meredith, and Montaigne were all self-educated, in the way you describe yourself. Is that significant?

VIDAL: Self-education is the point of education. But it is easier if you have escaped the stifling of the academy. I had only one interesting course at Exeter, on Plato and Milton, otherwise the boredom was complete. I tried to educate myself by writing down the events of history, in parallel columns, to learn what was happening in Assyria while events went forward in, say, France. I always wanted to know everything. And if I were a dictator, this is how I would require children to be educated, starting them out at whatever the best age is, with whatever the best theory is of the origin of the world, and bringing them along through history—in parallel columns—no black history or English history or other separatist nonsense—making them read the math, and philosophy, and literature of each period, so that when they are seventeen or so they would know the best that has been thought and said in the world, to appropriate Matthew Arnold's phrase.

JOHNSON: Your assumption, then, is that curiosity is an innate property of the human mind? It's a nice view.

VIDAL: I must believe that or I couldn't live. The whole reason I write those historical novels is to teach myself. Being a puritan, I believe it is good to know something. Still, regarding curiosity, there is some evidence to the contrary. Except Bellow, my celebrated contemporaries all seem to have stopped learning in their 20's. D. H. Lawrence said it all, in a review of Hemingway, when he pointed out that Hemingway was essentially a photographer—and photographers don't age well.

It was Virgil Thomson who advised a young music critic not to evaluate the music he heard but to describe it. The description would *be* the evaluation. But that requires that the critic, the describer, is an informed and evolving sensibility, not a camera. The biggest problem with our contemporary bookchat critics is that they are incapable of describing, or apprehending, or comprehending what they see. Is it the Taj Mahal? Is it a pavilion? A coliseum?

To comment intelligently on literature, you have to be used to reading, something that the generation under forty does not seem to like to do. On the other hand, they don't mind *writing* books and becoming legends. But they are ruled by ambition and envy, those two prevailing American passions which preclude comprehension. All distinction is resented, and that which has been distinguished is traduced, if not in the first flush of fashionable heat, then soon after.

OUI, 1975:   Do you feel that if your books had been accepted differently by American critics, you might be living in the United States today and not in Italy?

VIDAL: Ah, I see the interview! Bitter, disappointed, Vidal turns back on area and nation that rejected him! Hardly applicable, however, to a writer as much praised and read as I am—if for the wrong reasons.

STANTON, 1977:   If Henry James were alive today what might he say of your work?

VIDAL: James would find me puzzling.

OUI, 1975:   You have attempted to be both a popular and an intellectual writer. Do you find that intellectuals resent your popular success?

VIDAL: You must ask them. But then, there aren't many intellectuals in the United States. I have the impression that this happy few rather like what I do.

STANTON, 1977:   I recently read *Two Sisters*. On page 41 I hung over the following: "As for literature . . . it has no relevance to the young who were brought up on television and movies, and though they are doubtless happier for that whole experience, they are also quite unable to comprehend the *doubleness* of things, the unexpected paradox, the sense of yes-no without which there can be no true intelligence, no means, in fact, of examining life as opposed to letting it wash over one." A structural critic (pardon the thought) could have a field-day with such a fact. He would now have the answer to his primary question: What is at the very root of Vidal's art? Knowing this, our critic could now show how the concept of "doubleness" works in everything you do. I wonder if it will someday be done? Forgive me, but I think I should like to read it.

VIDAL: Don't get hung up on the idea that there is ever ONE theme to a writer's work (even if the ONE is TWO and so duality). Most bad criticism stems from the desire to make a case that all of the work of a given writer repeats a single theme. The best writers (and critics) are various. After all, what was Shakespeare's theme? Making that noun singular makes the question silly.

STANTON, 1977:   You do have one theme: America.

VIDAL: Well . . . America is a state of mind, as they say, and I pay state tax despite foreign residence. But a concern with the state I was born into and explore is not exactly A theme or One theme . . . just a point of reference. France was Flaubert's only subject. Proof? Only a Frenchman could have produced the dreadful *Salammbo* set in Carthage (Seine-et-Oise). By the way, he is an excellent example of the writer with many voices or, perhaps, tones. Difficult to link the *Temptation of St. Anthony* with *Madame Bovary*. Except for the Frenchness of it all! *L'Education Sentimentale* is a marvelous novel, by the way. . . .

DENNIS ALTMAN, 1977:   It's often said that the American literary establishment—you might argue whether there is such a thing—is relentlessly anti-gay.

VIDAL: I think that's quite true, at least during the thirty-odd years that I've been writing. Much of this reflects the general ethos of the country. Then there are special problems. *The New York Times* is essentially a Jewish newspaper. Until recently, the editors were a sort of rabbinate upholding Mosaic values. Fag-baiting was routine there. The fifties was a very bad time, in general. . . . The fact that 99.9 per cent of homosexualists haven't the slightest desire to be women, nor do they think of themselves as women, is still unknown out there in the wild American dark, and I can't think why. Old Testament canards, I suppose. The fact that all the so-called he-man occupations (warriors, sailors, athletes) are heavily populated by homosexualists is simply denied, even though anyone who has served in an army knows otherwise.

ALTMAN: How far have you suffered in terms of reviews, etc., from being known, in your phrase, as a "homosexualist"?

VIDAL: Contrary to legend, I have never discussed my private life in my work or in public—except once. As a result of something my old friend Jack Kerouac wrote about the two of us in *The Subterraneans*, I responded to it in *Two Sisters*. By temperament [I'm] not a self-revealer; on the other hand I've been an activist when it comes to changing laws and so on, and I'd say the reactions to that were pretty venomous. After two highly praised books, I published *The City and the Pillar*. Half the newspapers wouldn't review it and *The New York Times* would not take advertising for it. Orville Prescott (the daily reviewer for the *Times* and the most powerful bookchat writer in the country) said that not only would he not review that book, but he would never again review a book by me. So my next five novels were not reviewed in the daily *Times.* Silence is the great destroyer. That was how John Horne Burns was, in a sense, murdered by our literary homophobes. But I am not easily destroyed.

GERALD CLARKE, 1972:   Your reviews here [in America] haven't been all that bad.

VIDAL: Maybe one good review in ten. But then, are they really reviews? They usually read like Leonard Lyons' column, without Lenny's wit and polish. Our bookchat writers have heard about literary criticism, just as they know about books—they're something remote and faraway from school days. But when they have to actually describe a book, panic sets in. All those words to be read! Better to talk about the author: How much money does he make? What's his sex life? Politics? Life-style? Does he conform to what middle-class, middlebrow readers would think of as a really Good Person? I fear I'm not their idea of a Good Person. Worse, in *Two Sisters,* I said "classic" American literature wasn't much good. I dared suggest *Moby Dick* was not in the same class as *King Lear. Roget's Thesaurus* really hit the fan. After all, isn't America the greatest country on earth? If that's so, then its writers have to be the greatest—so Melville must be at least as good as Shakespeare. Actually, anyone who thinks Melville is in the same class as Tolstoy, George Eliot, Dickens, Flaubert, Stendhal . . . oh, well, you can't blame them. They're pumped so full of America the Beautiful laughing gas in school that they're kept permanently floating outside Western civilization.

We'll never know whether anybody was a good novelist or a bad novelist in this period because there's nobody left to do the necessary reading. . . . The bookchat writers haven't read Stendhal, much less me. There is a kind of galloping cretinism in the land which does not augur well for our shoddy civilization.

You see, if you don't share any of the cultural values of a country, you're immediately embattled. I have a militant nature, and I don't mind that at all, but it gets very tiring to live in continual conflict. I don't read the same books they do. I don't know the same culture, I don't have the same admirations, and I certainly don't have the same moral code as any of [our] contemporary writers. To me Norman Mailer is like the head of an American Legion post. His patriarchal attitudes toward sex are exactly the same, and his self-aggrandizing bullying is very much in the American tradition.

MONIQUE VAN VOOREN, 1976:   You've said that the critics in New York were not favorable to you yet you consistently keep getting good reviews. I just read in *The New York Times* a review of your book *1876* and it was extremely favorable.

VIDAL: I suppose after thirty years I've worn them out.

STANTON, 1979:   What makes American literary criticism so awful?

VIDAL: I've written so much about that. Most recently in my piece on V. S. Pritchett. I don't have much to add. Except, perhaps, that it is the American temperament to hustle. And the hustler—for obvious reasons—can never tell the truth about what he's hustling. And if you can't tell the truth, you can't be a critic.

STANTON, 1978:   Why do you have such a dislike of *The New York Times?*

VIDAL: Harvey Breit, the Assistant Editor of the *Times* Book section, told me in 1952 that I ought to use a pseudonym because nothing by me would be well-reviewed there. Incidentally, in your introduction [to *Gore Vidal: A Primary and Secondary Bibliography*—Vidal refers to an early introduction which was not used in the book] you don't seem to take seriously the blackout of my work. Because the books were widely reviewed around the U.S. (and very well in England) was not the point. The most important place in the country was closed to me from 1948 to 1964: the daily *New York Times* review. That was done by Orville Prescott (he came out of retirement in 1964 to review *Julian*) who proudly told Nicholas Wreden my editor at Dutton that he would never again read, much less review, a book of mine (after *The City and the Pillar*). So five novels were not noticed there or in *Time* or in *Newsweek*. You cannot remain a public novelist in the U.S. without the attention of those three places—at least then. So I wrote three books as Edgar Box—and *The New York Times* praised all three highly. Went to TV . . . the Prescott Ukase did not affect the *Times*'s TV reviewers or the theatre and film critics . . . for a time. Eventually, when I began to appear menacing, the reviews conformed. You may not criticize the American imperium and expect the *Times* to support you; particularly now when only the Pentagon stands between gallant little Israel and the Arab hordes. On homosexuality, the *Times* has been singularly vicious. They have slowly moved from hatred of the abominable (vide *Leviticus*) to alarm at an illness that endangers The Family. The in-house ax-job on Tripp's *Homosexual Matrix* is a recent example. Twice they prepared and carried off ax-jobs on me—on a major scale. When I was running for Congress they sent up a giggling reporter who followed me about and wrote a peculiarly mendacious account of what I was doing and what the campaign was all about. Shortly before that, Markel (the Sunday editor) approached several writers (mostly friends like Richard Rovere who reported to me what had happened), requesting an attack on *The Best Man* and *Advise and Consent,* by those two goy-fags who were traducing a Great Republic which alone stood between gallant little you-know-what, etc. I am not a favorite of American middle-class establishment Jews. Currently, the *Times* tries to get me to write for them while giving my books to ambitious, clumsy academics like the one who reviewed *Kalki* (getting the plot wrong . . . and a short book, too). Meanwhile Lehmann-Haupt usually gave me good but stupid reviews . . . until I wrote a letter to the *Times* explaining that my dislike of West Point and the rulers of the U.S. (a class I

know and they don't) was not the result of a Freudian conflict
with my West Point father, as Lehmann-Haupt stated confi-
dently on three occasions. The *Times* refused to print the letter, naturally. So it was printed in the *New York Review of Books.*
Now do you know why I dislike *The New York Times?*

PARIS REVIEW, 1974:   Why will you always get a bad
press?

VIDAL: That's more for you to determine than for me.
I have my theories, no doubt wrong. I suspect that the range
of my activity is unbearable to people who write about books.
Lenny Bernstein is not reviewed in *The New York Times* by an
unsuccessful composer or by a student at Juilliard. He might
be better off if he were, but he isn't. Writers are the only people who are reviewed by people of their own kind. And their
own kind can often be reasonably generous—*if* you stay in
your category. I don't. I do many different things rather better
than most people do one thing. And envy is the central fact of
American life. Then of course I am The Enemy of so many. I
have attacked both Nixon and the Kennedys—as well as the
American Empire. I've also made the case that American literature has been second-rate from the beginning. This caused
distress in bookchat land. They *knew* I was wrong, but since
they don't read foreign or old books, they were forced to
write things like "Vidal thinks Victor Hugo is better than
Faulkner." Well, Hugo *is* better than Faulkner, but to the residents of bookchat land Hugo is just a man with a funny name
who wrote *Les Miserables,* a movie on the Late Show. Finally, I
am proud to say that I am most disliked because for twenty-
six years I have been in open rebellion against the heterosexual dictatorship in the United States. Fortunately, I have lived
long enough to see the dictatorship start to collapse. I now
hope to live long enough to see a sexual democracy in America. I deserve at least a statue in Dupont Circle—along with
Dr. Kinsey,

DENNIS ALTMAN, 1977:   In the study of gay literature
that's going on now in the U.S. you've been classed along

with Williams and Capote and Burroughs as one of the important post-war American gay novelists. Do you reject that definition?

VIDAL: Yes. I deal in other subjects. Politics, history, theology. As a novelist I have dealt with The Subject on occasion. And, prematurely—1948 is a long time ago. But isn't *The City and the Pillar* really about sexual obsession? . . .

But, of course, the heterosexual dictatorship not only recognizes its enemies, but defines them in its own terms. In the last few months, I have been singled out not only as the National Fag, but as the creator of a new order that means to destroy The Family, The American Empire, Capitalism, and Warm Mature Heterosexual Relationships. This shit is being dispensed, variously, by Norman Podhoretz in *Harper's Magazine,* Joseph Epstein in *Commentary,* Alfred Kazin in *Esquire,* and what I take to be a Tel Aviv hotel named the Hilton Kramer in *Partisan Review.* All these fag-baiters are Jews who have swung to the right, to join Anita Bryant and the Jesus Christers who, officially, want us to prepare for that military showdown with international communism that will mean (as far as their American-Jewish allies go) security and victory for Israel. Of course, it will mean only death for all. But these people are fools, and dangerous. More to the point, they don't realize to what extent they themselves—the Jews—are hated out there in Goy-land. If they had any sense, they would ally themselves with us. But they don't so . . .

MONIQUE VAN VOOREN, 1976:   What do you think of John Simon?

VIDAL: Ah well, poor John Simon—what a nightmare, to wake up in the morning and realize that you are John Simon.

VAN VOOREN: Do you think he's a good writer?

VIDAL: No.

VAN VOOREN: Do you think he's accurate?

VIDAL: He's irrelevant. He's a peculiarly New York phenomenon. [New York] worships incompetence, particularly if it's combined with energy and paranoid self-confidence. Only in a city like New York could Truman Capote have made it, or John Simon.

STANTON, 1977:   Do you have any response to Seymour Krim's attack on your status as a serious artist in his "Reflections on a Ship That's Not Sinking at All" in *London Magazine* (May 1970)?

VIDAL: Did Krim attack my "serious" status? How would he know what was serious and what was not? A lively piece, as I remember. The only thing I really recall was his statement that *Dark Green, Bright Red* was my best novel. That was when I realized that he had never read any of my novels.

JUDY HALFPENNY, 1979:   You know I've never appreciated *Messiah* as it deserves, but, on the other hand, I've never written, as Michael Ross does in his *Literary Politicians,* "Vidal is no critic of ideas; he does not quarrel with Cave's doctrine of death." If you are not a critic of ideas, what are you? And how should a writer "quarrel" with a doctrine whose implications and results he is demonstrating?

VIDAL: Simple people like Ross always think that because a writer can embody a character or an idea that that is *his* character and idea. This is why we have so few literary critics. They do not know what or why literature is.

OUI, 1975:   You indicated that British critics had a better understanding of *Myra* than American critics. As a writer, do you feel more at home in England because of that?

VIDAL: No, it was a general observation. In America, bookchat has always been written by people who were not good enough to write about sports. Out in the provinces, books are often handed to somebody's wife or, worse, to a local academic. In England, the standard of all critical writing, whether it's bookchat or showbiz chat, is higher than it is in America because, by and large, the English write better and talk better than Americans. As Dwight MacDonald pointed out, any letter to *The Times* of London is better written than any editorial in *The New York Times.* The English just have a greater respect for language. And, of course, their reviewers have read more books than ours have. The British saw *Myra*'s relationship to world literature—that my origins are in Petronius and Apuleius, two writers no American journalist has ever read. One even remarked upon the resemblance to Choderlos de Laclos' *Les Liaisons Dangereuses.* I don't need to say that no bookchat hack at the *Times* has ever read that brilliant novel.

Even in Italy, where hardly anyone reads, the level of reviewing, though there's an awful lot of political ax grinding, is considerably higher than in the United States. And there are more good novelists working in Italy than in the United States, where all the bright young people want to be movie directors or, God help us, movie reviewers.

STANTON, 1977:   I've read *Matters of Fact and of Fiction* . . . and am very much aware of your dislike of academic critics, but I'm not sure of your reasons. I wonder if you sometimes confuse an academic critic with the average Sunday book reviewer. Aren't there large distinctions to be drawn?

VIDAL: If you have read with care "The Hacks of Academe" you will know why I dislike, in general, academic critics; obviously, in particular, there are a number that I have admired: Trilling, Dupee, Richard Chase. "Plastic Fiction" and "The French New Novel" also touch on the subject. At no point do I confuse those teachers of English concerned with something called Novel Theory with the writers of bookchat in newspapers—although *The New York Times* Sunday book section likes to have academic types comment on contemporary literature. I also say nothing at all about those English teachers who are engaged in scholarly and harmless (and sometimes useful) pursuits. Read Edmund Wilson on the tribe. I also quote somewhere Bellow on the arrogance of those English teachers who appropriate for themselves the prestige of those great figures that they teach. I suspect that most of your life has probably been spent in and around universities and it must seem to you that this is the whole of intellectual/literary life. I think that the American University has not much to do with either intellect or literature. And I do read (or try to read) some of the works that come out of the English departments. I also see what you probably don't see: the works of ambitious English teachers who submit pieces to the *New York Review of Books*. They can't write. This means that they have difficulty reading, that is, thinking. The *Review* is criticized for being Anglophile because so much of what it publishes is by English critics. But the reason is simple, and sad. The Americans don't write well enough. In the old racist days of my youth, the worst one could say of a writer was that he wrote like an educated Negro. As blacks achieved beauty (or what passes for same) and a black flow of language, "educated Negroes" in paleface have taken over the English departments. They are now trying to invent a new jargon for themselves, as if literary criticism ought to be as incoherent and paraphrastic, say, as the writings of the sociologists. In any case, I never confuse serious if misguided critics like Bloom or my friend Poirier who teach in universities with writers of bookchat like Alfred Kazin who looked, years ago, as if he might become a critic but has since settled for self-serving chat.

OUI, 1975:   Whom do the English departments admire?

VIDAL: Those academic writers who reflect the university itself, like John Barth. He writes novels to be taught in class. [Since] I aim at clarity, [I] need no one to mediate between me and the reader.

PARIS REVIEW, 1974:   How much do you think college English courses can influence a career? Or teach one about the Novel?

VIDAL: I don't know. . . . I have lectured on campuses for a quarter-century and it is my impression that after taking a course in The Novel, it is an unusual student who would ever want to read a novel again. Those English courses are what have killed literature for the public. Books are made a duty. Imagine teaching novels! Novels used to be written simply to be read. It was assumed until recently that there was a direct connection between writer and reader. Now that essential connection is being mediated—bugged?—by English Departments. Well, who needs the mediation? Who needs to be taught how to read a contemporary novel? Either you read it because you want to or you don't. Assuming of course that you can read anything at all. But this business of taking novels apart in order to show bored children how they were put together—there's a madness to it. Only a literary critic would benefit and there are never more than ten good critics in the United States at any given moment. So what is the point of these desultory autopsies performed according to that little set of instructions at the end of each text? Have you seen one? What symbols to look for? What does the author mean by the word "white"? I look at the notes appended to my own pieces in anthologies and know despair.

PARIS REVIEW: How would you "teach" the novel?

VIDAL: I would teach world civilization—east and west—from the beginning to the present. This would occupy the college years—would be the spine to my educational system. Then literature, economics, art, science, philosophy, religion would be dealt with naturally, sequentially, as they occurred. After four years, the student would have at least a glimmering of what our race is all about.

NEWSWEEK, 1974: Has the novelist lost his importance in America?

VIDAL: When I started, novelists were at the center of the culture. Now we're on the periphery; we're where the poets used to be. Now it's the film director or the trendy politician or the talking head on television, these are the hot people. . . .

PARIS REVIEW, 1974:   You have known a good many writers. Is there anything to be got from knowing other writers, personally?

VIDAL: I don't think so. When I was young I wanted to meet the famous old writers I admired. So I met Gide, Forster, Cocteau, and Santayana. I sent Thomas Mann a book. He sent me a polite letter with my name misspelled. I never expected to "learn" anything from looking at them. Rather it was a laying-on of hands. A connection with the past. I am perhaps more conscious of the past than most American writers, and need the dead for comfort.

PARIS REVIEW: Do you enjoy being with other writers? Henry James once said, for example, that Hawthorne was handicapped because he was isolated from other writers.

VIDAL: Yes, I like the company of other writers. Christopher Isherwood, Tennessee Williams, and Paul Bowles have been friends. But I am not so sure James meant that Hawthorne's isolation had to do with not knowing other writers. I think James meant that the American scene was culturally so thin that it was hard to develop intellectually if you had nobody to talk to. This explains the solipsistic note in the work of so many American writers. They think they are the only ones in the world to doubt the existence of God, say— like Mark Twain, for instance.

PARIS REVIEW: Who was the first writer you ever met?

VIDAL: Well, growing up in Washington, a lot of journalists came to the house: Walter Lippmann, Arthur Krock, Drew Pearson—but I did not think much of journalists. I was more interested in Michael Arlen who used to come and play bridge. A splendid, rather ornate, Beerbohmesque dandy. And by no means a bad writer. I was fascinated recently by *Exiles,* his son's book about him. One summer before the war we were all at the Homestead Hotel in Hot Springs,

Virginia, where Michael and Atlanta Arlen were much admired by everyone, including my mother and her husband
Hugh Auchincloss. But to my astonishment, I now read that
the boy was embarrassed by [his parents]—they were too
dark, flashy, exotic—not pink and square like the American
gentry. Like us, I suppose. Life is odd. Michael's son wanted
for a father a stockbroker named Smith while I would've giv-
en anything if his father had been my father—well, *step*father.

PARIS REVIEW: But later, on your own, whom did you
meet, know . . .

VIDAL: I was still in uniform when I met Anaïs Nin in
1945. I refer you to the pages of her diary for that historic encounter. I thought she was marvelous but didn't much like her
writing. Years later, reading her journals, I was horrified to
discover that she felt the same about me. In '48 I met Tennessee in Rome, at the height of his fame. We traveled about in
an old jeep. I have never laughed more with anyone, but can't
say that I learned anything from him or anyone else. That
process is interior. Paradoxically, in the ten years that I wrote
for television, theater, movies, I learned how to write novels.
Also, writing three mystery novels in one year taught me that
nothing must occur in narrative which is not of use. Ironic
that the lesson of Flaubert—which I thought that I had absorbed—I did not really comprehend until I was pot-boiling.

PARIS REVIEW: You have described meeting E. M. Forster at King's College . . .

VIDAL: I met him first at a party for Isherwood. London, '48. Forster was very excited at meeting Tennessee and
not at all at meeting me—which I considered unfair since I
had read and admired all his books while Tennessee, I fear,
thought that he was in the presence of the [creator] of Captain
Horatio Hornblower. Part of Tennessee's wisdom is to read
nothing at all. Anyway Forster, looking like an old river rat,
zeroed in on Tennessee and said how much he admired *Street-
car.* Tennessee gave him a beady look. Forster invited us to
King's for lunch. Tennessee rolled his eyes and looked at me.

Yes, I said quickly. The next day I dragged Tennessee to the railroad station. As usual with Tennessee, we missed the first train. The second train would arrive in half an hour. Tennessee refused to wait. "But we *have* to go," I said. "He's sitting on one of the lions in front of the college, waiting for us." Tennessee was not moved by the poignant tableau. "I can't," he said, gulping and clutching his heart—when Tennessee does not spit blood he has heart spasms. "Besides," said Tennessee primly, wandering off in the wrong direction for the exit, "I cannot abide old men with urine stains on their trousers." I went on alone. I have described that grim day in *Two Sisters*.

PARIS REVIEW: You seem to still see this scene vividly. Do you think of the writer as a constant observer and recorder?

VIDAL: Well, I am not a camera, no. I don't consciously watch anything and I don't take notes though I briefly kept a diary. What I remember I remember—by no means the same as remembering what you would like to.

GERALD CLARKE, 1972:   How about Truman Capote?

VIDAL: Truman and I have known each other since I was nineteen and he was twenty. His first short story and my first novel came out in the same year. All through the forties we were linked together by the press, I suppose just because we were the two youngest writers. Neither of us much enjoyed the linking together. Capote always had a passion for knowing the rich and famous. [I] didn't [—and I don't.]

PARIS REVIEW, 1974:   How do you see yourself in an age of personality-writers, promoting themselves and their work? For instance, Capote says he is an expert at promoting books and gaining the attention of the media.

VIDAL: Every writer ought to have at least one thing that he does well, and I'll take Truman's word that a gift for publicity is the most glittering star in his diadem. I'm pretty good at promoting my views on television but a washout at charming the bookchatters. But then I don't really try. Years ago Mailer solemnly assured me that to be a "great" writer in America you had to be fairly regularly on the cover of the Sunday *New York Times* Book section. Nothing else mattered. Anyway, he is now what he wanted to be: the patron saint of bad journalism; and I am exactly what I set out to be: a novelist.

STANTON, 1978:   I should like to know why Mailer is so crazy. I read his article in the November, 1977 issue of *Esquire,* and saw you and him on the Dick Cavett show. I'm going to write him a letter to see if he can come up with an explanation of his strange behavior.

VIDAL: I'd be interested to see what Mailer writes you, if anything. I don't think he is likely to admit to envy, that chief emotion of all United Statespersons. "When I first heard of you, I thought you were the devil," he said to me when we met in the early '50s. I suspect he has now gone back to his original superstition. For decades Capote was reviewed as if he were Goethe. Now Mailer would have hated Capote for his success. Not I. I had—and have—perfect contempt for these writers of bookchat who were not able to see how very bad Capote's work was (and, obviously, how good mine was!). You might have some fun trying to figure out the reason why I create such a storm of rage from so many odd types . . . even, on those rare occasions, when I am innocent of provocation.

STANTON, 1978:   Alas, Mailer never answered my letter.

VIDAL: Mailer is too great a writer to read anything at all.

MONIQUE VAN VOOREN, 1976:   Have you seen Capote lately?

VIDAL: I've seen him about once in twenty years and I had an impression that the one time was probably too often. It was at Dru Heinz's. I didn't have my glasses on and I sat down on what I thought was a poof and it was Capote.

FAG RAG, 1974: Truman said you took him to the Everard [Baths].

VIDAL: I did take Truman to the Everard. Couldn't have been funnier. "I just don't like it," [says Vidal in Capote's voice].

FAG RAG: What is it about that man that interests him in murder?

VIDAL: Peculiar.

FAG RAG: Will Capote be very rich when he dies?

VIDAL: Capote has no money.

FAG RAG: Really? Living at UN Plaza?

VIDAL: This is one of the reasons why he has no money. He thinks he's Bunny Mellon. . . . He thinks he's a very rich Society Lady, and spends a great deal of money.

FAG RAG: So Mailer went after you?

VIDAL: They all did. However, Capote never really touched on the subject. He is a Republican housewife from Kansas with all the prejudices. Just as Norman Mailer is a VFW Commander in Schenectady.

STANTON, 1979: What ever happened to Capote's *Answered Prayers?* He claims that he started the work in the mid-1950s. I notice that in a recent interview with Capote, David Susskind did not ask him about the work. He won't answer any of my letters to him. Does anyone know if his "swan song" (his words) will ever be finally sung?

VIDAL: I gather that Capote has written nothing since those pieces that he composed in 1968 and published in *Esquire* as parts of something called *Answered Prayers.* I have never found him an interesting writer. No, this is not because of my distaste for him personally. An hour with a dentist without novocain was like one minute with Carson McCullers but I admired her work. It is never wise to allow personal feelings to affect one's critical judgment. If they do, then avoid any mention of the one disliked. After all, if a critic is not personally disinterested, he's simply another literary gangster, grinding axes.

JUDY HALFPENNY, 1979:   I have never known a book to disappear as fast as *Answered Prayers.*

VIDAL: Mr. Capote never wrote *Answered Prayers.* It is the Madonna of the Future all over again. But as this is America, if you publicize a non-existent work enough, it becomes positively palpable. It would be nice if he were to get the Nobel on the strength of *Answered Prayers* which he, indeed, never wrote. There were a few jagged pieces of what might have been a gossip-novel published in *Esquire.* The rest is silence; and litigation and . . . noise on TV.

GERALD CLARKE, 1972:   William Styron once told me that there are only five big writers in the country today. He included Mailer, of course, Truman Capote, and himself. You, I'm sorry to say, were not on his list. . . .

VIDAL: There are some writers who are more written about than others. . . . I'm more written about than most. Is this bigness? The books of Styron's "big" writers aren't very good. *A Separate Peace* by John Knowles is better than any novel by William Styron. The novels of Louis Auchincloss are better than the novels of Truman Capote. But Capote and Styron are big, Knowles and Auchincloss are small. Bill *looks* like a great writer, and he sounds like a great writer. Will anybody ever sort this out? In the absence of literary criticism, probably not.

JUDY HALFPENNY, 1977:   In general, I dislike short stories but I enjoy those of Louis Auchincloss more than his novels, and I even think they are better written.

VIDAL: You're right about Louis's stories. They are infinitely better than the novels and I can't think why. He has the architectural sense which makes novel-writing possible. Not many writers have the capacity. I think he gets bored too early with his characters.

STANTON, 1978:   Do you have any reactions to John Knowles' use of you as a model for Brinker Hadley in *A Separate Peace?* Did he give us an accurate portrait of you as a young man? How well do you know Knowles? Where did he stand in relation to you at Exeter?

VIDAL: I don't remember Jack at Exeter. I was a year or two ahead of him. He knew me because I was a busy politician; and wrote for the *Review.* The character is not me at all; in fact, Jack is more interesting in *Look* magazine in '68, when he describes me to Laura Berquist. I liked his book enormously. I see him from time to time.

MICHAEL DEAN, 1968:   You are regarded, from this safe distance [in England] anyway, as a rather patrician figure, as a kind of fugitive from the French court.

VIDAL: Which court? Not Malraux's anyway. I never much liked the classical canon in American literature. I always thought that our great novelists were minor provincial writers. Our great classic canon now being taught at Sussex and so on really isn't much good, and I think I have known this all along—that's part of my loneliness, you know, that *Moby Dick* is a very bad novel. I think I could prove it, given 5,000 words.

STANTON, 1977:   You have not really said much of importance on early American literature, have you? Perhaps Henry Adams is the one exception, and maybe Washington Irving. . . . Do you see yourself in line with any particular American writer or writers?

VIDAL: No, I don't feel any particular kinship with the early American writers. Obviously James and Henry Adams have been influences but since I do not write romances I was not influenced by Hawthorne & Co. who were all romancers rather than novelists. Late in life, I've developed a taste for Howells. And, of course, Edith Wharton.

EVE AUCHINCLOSS & NANCY LYNCH, 1961:   Can a democracy produce great literature?

VIDAL: Well, [so far] it hasn't, not in the large tradition. Literature comes out of a civilization, not the other way around. And this is hardly a civilization yet. We've produced many enormously talented writers, whom we have tended to inflate, but we've produced no literature. You can make literature out of anything, but there must be a proper climate to make the best things possible. We may now be on the verge of having a civilization—small, but all our own—but it looks like it may not be interested in novels.

CURTIS BILL PEPPER, 1974:   What is the aim of art?

VIDAL: It used to be perfection, whatever form you were working in. What is perfection? We don't know, but we certainly know what is *less* than perfection, so that's how you can, in a sense, be a critic. For the last fifty years, however, the aim of art has been novelty—which, by and large, is repellent. So the result is a kind of vicious circle, with people trying to think up something that nobody else has thought up because they think that's the way Masaccio discovered perspective. They think he sat and thought and thought . . . and, by God he came up with perspective. Well, everybody knew about perspective. It just happened that in the evolution of Masaccio's way of looking at things—and in the situation in which he was when he was given a couple of walls to paint on—he made something of his own. That's how it happened, how it always happens. The great artist is original without trying to be.

STANTON, 1978:   I hope one day to be able to recreate Hawthorne's world in a novel. Although I have been studying Hawthorne for fifteen years, I am not ready to put him into a novel yet. But I am learning through your example, and what I'm writing now is quite good I think. The only clumsy thing about Hawthorne was his use of dialogue. He had, as he was told by a one-armed lawyer, the eye of a hawk. Have you read the letters and notebooks? It was impossible to fool him; he was a brilliant observer and his art is rich and deep, especially his descriptive powers. *Our Old Home* will delight you, if it hasn't already.

VIDAL: The world of Hawthorne ought to be a fascinating thing to reconstruct. There is something awfully wrong with his writing. Partly, no ear for dialogue. Partly too much Romance? I've read *Our Old Home,* and borrowed from it for *Burr:* the description of a consul's tasks vis-à-vis ships in port. The Franklin Pierce connection is also interesting. And Melville. . . . You have, indeed, a Subject.

STANTON, 1977:   Three outstanding writers—Stephen Crane, Joseph Conrad, and Hemingway—have written about the test of men (and their honor) in face of an overwhelming challenge and/or death. We know that Hemingway has been an influence, but what about Crane and Conrad? Is their theme in your work? If so, how have you handled it differently? Did you ever meet Hemingway? If so, what was your reaction?

VIDAL: I don't see Hemingway as an influence after the first three books. And Crane was more of an influence in *Williwaw* than Hemingway; also, Dos Passos's *Three Soldiers.* Crane and Hemingway are external writers; Conrad internal. I don't think their themes are mine. Just read *The Secret Agent,* not bad, and *Under Western Eyes,* really bad . . . no focus, art. I never met Hemingway.

STANTON, 1977:   Are you still influenced by Marshall McLuhan? What do you think of his literary criticism?

VIDAL: I have never read Marshall McLuhan; I've read about him . . . as did Myra. She was a great one for the second-hand quote. I hear he is good on the 18th century literature.

PARIS REVIEW, 1974:   You came out of the Second World War. What do you think of the writers of the previous generation—Hemingway, for example?

VIDAL: I detest him, but I was certainly under his spell when I was very young, as we all were. I thought his prose was perfect—until I read Stephen Crane and realized where he got it from. Yet Hemingway is still the master self-publicist, if Capote will forgive me. Hemingway managed to convince everybody that before Hemingway everyone wrote like—who?—Gene Stratton Porter? But not only was there Mark Twain before him, there was also Stephen Crane who did everything that Hemingway did and rather better. Certainly *The Red Badge of Courage* is superior to *A Farewell to Arms.* But Hemingway did put together a hypnotic style whose rhythm haunted other writers. I liked some of the travel things—*Green Hills of Africa.* But he never wrote a good novel. I suppose, finally, the thing I most detest in him is the spontaneity of his cruelty. The way he treated Fitzgerald, described in *A Moveable Feast.* The way he condescended to Ford Madox Ford, one of the best novelists in our language.

EVE AUCHINCLOSS & NANCY LYNCH, 1961:   Is there a clue to the future of literature in the writing of the Beats?

VIDAL: Their kind of run-on writing is, in a sense, a farewell to art. Whatever comes into your head, you put it down on the grounds that since you found it there in your head—which is an enormously valuable head, because all things are equally valuable under the sun—[so] it must be recorded.

DANIEL HALPERN, 1969:   Do you enjoy the writing of the Beats: Jack Kerouac for instance?

VIDAL: Oh, there was a great sweetness about Kerouac's writing. He was so innocent and so dumb, but very appealing. I wouldn't say that I would ever reread it, or that I've read it all, but I liked *On the Road,* and I liked *The Subterraneans,* and I liked Jack. Either you liked Jack or you didn't. If you liked him you liked his books. If you didn't, you couldn't read them. But as literature it's sort of—well, James Whitcomb Riley. It's just popular . . . *Kitsch,* I think, is the word.

HALPERN: How do you feel about the Ken Kesey books?

VIDAL: I haven't been able to get through one yet.
I've tried. That hippy drug culture! In theory I approve of it.
I'd much rather have them sitting around passively misquot-
ing Zen and keeping out of the way than getting drunk and
smashing up automobiles. After all, there are too many people
in the world, and since we haven't got much of anything for
them to do, they might just as well be stoned. I think they
should be supported by the state. But they do bore the absolute *hell* out of me, and I can't talk to one for more than five
minutes. *Man. Like. Groovy. Cool.* The vocabulary of the average
American is not very large to begin with. For the heads, vocabulary has shrunk to less than basic English. They have
about three hundred words, but you see, they're *like* non-ver-
bal, *man. Like you don't need it. Like blow your mind. Like fuck.*

HOLLIS ALPERT, 1977:   Is there a method you prefer in
telling stories?

VIDAL: Godard once made a marvelous remark to
Clouzot. Clouzot was criticizing Godard's work and his methods, and finally Clouzot said, "You've got to admit, Mr. Godard, that a movie has to have a beginning, a middle, and an
end." And Godard said, "Yes, but not necessarily in that order." There are many different ways of skinning a cat. The secret is that you must be very interesting. I don't know how
you translate that into action, but one way of being interesting is to be interested. I've found that writers I've known for a
long time whose work starts to fall off have first lost interest
in the world. My old and dear friend Tennessee Williams is a
great playwright. But Tennessee's work has been fading for
some years, which he puts down to drink and pills and so on,
but that is only part of it. He's got a very strong talent and a
very strong physical structure. Unfortunately, he's lost interest in people. He doesn't read a newspaper, doesn't read a
book, doesn't know what country he's in. He's a romantic
writer who is essentially working out of his own past, and
that kind of writer has just so many cards. He has the sister,
he has the mother, he has the father, he has the piece of trade.
He keeps playing with this same deck of cards, and at his best

he's the best around. But you cannot keep on using your own youth, particularly if you're going to have a career that lasts forty or fifty years. You wear out the deck.

Mailer is another case. Norman doesn't read much of anything. Yet when he does get outside of himself and looks at something, he's marvelous. He got interested in—and therefore he was interesting on—the moon shot. He suddenly started describing machinery. He was trained as an engineer, and he has a convergent as opposed to a divergent mind, which means he's always trying to connect one thing to another. I'm just the opposite—I see no connections. There's poor Bill Inge, who died out here. Absolutely nothing was going on in Bill's life or in his head after about the age of thirty-five. He couldn't take in anything new. So the object is to stay interested and to try and pick up new things. Certainly, it's very dull if you don't, and failure isn't much fun, though I am told that there's plenty of room at the bottom....

PARIS REVIEW, 1974:   What are your feelings about the so-called great writers of the 20th century, Hemingway aside? You didn't like Faulkner, I take it.

VIDAL: I like mind and fear rhetoric—I suppose because I have a tendency to rhetoric, I also come from a Southern family—back in Mississippi the Gores were friends of the Faulkners, all Snopeses together. In fact, when I read Faulkner I think of my grandfather's speeches in the Senate, of a floweriness that I have done my best to pluck from my own style—along with the weeds.

PARIS REVIEW: How about Fitzgerald?

VIDAL: If you want to find a place for him, he's somewhere between Maurice Baring and Evelyn Waugh. I like best what he leaves out of *The Great Gatsby*. A unique book. Incidentally, I think screenwriting taught him a lot. But who cares what he wrote? It is his life that matters. Books will be written about him long after his own work has vanished—again and again we shall be told of the literary harvest god who was devoured at summer's end in the hollywoods.

PARIS REVIEW: Were you influenced by Waugh?

VIDAL: Perhaps. I was given *Scoop* in 1939 and I thought it the funniest book I'd ever read. I used to reread it every year. Of the American writers—well, I read Saul Bellow with admiration. He never quite pulls off a book for me but he's interesting—which is more than you can say for so many of the other Jewish Giants, carving their endless Mount Rushmores out of halvah. Calder Willingham I've always liked— that frantic heterosexuality. There must be a place for this sort of thing in American literature. I've never understood why he was not an enormously popular writer.

PARIS REVIEW: You said you thought you had been influenced by Waugh, but weren't quite sure how. Who else has influenced you? Either now or years ago.

VIDAL: Oh, God, it's so hard to list them. As I said, by the time I got to *The Judgment of Paris* I was myself. Yet I'm always conscious that literature is, primarily, a chain of connection from the past to the present. It is not re-invented every morning as some bad writers like to believe. My own chain of literary genealogy would be something like this: Petronius, Juvenal, Apuleius—then Shakespeare—then Peacock, Meredith, James, Proust. Yet the writers I like the most influenced me the least. How can you be influenced by Proust? You can't. He's inimitable. At one point Thomas Mann fascinated me; thinking he was imitable, I used to compose Socratic dialogues in what I thought was his manner. One reason for re-writing *The City and the Pillar* was to get rid of those sombre exchanges.

EUGENE WALTER, 1960:   Who gives you the greatest pleasure?

VIDAL: Well, different works at different times and in different moods. I suppose my greatest pleasure still comes from Apuleius and Petronius, "the bright pagan world." Then I've read all of Flaubert, Proust, Henry James, Meredith, and Peacock, who for a certain kind of thing I often try to do, is the most relevant model. The novel of ideas: a most imprecise designation. Everybody, of course, would like to have written *Le Grand Meaulnes.*

EVE AUCHINCLOSS & NANCY LYNCH, 1961:   Is it a coincidence that the writers you admire describe life on a highly civilized level?

VIDAL: No. The novel is largely a middle-class form, but to me its highest points were always reached by those who set their characters free from making a living and were then able to carry forward the debate, the interplay of character. Thomas Love Peacock would set everything in a country house and the characters would just talk all weekend. Nothing much happened, but it was brilliant talk and things happened intellectually. This is a kind of novel I like—and in *The Judgment of Paris* approached.

EUGENE WALTER, 1960:   Any others who have been signposts for you?

VIDAL: I don't know. One's tendency is to fake influences later, to rearrange history. I suppose Gibbon has had as profound an effect on me as any writer. I don't mean stylistically so much as the effect of his attitude. Then one goes through phases: Lawrence's *Women In Love,* and Mann's *The Magic Mountain* and *Tonio Kröger.* When I was very young the greatest influence . . . was Shakespeare. I read all Shakespeare when I was fourteen at Los Alamos. *The Yale Shakespeare,* a play to a volume, I read the lot.

STANTON, 1978:   Do you recall what you read of Swift's work thirty years ago?

VIDAL: I draw a blank on Swift. *Gulliver* is on the memory tablet; some of those odd letters to . . . Stella? The baby talk? I should think that his kind of satire came to me in childhood from Twain and *Brann the Iconoclast* and Bierce. I also started reading at twelve or thirteen Evelyn Waugh, a novelist unknown in the U.S. in the thirties and never popular until the awful *Brideshead.* Also, on both sides of the family there was dark wit. T. P. Gore: "If there was any race other than the human race, I'd go join it." E. L. Vidal also had a way of observing human folly aslant.

OUI, 1975:   Do writers of your generation read one another?

VIDAL: It's my impression that most of my contemporaries never read books at all. I know that twenty-five years ago, you could never talk about a book to any other writer unless it was a new book by a contemporary. There was also no interest in any literature except the home-grown. They thought if you had read Herman Melville, you knew all there was to know about great writing. As a result, our writers have had very little connection with Western civilization, and that's what the game's all about.

But genius is not enough. You also have to be good. And since we are a nation of hustlers and self-promoters, forever lying about ourselves, we have a situation where nobody tries to be good, only great. The result is our writers are neither. . . .

One of the problems the American writer has always had is that there's no one to talk to. Mark Twain finally decided there wasn't a God and confided his terrible discovery to a secret journal. Poor Mark Twain thought he was the only person ever to have thought this thought, because he had never really read much of anything and had no one he could talk to honestly.

MICHAEL S. LASKY, 1975:   I think I once heard you say that writers in America grow old too quickly and lose their ability.

VIDAL: Quite the contrary. I don't think they grow old at all—they don't grow up. The age of forty is morning for a novelist, almost without exception. The great work is done after forty. . . . The novel is peculiarly the work of, if not middle age, of maturity; but Americans are *forced* by the general competitive atmosphere. . . . [They] tend to be overpraised for their first efforts and then, I would say, ninety per cent

take to drink. And between the drink and the pressures of society, and perhaps their own lack of ability, they don't go on.
And when [, finally, it is] the morning of their career—in other words, the forties—they are either hung-over—or dead. So
it's no accident that our greatest novelist, Henry James, and
our greatest poet, T. S. Eliot, left our shores and they survived. The ones who stay here don't have a very good time.

STANTON, 1977:   You know about my life—the poverty,
the struggle for education, the writing of poetry, novels, critical and bibliographical studies, my numerous working positions, the censorship I encountered in St. Augustine,
Florida. . .

VIDAL: Well, your life has been full; and you have by
now, perhaps, too much matter for fiction though an uncommonly wide range for a sort of social-historical-critic in the
Wilson style. Later comes *Memoirs of Dade County,* or wherever
St. Augustine nestles. I still think that the University is still to
you a center for whatever civilization we have because (like
most Americans) you've encountered no other. There is a
world elsewhere . . . and not on Morningside Heights, to the
amazement of the Trillings and Co. But they do their best. In
theory, there is nothing wrong with a school acting as refuge
for those who want . . . to talk and think and write. But then
consider the English Departments! Their bad notices are not
entirely undeserved. Only the dread high moralist John Gardner seems to think he has found the great good place instead
of the distinguished thing itself.

FAG RAG, 1974:   Regarding the issue of censorship, I
[John Mitzel] am doing an article on John Horne Burns, particularly the job the critics did on him. Did you know him?

VIDAL: Yes.

FAG RAG: I find in researching him that there are only
three pieces still extant since his death: your piece in *The New
York Times Book Review,* Brigid Brophy's piece in the Sunday

London Times Magazine, and a piece in *One* Magazine, a Los Angeles based homophile publication.

VIDAL: He was obliterated by the press.

FAG RAG: In rereading him, there is a certain circumspection that comes through. I can feel . . .

VIDAL: He's being careful in the first one, *The Gallery*. *Lucifer with a Book,* however, is when the critics let him have it. I think *The Gallery* is certainly the best of the "war books." It was much applauded, much admired. You see, he did six or seven books before *The Gallery*. He was an awful man. Monster. Envious, bitchy, drunk.

FAG RAG: Another Irishman.

VIDAL: Yeah. Bitter. Which was why *The Gallery* was so marvelous. It was his explosion into humanity at a fairly late date. I think he was in his early thirties, after a half-assed career as an English teacher and writing unprintable novels.

FAG RAG: Have you seen any of the manuscripts?

VIDAL: No. But I've been told about them by Freddie Warburg who published him in England; [he] said they were all pretty bad. They must be around somewhere.

FAG RAG: How did he die? I can't find that out. Was he killed?

VIDAL: No, no, no. He was drinking himself to death in Florence. Every day he would go to the Grand Hotel and stand in the bar and drink Italian brandy, which is about the worst thing in the world. And chew on fruit drop candy. He always said that it would counteract the drunkenness. . . . One day he was drunk at a bar, wandered out in the hot midday sun and had a stroke. Cerebral hemorrhage.

FAG RAG: At age thirty-seven?

VIDAL: I think he wanted to die. They really wiped him out on *Lucifer with a Book*. Same thing happened . . . it's very funny . . . we were both, in 1947, the two leading writers in the country. The ineffable John W. Aldridge began his career with a piece in *Harper's Magazine* ["The New Generation of Writers: With Some Reflections on the Older Ones," November, 1947], out of which came his book *After the Lost Generation* [in 1951]. He reversed all his judgments [between the two publications, including two favorable reviews of Vidal in 1949]. He began his career as our great admirer. [Later] he discovered we were dealing with the horrors of homosexuality. He then exactly reversed himself and began to applaud the Jewish Giants who are still with us today. Aldridge is nothing if not a rider of bandwagons. So Burns was absolutely at the top then. We were both admired as War Writers. To be a War Writer was pretty gutsy. You can't knock off a War Writer. Then *City and the Pillar*. Then *Lucifer with a Book*. They said: "Oh, my God! What is this we've been admiring?"

FAG RAG: Did the straight critics pick up on the homosexual themes in *Lucifer with a Book* and *The Gallery?*

VIDAL: They got it in *Lucifer with a Book*. He hit you on the head with it.

FAG RAG: One never knows the mentality of reviewers.

VIDAL: We wrote differently in those days, but it was perfectly plain what was going on at that school [Burns described in *Lucifer*].

FAG RAG: And was that the reason to condemn the book?

VIDAL: Entirely. Any writer suspected of being homosexual. . . . The only thing that they respect, that they put up with, is a freak like Capote, who has the mind of a Kansas housewife, likes gossip, and gets all shuddery when she thinks about boys murdering people.

JUDY HALFPENNY, 1976: It's the adolescents who write confessions; the 'mature,' well-adjusted, married fags keep quiet. Which leaves me with one burning question: what about the wives? Do they know? Do they accept it? Would they sue for divorce if they discovered their husbands were fags, or do they keep quiet for fear of the neighbors? I wish someone would find out.

VIDAL: Do fags' wives know? Generally, yes (I speak of the generation before and just after me, as well as my own), but the subject is often tabu. In Paris and Rome it is the ladies who are the bisexuals with a passion, and the husbands who do not know, even though Marcel tried to tell them.

ISRAEL SHENKER, 1968:   Have you read any bad books lately?

VIDAL: I've just finished a book that I thought I was going to like—Flann O'Brien's *At Swim-Two-Birds,* which first appeared in the 1930s, was much admired by James Joyce; Graham Greene wrote a great review of it, comparing it favorably to Laurence Sterne; and I must say I disliked it intensely. It's very Irish, and in a rather interesting Pirandello way it works together Irish myths, past and present. But unless you're interested in Irish myths, past and present, it doesn't work as literature. I'm not much interested in Southern writing, or Jewish writing, or Russian writing, if it's just that. I think it's a strange phenomenon in this particular time. There seems to be provincialization of literature rather than the opposite—urbanization? universalization?

SHENKER: What kind of books do you like, then?

VIDAL: I suppose that which engages the imagination. The problem with the ethnic or provincial novel is that unless it's really a work of genius you don't respond to it unless it's your province or your race that it's dealing with. You can look at it and say, "Well, that's worthy work." But when Flaubert puts himself into the French provinces and writes about Madame Bovary, he's able to make it considerably larger as a theme than I would suppose somebody describing what it's like to be Irish on the South Side of Chicago in the 1920s. If it's just that, there's nothing for me as reader to grab on to, and I would prefer reading journalism or history.

SHENKER: You don't think Flaubert has done about as much as can be done with that kind of universal theme?

VIDAL: We're living in an age of revolution now. Whether it's 1830 again or 1848 seems to be in dispute, but I think that the first really modern book was Flaubert's *L'Education Sentimentale,* which not only concerned that revolutionary year '48, but was the first book to deal with the great modern theme which is drift. So in that sense, whether he's writing about 1848 in the year 1880 or what have you, he's struck something that's considerably larger than just the immediate problems and what is in effect the gossip of the day.

SHENKER: When you say the great modern theme is drift, aren't you ignoring a lot of other themes with equal weight?

VIDAL: No, I think "drift" sums it up. Perhaps it's not the happiest word. There are certain other words to use. It includes lack of any sense of identity, which is again very much a modern theme. I think it's an age in which, due to mobility, people do literally drift from place to place, particularly Americans. This is an age of overpopulation, where people are crowded together in cities, and they're beginning to react just the way rats do when overcrowded during a laboratory experiment. They go berserk. I think that there's a great sense in modern life of people simply not knowing who they are and of drifting from point to point not only geographically but also psychologically.

SHENKER: Who would you say are the masters of drift these days?

VIDAL: I think, in a very romantic way, Tennessee Williams, at points in his plays, has always dealt with the drifter. I would say that in a somewhat different fashion you could say that Beckett deals in this same kind of thing, though he's drifting toward night and silence, while Tennessee is drifting toward greater fulfillment and day. I think we all, in a given period, cannot help but reflect the period in which we live. We're each born into a cage, and like that poor chimpanzee who became a painter—the first thing the chimp painted was the bars of the cage, knowing nothing else—well, we often do the bars of the cage without even knowing they're there.

SHENKER: What about people like Nabokov?

VIDAL: Well, I enjoy him—not as much as he enjoys himself, but I do enjoy him. I like the game he plays. It fascinates me how he's been taken up by certain young critics who don't seem to realize that they are everything which he detests, that he is really a displaced 19th-century dandy, and quite alien to their normal interest. It's a good sign they like him. He writes well, which is very rare now.

I think that one of the problems is that we are at the end of a great, great literary art, the novel, [at] the end of a rather weighing-down culture. Too much has been written, too much is remembered, and so there is a kind of Alexandrianism affecting all of the arts now. The more one knows of the past, the more convinced one is there is nothing new to be said. So this leads us to the "vice," as Goethe called it, of novelty. But since there is nothing new to be said, then you must continually find new ways of saying it. Well, that's sort of been the problem of art from the beginning. But now we live in this huge library, this vast museum, and in a sense the people who have the easiest time are the barbarians, the writers who have never read anything, the painters who have never looked at a picture, who flaunt their personalities on the grounds that that's all they have. So I suspect in a way we may be moving more toward happenings, toward the random, to a breaking down of the formal. But to the extent that you're going to say that there is such a thing as art, you must say that it is made and there are better ways and worse ways of making something, and that is style.

PARIS REVIEW, 1974:   Where do you place Nabokov?

VIDAL: I admire him very much. I'm told he returns the compliment. We do exchange stately insults in the press.

Shortly after I announced that I was contributing $100 to the Angela Davis Defense fund in Nabokov's name—to improve his image—he responded by assuring an interviewer from the *New York Times* that I had become a Roman Catholic. It is curious that Russia's two greatest writers—Nabokov and Pushkin—should both have had Negro blood.

PARIS REVIEW: Have you read *Ada?*

VIDAL: No one has read *Ada*. But I very much admired *Transparent Things*. It is sad that the dumb Swedes gave their merit badge to Solzhenitsyn instead of Nabokov. Perfect example, by the way, of the unimportance of a writer's books to his career.

STANTON, 1978: Any response to Solzhenitsyn's commencement address to Harvard?

VIDAL: I stand by my comments on Solzhenitsyn in the "Ten Best Sellers" piece [reprinted in his *Matters of Fact and of Fiction*]. He is a bad novelist and a fool. The combination usually makes for great popularity in the U.S. The Russians displayed uncharacteristic humor in letting this nut come to our shores.

MICHAEL S. LASKY, 1975: In your case, what are the risks for a writer who takes sharply critical swipes at individuals?

VIDAL: I usually never attack individuals. It's usually an idea I'm after or what I think is a false or dangerous attitude. I never attacked Richard Nixon, the man, because I don't know him, and [I've] never attacked anyone personally that I did know—for personal reasons. I certainly gave it to Norman Mailer for what he had written about women. [But] it had nothing to do with him personally. [Naturally,] he took it personally. . . .

MONIQUE VAN VOOREN, 1976: What is the reason you don't like Norman Mailer?

VIDAL: I don't like what he stands for—

VAN VOOREN: Which is?

VIDAL: That women are put on earth only to provide men with sons—that's a quote. He's against masturbation, he's against homosexuality. He believes that murder is essentially sexual. I think he's rather an anthology of all the darkest American traits.

VAN VOOREN: What do you think of him as a writer?

VIDAL: He comes and goes. Sometimes he's better than other times, like the rest of us.

PLAYBOY, 1969:   You have characterized Norman Mailer's *The Naked and the Dead* as "a clever, talented, admirably executed fake" and said of his subsequent work, "I am not sure, finally, that he should be a novelist at all, or even a writer, despite formidable gifts. He is too much of a demagogue." Are the roles of writer and demagogue really mutually exclusive?

VIDAL: I think in the ten years since I wrote that piece, Mailer has borne me out. He has almost ceased to be a novelist and has become a superb journalist, with himself as subject, pluckily taking on the various occupants of the American pantheon, from Sonny Liston to the Pentagon. Yet to be a novelist is not to be more worthy than a journalist of the highest order, particularly one with a messianic desire to change society. We may not need Norman's novels at this time, but we certainly need his rhetoric.

PLAYBOY: Isn't the central political concern of writers such as yourself and Mailer a relatively new development in American letters?

VIDAL: Yes and no. In the 1930s, writers were much involved with politics. Yet there has always been a high romantic view of the serious, dedicated artist as being a sort of divine idiot—like William Faulkner, mumbling he was just a farmer and didn't know much about them things. For most of the country's history, our serious—as well as our solemn—writers were terrified of being thought politically engaged.

For one thing, few of them knew much about politics, ideas, or even the actual everyday life of the country. For another, in this century, they were much attracted to the Flaubert-Joyce-Eliot sacerdotal tradition: the writer as holy man, too pure for the agora. This attitude was useful to Flaubert, who was actually not all that apolitical, but I don't think it has done Mr. J. D. Salinger much good. Of course, if political novels mean Allen Drury and social engagement means Dalton Trumbo—in other words, artless work—then one can see why the ambitious writer would steer clear of that sort of commitment or genre. He would be making a mistake, however; much of the best writing has been passionate and worldly, and most of the worst, in our time, private and proud—those dread exercises, usually taking place on campus, where last summer's adultery turns out to have been a re-enactment of *Alcestis.*

STANTON, 1979:   Do you favor the upsurge of political writing that has resulted since Watergate?

VIDAL: There is no art to political writing as practiced by today's journalists. For one thing, the newspapers are owned by the same people who own the banks who own Boeing who provide the weapons for the Pentagon, etcetera. A fearless critic of the society will find himself writing for something like *New Times,* which went out of business, sad to say. *The Nation* is good but its circulation is too small. Meanwhile, Mr. James Reston has never really met a President he did not like, who did not grow in office, who was not as good and as fine as the people who elected him . . . this last is, of course, true. Napoleon called the English a nation of shopkeepers. The Americans of today are a nation of shoplifters. They knew Nixon was a crook and they liked him until he was caught.

MICHAEL S. LASKY, 1975:   Does political writing affect politics at all?

VIDAL: Well, it affects politicians because they are very sensitive. They read everything that is written about them and they are *very* sensitive when attacked.

JUDY HALFPENNY, 1978:   Tell me something interesting about Anthony Howard.

VIDAL: Tony Howard is very bright—and much missed. A good editor; a better journalist. He used to cover Washington for the *Observer*. In '68 we attended a Ronald Reagan press conference at Miami just before Nixon was nominated. Reagan was running hard while trying to appear stationary. I wanted Howard to ask him if he, as the Moral Candidate representing American Virtue and Moral Rectitude, thought that the fact that he had divorced his gallant first wife to remarry a rich lady would somehow make him seem less pure to those who saw him as Savior? Tony thought I should ask the question. But I was too well-known to the press *and* Reagan (Buckley and I were on every night at that time). So our moment passed. But the answer would have been marvelous.

MONIQUE VAN VOOREN, 1976:   What's your opinion of Mr. Buckley?

VIDAL: Buckley? . . . I suspect he is not as nice as he looks.

MICHAEL S. LASKY, 1975:   Why do you think people were still interested in your year-long [1968–1969] feud with Buckley to the point where *Esquire* published those essays by the two of you?

VIDAL: Well, twenty million people watched it. It was a television event and [television] is the only thing that binds our people together. Literature doesn't. [People] are interested in personalities and not ideas.

LASKY: How did that article in *Esquire* about Buckley ["A Distasteful Encounter with William F. Buckley, Jr." in September, 1969] come about almost a year after the ABC telecast at the convention?

VIDAL: Buckley. . . . arrived at *Esquire* one day with a 10,000-word piece that he had written attacking me, a piece more suitable for the pages of *Krafft-Ebing* than for *Esquire*. And they, being opportunists, journalistic ghouls—took it. . . . *Esquire* asked if I would answer it. And I said yes, but not at such length. Buckley read my answer and became angry and threatened to sue the magazine. They said they were printing it anyway and he did sue them. And he sued me but dropped [the suit against me] after four years of litigation rather than go into court. The only thing I disliked about [all this nonsense] was that it put me at his level. He's not a writer. He is not anything except a right-wing TV entertainer.*

EUGENE WALTER, 1960:   What would you consider the perfect novel: the novel you'd most wish to read?

VIDAL: The terrible thing is, I don't want to read *a* novel—I never have. When I read fiction with any delight it has always been when I've the time to read the whole of a man's work, rather than one book.

FAG RAG, 1974:   Among American fiction writers, whom do you read for enjoyment?

VIDAL: Calder Willingham. Southern writer. Very funny.

FAG RAG: I couldn't get through *Providence Island*.

VIDAL: No. That's bad. But *Rambling Rose* is new and rather good. I love *Geraldine Bradshaw*. They're pussy novels, you're right. Just this terrible, relentless quest for pussy. [Also,] full of failure, which is like life, which is what I like about [his work.]

STANTON, 1977:   C. P. Snow and Anthony Powell are excellent novelists. I have read all of their work. Snow says that *Homecoming* is his best novel; I think *The Masters* is just as good. Powell lacks the psychological depth of Snow—I doubt that any other living writer can match him in this area—but

---

*Had I but known then the wicked things that Bill was doing to his fellow directors in Starr Broadcasting! [G.V., 1979]

Powell is probably the superior artist. Like you, he is classy and a classicist. . . .

VIDAL: I have read nothing by Snow and only a book or two by Powell. I mean to get to both one day. I'm somewhat intimidated by huge sequences of small books. One's life gets used up by the author, in the act of reading him.

MONIQUE VAN VOOREN, 1976:   What do you think of Muriel Spark?

VIDAL: Muriel, well she's very interested in her own work, I'll say that.

VAN VOOREN: Did you like [Spark's novel] *The Driver's Seat?*

VIDAL: I didn't read it. Yes, I did read it. I did like it. I didn't see the movie.

ISRAEL SHENKER, 1968:   A friend told me recently he thought Malcolm Lowry's *Under the Volcano* was the greatest book since World War II.

VIDAL: I found it dreadful. But there's a whole line of writing that I dislike, most of it American, and most of it the great line of our imperial American literature from Melville through Faulkner, windy, bombastic, imprecise, self-indulgent, self-loving. I cannot bear [all those] infinitely windy writers who use words without knowing what they mean, who are continually inflating themselves with air so that they'll be larger than they are. I went all the way through a book of Faulkner's and he kept using the word "euphemistic" thinking it meant euphonious. That is provincial writing at its most ungodly. And the pretentiousness: Herman Melville wanting to write *King Lear.* He was better off writing about the South Seas and doing little whaling stories.

DANIEL HALPERN, 1969:   Are there any writers whom you feel are completely overrated? Writers who have achieved great notoriety and write, in your opinion, very poorly.

VIDAL: Susan Sontag certainly is as bad a writer as I've ever read . . . and a fifth-rate mind.* But her reading is enormous. She really has read a great deal, and, of course, Americans don't read very much, particularly the ones who write about books. And what they have . . . I mean they think if they've read *Moby Dick* they've mastered literature. They know nothing of French literature, Italian, German, or even English. Well, Susan doesn't know much about English or American; but she has read the French, she has read the Germans, and this makes her very impressive to them—impressive to me, too. But I would say she was monstrously overrated. Mr. Vonnegut is very much overrated at the moment. There's always a writer that the kids like at any given moment, who because of that gets all sorts of attention that normally he wouldn't, and then when the kids abandon him, nobody mentions his name again. J. D. Salinger was such a case.

HALPERN: Do you think Salinger is a bad writer?

VIDAL: No, I think he's a good writer. I don't like what he's up to. Feeding the self-pity of the young. But he does it very well.

HALPERN: And J. P. Donleavy?

VIDAL: I've tried with the best will in the world to read him, but can't.

HALPERN: You do like Borges.

VIDAL: Yes, I like Borges very much. I also like Gadda. . . .

HALPERN: I'm thinking now of the large bookstores with their great displays of popular writers.

VIDAL: There's Bernard Malamud, whom I find unreadable. Philip Roth—I liked very much *Portnoy's Complaint.* It

---

* Since 1969, I have come to admire Sontag. I have changed? No, no. She has! [G.V., 1980]

was a good joke and it didn't go on too long. It was a good joke *well told.* But *Letting Go* I thought terrible. I like J. F. Powers: he's not very well known. By and large, the "Jewish Giants," as I call them, leave me cold. Now we're in for an age of "Black Giants," whom we're not supposed to criticize because they've suffered so much.

HALPERN: And James Baldwin?

VIDAL: Jimmy writes very well. The novels are a bit on the gushy side, but his prose is often quite eloquent, and, as we know, he's a very good polemicist.

HALPERN: His *Giovanni's Room* was very special.

VIDAL: But I fear he believed in love when he wrote that book. Young writers often believe in love—a subject which they tend not to work much in later years. . . .

ISRAEL SHENKER, 1968:   I get the impression that there aren't many things that give you positive pleasure when you read them.

VIDAL: Oh, I think a lot of things give me positive pleasure. I read a great deal of history. But the pleasure *is* often negative, rather than positive. Negative pleasure is having one's worst fears confirmed about human history and human behavior. And now I've been reading anthropology, trying to fathom Lévi-Strauss and [his antagonist] Barthes, and trying to keep up with those debates, and very difficult they are for what General De Gaulle laughingly calls [us] Anglo-Saxons.

PARIS REVIEW, 1974:   You once said the novel is dead.

VIDAL: That was a joke. What I have said repeatedly is that the *audience* for the novel is demonstrably diminishing with each passing year. That is a fact. It is not the novel that is declining, but the audience for it. It's like saying poetry has been declining for fifty years. Poetry hasn't. But the audience [for poetry] has. The serious novel is now almost in the same situation as poetry. Eventually, the novel will simply be an academic exercise, written by academics to be used in classrooms in order to test the ingenuity of students. A combination of Rorschach test and anagram. Hence, the popularity of John Barth, a perfect U-novelist whose books are written to be taught, not to be read.

PARIS REVIEW: As long as we're on Barth, let me ask you what you think of-your contemporaries, people in your generation, people in their forties?

VIDAL: You must realize that anything I *say* (as opposed to write) about other novelists is governed by my current mood of jaunty disgust—which is quite impartial, cheerful, even loving. But totally unreliable as criticism—putting me in the great tradition of American journalism, now that I think of it.

MICHAEL S. LASKY, 1975:   What do you think of the current state of American writing?

VIDAL: There are an awful lot of books by dead writers I am still catching up on. I am now reading all of the work of George Eliot; last summer I did all of Turgenev. There are some interesting younger writers today: John Gardner,* Robert Coover's short stories, Grace Paley.

DANIEL HALPERN, 1969:   How do you feel about the "best-seller" group?

VIDAL: Which ones?

HALPERN: The writers who are consistently one through five on the *Times* best-seller list each week.

VIDAL: Except that I'm very often one, sometimes two, sometimes three, and sometimes four. You mean the *other ones?*

HALPERN: The other ones.

VIDAL: I don't read them. I read one book by Harold Robbins once, because I was told I was in it. *The Adventurers.* It

---

*I liked *Grendel* then. But since. . . . [G.V., 1979]

reads like a gossip column, in which you know he's really writing about Jack Kennedy and Joe Kennedy, but they're called Callaghan. What did fascinate me was how very little he knew about what he was writing about; he knows as little about these grand jet-set people as his readers, and I suppose this is an interesting symbiosis: to be as stupid as your reader makes for a perfect union. I have not read Miss Susann or Mr. Slavitt.

PARIS REVIEW, 1974:   Do you read new works by your contemporaries as they come out?

VIDAL: I wouldn't say that I am fanatically attentive. There's only one living writer in English that I entirely admire, and that's William Golding. Lately I've been reading a lot of Italian and French writers. I particularly like Italo Calvino.

PARIS REVIEW: Why do you think Golding good?

VIDAL: Well, his work is intensely felt. He holds you completely line by line, image by image. In *The Spire* you see the church [as it] is being built, smell the dust. You are present at the event that exists only in his imagination. Very few writers have ever had this power. When the priest reveals his sores, you see them, feel the pain. I don't know how he does it.

PARIS REVIEW: Have you ever met him?

VIDAL: Once, yes. We had dinner together in Rome. Oxford Don type. I like his variety: each book is quite different from the one before it. This confuses critics and readers, but delights me. For that reason I like to read Fowles—though he is not in Golding's class. Who else do I read for pleasure? I always admire Isherwood. I am not given to mysticism—to understate wildly, but he makes me see something of what he would see. I read P. G. Wodehouse for pleasure. Much of Anthony Burgess. Brigid Brophy. Philip Roth when he is at his most demented. I like comic writers obviously. I reread Evelyn Waugh . . .

FAG RAG, 1974: Did you get through [Thomas Pynchon's novel] *Gravity's Rainbow?*

VIDAL: I don't think I'm going to get to that. . . . * I'm sure there is a place for . . . novels which are written to be used in the classroom. Since I think that's where the novel is going to end up, I think of myself as an anachronism, and *that* is the future. Someone like John Barth to me is just cement. Pynchon. I read *V.* Some of it is fun, but so heavy-handed. The jokes are so heavy, such awful names. Nabokov remembers him.† He was once in one of Nabokov's classes. . . .

DANIEL HALPERN, 1969: Do you think there is anyone writing today who is saying anything important? Even in bad English?

VIDAL: I think that, oh, there's as much talent now as at any given moment in the history of the world. I would say, slightly to shift my ground, that the general competence of novel-writing is probably higher today than it ever was, possibly just because there are more people, particularly more people going through what we laughingly call the educational process. So they're told about novels, those few who show a sign of some sort of affinity for them, and I think there's a degree of competence. Vonnegut? He writes prose as bad as I've come across in some time. But it's easy to read, particularly for kids who can't cope with dense paragraphs or unfamiliar word-constructions. Their eyes are repelled by a page that isn't much broken up with type, quotation marks, indentations, and tiny paragraphing, because they've come, really, from comic books, television, and, perhaps, newspapers, to books. Right off, books have a very bad association: they mean school. Vonnegut looks interesting on the page, like the prose you read in balloons over comic strip characters' heads. Now that's his prose. His imagination, on the other hand, is first rate. I love science fiction, and I liked that book, *Sirens of*

---

*I did, finally. My report can be found in "Plastic Fiction" [G.V., 1979]
† No. Mrs. Nabokov remembered him. [G.V., 1979]

Titan. Cat's Cradle was a bit heavy-handed, but there were a lot of very funny things in it. I've read a lot of science fiction, so Vonnegut is not as startlingly new to me as he would be for people who haven't.

ISRAEL SHENKER, 1968:   What about the "new novel"?

VIDAL: I think some of the books are more successful than the theory, and in spite of the theory or theories. One or two books by Nathalie Sarraute I think are very good. I like one book by Robbe-Grillet: *Jealousy.* Robbe-Grillet, being a true 20th-century man and profoundly innocent, thinks this is the age of science, the great achievements are in science. How does science get these great events? Through experiment. Ah! Now let us go into the laboratory and bring out the "new novel." Well, this is naïve, and this is not the way art is made. As he has discovered.

SHENKER: Although he insists that his audience is growing.

VIDAL: I think every writer lives by such delusions. You have Harold Robbins whose audience grows even greater. That means nothing. I'm often struck by literary naiveté even in a great writer like Stendhal, who said "I'm writing for the year 1935." So what? Why is 1935 a better year than 1835 or 1882? [The people then are] just as stupid or just as intelligent [as] in 1935. It is true that some works take time to find an audience. So you've had a good year in '35 and in '36 you're finished. The only pleasure I find in a long literary career is seeing various books of one's own taking on new life, books that failed entirely when they came out. My career has lasted long enough now for [me to read a book about me.]*

SHENKER: Does it include *Myra Breckinridge?*

VIDAL: No. Lucky man or unlucky man, he stops with *Washington, D.C.*

---

*Gore Vidal (Boston: Twayne, 1968), by Ray Lewis White.

STANTON, 1977:   Do you ever read poetry?

VIDAL: I think a lot about reading poetry again (I stopped at the end of my twenties). This winter I hope to read, for the first time, *Paradise Lost*. On the other hand, I recall from memory yards of Pope. And the Byron of *Don Juan*.

DANIEL HALPERN, 1969:   What about the "street poetry" and the "black poetry" that's being turned out?

VIDAL: Yes, I've seen it and heard it. . . .

HALPERN: It has quite a large audience.

VIDAL: Everything has an audience. With a loud and simple-minded beat you can get quite a crowd. It doesn't interest me; it may well be the future. Rock music and lyrics.

STANTON, 1977:   I greatly admire the trilogy of novels— *White Mule, In the Money,* and *The Build-Up*—by the poet William Carlos Williams. Have you read them? If so, did you learn anything from them?

VIDAL: I read almost nothing by W. C. Williams. No, I read *In the American Grain* years ago. He was a friend of Anaïs. I was astonished that he was well into middle age before he figured out that the word "venereal" came from Venus. And he was an M.D. Small things like that put one off.

PARIS REVIEW, 1974:   How about some of the younger writers? What do you think of John Updike, for example?

VIDAL: He writes so well that I wish he could attract my interest. I like his prose and disagree with Mailer who thinks it bad. Mailer said it was the kind of bad writing that people who don't know much about writing think is good. It is an observation that I understand, but don't think applies to Updike. With me the problem is that he doesn't write about anything that interests me. I am not concerned with middle-class suburban couples. On the other hand, I'm not concerned with adultery in the French provinces either. Yet Flaubert commands my attention. I don't know why Updike doesn't. Perhaps my fault.

DANIEL HALPERN, 1969: To go back for a moment to style and content, you do, then, make the distinction with John Updike between what he says and how he says it. You enjoy his prose but lose interest in what he is saying.

VIDAL: Yes, but I would say that with my interest in language, in style, I can certainly read him with a degree of pleasure if not profit, whereas somebody whose subject matter theoretically is a good deal more interesting, like Bill Burroughs, I can hardly read at all because of that cretinous style he's put together.

HALPERN: So you would rather read something that is, stylistically, well done, than something dealing with very interesting subject matter, but which is written poorly?

VIDAL: Yes, I would, because there aren't that many stories and there's not that much experience in the world. It's how you arrange it and how you filter it and how you make art of it that matters. I mean, to fuck is to fuck; we all know what it's like, and for Hemingway to do it was no different from the way Balzac did it, but it's how they manage to render that thing on the page that's important. Subject matter is much overrated.

PARIS REVIEW, 1974: Are there others of the younger generation who are perhaps less well known whom you like?

VIDAL: Alison Lurie. Viva's autobiography...

PARIS REVIEW: Andy Warhol's superstar?

VIDAL: Yes. And it's marvelous. Part fiction, part tape recording, part this, part that, gloriously obscene. Particularly interesting about her Catholic girlhood in upstate New York. Her father beating her up periodically beneath the bleeding heart of Jesus. And those great plaster Virgins that he had all over the lawn, lit up at night with 3,000 candles. That kind of thing appeals to me more than stately, careful novels.

DANIEL HALPERN, 1969:   Many of the new writers in America have adopted a new gimmick style of writing: using an altered syntax and various other tricks to liven up the language. How do you react to this experimentation?

VIDAL: There's a theory that any experiment in form is better than no experiment. Susan Sontag deeply believes that. I see the point to breaking up old forms. After all, we don't want another novel like John Galsworthy. On the other hand we don't want another novel like James Joyce. But I think this comes back to the word . . . *authenticity*. The *authentic* writer is an innovator without effort. He is himself. Bowles's short stories did not come out of any desire to: "Oh, let's shock them, let's really give them a shocker this time, something no one's ever thought of. Now, let me think." They came right out of him, and at the time they were first published they were very startling, and in the best sense of the word they were *avant-garde*. I feel with Pynchon and some of these others that they're straining; they're trying to be more interesting than indeed they are. Because they don't know who they are, they play around with form. In a sense, they're doing what Picasso in a great way did, but there are not many Picassos, not many who have that kind of all-encompassing view and mischievous desire to fiddle with form. Language is a very difficult thing to play with. I'm not saying it shouldn't be done, but you must understand it to its *roots* before you start inventing. If you're a poet you don't begin by writing sestinas, and I would suspect if you're a novelist you don't begin as some of these young writers do, by smashing every known form and hoping to God that the pieces will coalesce into something superb. Nowadays everybody wants to be great and nobody wants to be good. The result is, they're neither.

HALPERN: Do you feel that it is perhaps better for a young writer to hold off attempting to publish until he's at least thirty?

VIDAL: I don't think it makes much difference. Though there is this danger: he might become successful, and so think that he was better than he is, and not develop. I always knew that I was not much good when I began, that I had a range, but it wasn't very wide, and that to align my ambition (for my prose) with what I was able to do ... well, I didn't even get anywhere *near* it until I was into my thirties. And now I find that with each book it gets more and more difficult to write well, which of course makes me more and more interested. You never get to the bottom of it. But I suppose I could have gone on doing *The City and the Pillar* over and over and over again the way Kerouac did *On the Road* over and over and over again, and I might have had a better reputation in America than I have now.

AMERICAN FILM, 1977: Do you think films are affecting the writing of novels?

VIDAL: Yes. Mine is the first generation of writers brought up on talking films and I think we were more affected by films than any of the other narrative forms. Tell me somebody's favorite actor when he was ten years old, and I'll tell you who he is. Could Norman Mailer have existed without John Garfield? He's been playing Garfield, and I've been doing George Arliss. You get hung up with an image. Now, today's generation is being brought up on ninety-second television commercials. That might make for a certain oddness. Twenty years from now a girl might break down and discover that she's an Oil of Olay commercial. Or a detergent. Today's models for the young are not as gorgeous as ours were.

MICHAEL S. LASKY, 1975: What about nonfiction?

VIDAL: What is nonfiction?

LASKY: Journalism—do you read any magazines regularly?

VIDAL: I *look* at a lot but I don't think about them much. I read altogether too many newspapers and magazines and after I read them I try to blot it all out. I think it is bad for the head to put all that . . . stuff . . . in it. But I am . . . addicted to magazines and newsprint.

STANTON, 1977: Have you been influenced by the methods and means of New Journalism?

VIDAL: No. But I wish to God they had been influenced by me.

DANIEL HALPERN, 1969: Why do you think so many people who used to read novel after novel have turned to nonfiction?

VIDAL: Well, journalism has improved a lot, and there's the first person narrative. Everybody is interested in *writers* because they have a somewhat romantic and demonic aura, but nobody is really interested in their *books*. Norman Mailer learned this great truth, so he made himself his book. Then *I* went to the Pentagon, then *I* went to the convention, then *I* was busted . . . and that has great fascination for readers. It's been going on since Rousseau. There's always been that I, I, I tradition. High Romanticism. And irresistible in an age like ours, of instant fame and publicity. It's quite possible to be world-famous in twenty-four hours and forgotten, mercifully, in forty-eight.

PARIS REVIEW, 1974: Has anyone else done such a wholesale revision of his past work [as you have done]?

VIDAL: I shouldn't imagine that any other American writer would want to do anything that reflected on the purity and the spontaneity of his genius at any phase of his sacred story. In the land of the free, one sentence must be as good as another because that is democracy. Only Henry James set out methodically to rewrite his early books for the New York Edition. Some works he improved, others not. Tennessee, come to think of it, often rewrites old plays, stories . . . it's sort of a tic with him. Returning to an earlier time, different mood.

PARIS REVIEW: You find other writers proficient technically but don't have much to say?

VIDAL: They appear to rely on improvisation to get them to the end of journeys that tend to be circular.

PARIS REVIEW: Which works and which authors are you thinking of?

VIDAL: Well, as I was talking I was thinking of a book—any book—by someone called Brautigan. I can never remember the titles. The last little book I looked at is about a librarian. Written in the See Jane Run style. Very cheerful. Very dumb. Highly suitable for today's audience. But he's not exactly what I had in mind. There is one splendid new—to me—writer. Robert Coover. He, too, is circular but the circles he draws enclose a genius of suggestion. Particularly that story in *Pricksongs and Descants* when the narrator creates an island for you *on the page.* No rude art his. Also *Omensetter's Luck* by William Gass. A case of language doing the work of the imagination, but doing it very well.

MONIQUE VAN VOOREN, 1976:   What would your advice be to upcoming writers who look to you as the utmost in your field?

VIDAL: There is room at the top for only one. STAY AWAY!

CURTIS BILL PEPPER, 1974:   Do you think, at forty-nine, that your creative powers are as strong now as when you wrote *Julian*—twelve years ago?

VIDAL: Oh sure, but whether my will to continue is as great as it was is doubtful. You can't really be an artist if you have no sense of future time. As ridiculous and abstract as that is, it's still important to the maker of things. Well, I don't believe that in a century there will be anything remotely like Western civilization as we have known it. The crack-up may come even sooner.

All the arts reflect this state of mind, this waiting for the end. A kind of interior deterioration is taking place, a drive on the part of almost every artist to blow up his own art form, sometimes in the interest of novelty . . . to explode it, to shit on it.

A lot of this comes from the dreadful effect of science on the humanist tradition. In the twentieth century, science has been everything and the arts almost nothing by comparison. As a result, many artists now pretend to be scientists. They try to imitate the strategies of science. Paintings that talk. Sculpture that swims. Books that turn to ash. New formulas—just like the scientist. But that isn't science of course, nor is it art. Just the end of the road.

DANIEL HALPERN, 1969: Are you disappointed in the present state of literature?

VIDAL: No. I see the end of the world, so . . .

HALPERN: You expect things to get worse.

VIDAL: I expect *everything* to get worse. That's the second law of thermodynamics: everything is running down.

HALPERN: Do you see any way that the present state of affairs can be . . .

VIDAL: Reversed? No. I think literature as we have known it is pretty well at an end. . . .

HALPERN: Even if in some way people could be taught to write and speak proper English, you feel there is no hope for literature as we have known it?

VIDAL: No. It's a kind of feedback. If you hear a terrible language while you're growing up, and you grow up in a house with no books, which 99 per cent of the Americans do, and your parents can barely talk (and I'm not just speaking about immigrant parents—any parents), this feeds back, and how are you going to break the circle? Your language is formed by what you hear around you in the first dozen years of your life. And your reading habits are formed then, if they're ever formed. Well, if you read rather bad books, and you hear a bad language around you, a meager language . . . I suppose with an enormous effort of will and some natural talent you could pole-vault out of that, but where are you going to go? Nobody talks and writes worse than university professors. So, if the academic world can't shelter you, give you an audience, I don't know where you go. I was brought up in a fairly literary household of rather eloquent politicians, so we all had the gift of gab, and took pleasure in language. Particularly my grandfather, who was a professional orator. Also I went to the sort of schools where people *did* read for pleasure—but that was in another time.

HALPERN: Is it possible that a new art form can come out of this bastardization of the language?

VIDAL: It has—television! A written one . . . I don't know. What would you do, write mottoes on silk scarves or something?

HALPERN: So then you think literature in the classical sense is finished?

VIDAL: Oh yes. All over. If the human race does survive . . . we need a complete bust-up of this particular civilization. It's not working very well. And we need to reduce the world's population by about two-thirds. Then with our technological knowledge, the survivors could have a very good time. There would be less onerous work to be done, and more time to use our little monkey brains to make new things. Until then, everything is bloated and running down.

5

Sexuality

RICHARD GRENIER, 1975:   The plaque on the church says in Italian that Saint Francis of Assisi stopped here in 1222 and founded something. Then the footpath resumes—up, level, more steps up, twistings to the left, twistings to the right, stone walls on either side masking vineyards and lemon groves. Suddenly, the path drops away and there is a dizzying view of the coast and the Bay of Salerno eleven hundred feet below. The height is so great, waves in the blue Mediterranean seem frozen, as if seen from an airplane. Over the water hovers a faint haze, and the horizon is barely perceptible. The steep olive-green hills are banked with centuries-old terraces and gray-stone retaining walls, dotted with little white houses with orange roofs. The sun is blazing, the air cool, the sky a brilliant blue. The smell of cypress and stone pine is in the air. Miles and miles away a country dog is barking. Far out on the bay a motorboat makes a faint *put-put-put.*

The sumptuous five-story white-stucco villa seems to be bolted horizontally to the side of the gray cliff. Charlie, the narrator of Gore Vidal's best-selling *Burr,* confessed it was his ambition to live in Spain or Italy, like Washington Irving, and write stories. And Gore Vidal has achieved his character's ambition: lives in Rome and in this palatial Swallow's Nest in Ravello, on the Amalfi Coast south of Naples, and writes "stories." Approaching the house is like crossing a catwalk in

217

the sky. Birds wheel and swoop below. Leaning over a black iron railing in front is an affable, freckle-faced man in a trench coat gazing across the bay: Howard Austen, Gore Vidal's companion for some twenty-five years. "You didn't come over the mountain!" says Howard, alarmed. "All these days you've been coming here, you've come over the mountain? Gore! Richard's been coming over the mountain!"

Gore Vidal appears at the door of his manor, dressed in a brown tweed jacket, brown slacks, tieless white shirt with an orange pattern. He is in one of his overweight periods, moving carefully because of a broken rib. His hair is longer and more rumpled than in his pictures, with just a sheen of gray. The face is stern, unsmiling.

VIDAL: I explained it perfectly to you the first day. . . . I showed you where you come in the gate onto the private road.

GRENIER: I got it mixed up with all the steps.

VIDAL: What steps? There are no steps but right over there. . . . The rest is entirely flat. The first day I told you to go back through the black gate.

GRENIER: I'm sorry, Gore. I got it mixed up with the other black gate.

VIDAL: I explained to you about the private road the first day when we walked here.

GRENIER (aside): There is nothing personal in all this. It is, no doubt, intended for my improvement. Gore Vidal favors radical change. He wants people to get better.

He walks back into the house and I follow. . . . Vidal and I are on the main floor, handsomely proportioned, white walls. He is not angry with me. He had hoped I was more intelligent perhaps, quicker to grasp new things, but the world was ever thus, filled with dolts, semidolts. He accepts, perforce. In fact, he seems rather well-disposed toward me today. But you have to be very careful with Gore Vidal, make sure you don't say anything stupid.

※

NEWSWEEK, 1974: You've long advocated complete sexual freedom. Is it happening?

VIDAL: There is sexual blurring. The boys are looking more feminine—their pelvises are wider and their shoulders are narrower and they tend more to fat. There is a kind of "caponizing" going on. I thought at first they were just not sexually inclined toward me, which is always a grievous blow. But they aren't sexy. Maybe it's like those rats who when overcrowded get very bland and lose all interest in sex. But I do take seriously what you do hear about impotence in the male. While I don't see much difference between male and female in character, yet there is something. Now whether this is innate in the male I don't know, but if the male is not the sexual aggressor he can't get it up. This is certainly true of me; when anyone else is the aggressor, male or female, I can't respond. I have always been extremely selfish in sexual matters. I was told by one woman that I made love just like Picasso and I said, "Oh, I'm a genius too?" and she said, "Yes, and a very bad lover. In and out and back to work."

JUDY HALFPENNY, 1978: Have you read Sarotte's book *Like a Brother, Like a Lover?*

VIDAL: I glanced at Sarotte's book when it first came out in French. *Le Monde* hailed it as a masterpiece, no doubt wanting to prove that the declining Americans are *and* were nothing but a bunch of fags. I read the parts about me and was a bit bewildered. He is so busy making his sub-Freudian case that he ignores the main line of my work which has nothing at all to with sex unless sex is *everything*—which some like to say, but not in my presence.

FAG RAG, 1974: Are you sexually active when you write?

VIDAL: The more active I am the better I write. I'm much more interested in economics and class than sex. All this is part of the middle class, part of the Puritan work ethic. You keep your seed in your bank and it collects interest; you have too many drafts on it you weaken it. This is a Protestant, middle-class thing. It was my very good fortune not to be born middle class. So I'm at a completely different vantage point.

FAG RAG: Do you think you're similar to the working class, in this respect?

VIDAL: Well, that's what's always been claimed by the British, and I think so. The fact is that for us there was really no fuss about sex. You did as much as you could. I'm fascinated by this book [*Portrait of a Marriage*] about Vita Sackville-West and Harold Nicolson. . . . He was a relentless chaser of Guardsmen and she of cunt. This is the condition of people who are not trapped into that economic middle-class tightness, and the worry of always keeping up appearances, the worry that they're always going to be 'done in' by somebody. The working class, God knows, they're filled with terrible passion and prejudice, but give them a sexual act to perform that seems amusing . . . In Texas—that relentless Bible belt—there's nobody who's not available. It's like Italy.

FAG RAG: Is there legal prostitution in Italy? Are there bordellos?

VIDAL: No. Rome is actually very Puritan. That's because the Pope lives there.

FAG RAG: . . . Are there sex toy shops in Rome? And how do you contrast the sort of decadent Puritanism with sensuality—of which you've always been an advocate —in Italy?

VIDAL: The Italians are naturally sensual and opportunistic about sex. They don't fuss. That's one of the reasons why there are really no queer bars. Pornography is really outlawed,* though there probably would be if the law allowed it.

FAG RAG: Do all middle-class [Italian] men have mistresses?

VIDAL: Yeah. Till the traffic got so you couldn't get across town.

OUI, 1975:   Do you think pornography, which we are seeing more of, is good for us?

VIDAL: Yes, it's an aid to masturbation. I think it's particularly useful for the young, to educate them, to find out what it is that turns them on—also, to learn what an extraordinary variety there is in the world. The heterosexual dictatorship in this country requires us to marry early and have lots of babies—and everything else is, as Mailer would say, dirty. This is not true. When I see movies that are not allowed to those under eighteen—most of them shouldn't be seen by anyone *over* eighteen.

OUI: In an essay you wrote on pornography, you described it as a middle-class phenomenon.

VIDAL: It's a cultural thing, really, and there's always a lag between the people at the top of the society, who are traditionally freer sexually, and those at the bottom. After all, one way of controlling the lower orders in our industrial society is to con them into marrying young and having children. The people who *own* the society, on the other hand, are perfectly free to fuck anybody they want, eat anything they want, read pornography, take drugs, what have you. For another, they own the police. Now, thanks to that beautiful word *media,* the lower economic orders are discovering what fun their masters are having. A magazine like *Playgirl* is, in a sense, blowing the minds of a lot of middle-class women who never thought they'd ever see a photograph of a cock. Now

*In 1979, pornography is now sold—in cellophane wrappers—to the residents of the peninsula. [G.V.]

they're getting a look at some very famous ones and this must make them fairly . . . well, thoughtful.

OUI: What still shocks us in America?

VIDAL: At heart, everybody is still shocked by everything. After all, most people still believe that man was destined to impregnate woman in order to have babies. Yet marriage is not a biological necessity, it's an economic one. When the economic *need* for marriage goes, then marriage will vanish. In highly industrialized Western countries, it's beginning to wither away. People are crowded, live in too small an area. So families are getting smaller; the birth rate is dropping. Suddenly, it will occur to the advanced societies: We don't have to get married! When we want to have sex, we'll have sex. When we want children, well, we should be together until they're grown. Meanwhile, the true revolution began when Nora slammed the door—and got a job. When a woman can support herself and her child, the family begins to die. But it's a slow process.

MICHAEL DEAN, 1974:   . . . You wrote in one of your essays that sex was something you felt which was probably the most existential thing in the world, something that was neither good nor bad but simply *was*. You said you could quite easily envisage a circumstance in which you made love to a man on the Monday, a woman on the Tuesday, and both on the Wednesday . . .

VIDAL: I was young then!

DEAN: Would you see pursuit of pleasure as quite a worthwhile aim in itself?

VIDAL: Indeed I would. I would include it among those things which are good. I don't believe that sex should be restricted entirely to procreation—in fact, we have taken a rather dim view of procreation. Sex is one of the few pleasures that practically everyone can indulge in, and [so, naturally,] it's one of the things that our Puritan masters here in the West, in order to keep the workers at their jobs carefully married, [try to deny us].

MALCOLM MUGGERIDGE, 1974:   Well, here we hold fundamentally different views. My own feelings about sex are perfectly expressed by St. Paul, when he says that to be carnally minded is death and to be spiritually minded is peace. I dislike intensely being carnally minded. I think all that's most horrible in human beings is stirred up by being carnally minded, and that sex detached from its purpose and its condition, which is love, is a very horrible thing, not a pleasure at all.

MICHAEL DEAN, 1974:   Do you think people should be free to make some kind of sexual choice?

MALCOLM MUGGERIDGE, 1974:   Absolutely. I wouldn't impose that view by law or anything like that. I wouldn't even impose it by means of censorship. The furthest I'd ever advocate in censorship is to protect the young from the excessive propagation of erotic literature. But if the uninhibited pursuit of sex as a pleasure is a civilizing, tranquilizing and happiness-producing activity, why is it that in the countries in which this process has gone furthest, for instance the Scandinavian countries and certain parts of the United States, they are also by universal consent the places in which this 20th-century despair is most manifest?

VIDAL: The last person I heard say that was Barry Goldwater in America. As for the melancholia that is supposed to show itself in suicide statistics, I don't find the Swedes particularly wretched, or any Scandinavians. Sex is a part of their lives in Sweden, like eating, and they don't really attach the enormous importance to it that Puritans on these [British] islands or in parts of the United States do. It's a much healthier thing, and I would say that the pursuit of eros is certainly better for the character than the pursuit of certain ideas of God. And, of course, Mr. Muggeridge is not in the censorship business except for the young . . . I think the only people

who should really [read this sort of] literature are the young—
they're the ones who [need to] learn.

MICHAEL DEAN, 1974:   If you had to nominate one
thing that made the whole liberal permissive movement
worthwhile, what would it be?

VIDAL: I would say openness of attitude. The Kingdom of Heaven is here, it's within our own skulls, it is not
somewhere else, and if you're going to make any sort of a decent society it is going to be here, it's not going to be through
personal relations with the deity. I would say that sexuality,
which I don't regard now that I'm middle-aged as all that central as I might have done twenty years ago, is, however, an
extremely important part of living a human life. The idea that
a man becomes happy on earth through [sublimating or deny-
ing his natural desires] is a form of lunacy.

EVE AUCHINCLOSS & NANCY LYNCH, 1961:   Why do you
think there's so much repressive legislation over sexual mores?

VIDAL: Well, it's our inheritance from a Judeo-Chris-
tian ethos which was seized on delightedly by the northern
barbarians from whom we descend. It is a curious subject to
make such a fuss over. Imagine, if instead of having all the
terrified and terrifying responses we do to sex, that we felt
this way about food. For instance, you could not eat in public.
You could never mention what you ate without being thought
to be terribly daring and just a bit obscene. And certain kinds
of food would be forbidden you. You could have brown
bread, but not white bread *under any circumstances.* And if you
were caught with a loaf of white bread, you would go to prison. I think you could work out a fine analogy in Samuel But-
lerish detail. If all the sex laws that are on the books were put
into practice, ninety-nine per cent of us would be in prison, or
so we've been told.

AUCHINCLOSS & LYNCH: Have you seen any signs of
change?

VIDAL: Most people's sex lives, at least in the urban parts of the United States, are coming into closer accord with [their true desires]. I've often thought one attack that could be made [on the sex] laws [is that they] are unconstitutional. The Constitution does guarantee us the pursuit of happiness . . .

AUCHINCLOSS & LYNCH: And liberty.

VIDAL: Yes, and the freedom to assemble might also be regarded as freedom for sexual assembly. We may very well find that common law is unconstitutional, in which case we could change it. I've been reading an inadvertently funny book about the sex lives of male college students and it is fantastic, the taboos and general terror of sex that have been carefully inculcated in them. Yet, perhaps the curious genius of our race—unlike the non-sadistic, hedonistic Polynesians, for instance—is derived from the fact that by blocking most sexual drives, we have managed to keep ourselves in a state of irritability out of which have come the combustion engine and lyric poetry. Certainly German philosophy could only have come out of complete sexual frustration. No Greek could have written that way, no Polynesian could have *conceived* such things. But I'm not voting for further sexual frustration.

AUCHINCLOSS & LYNCH: What connection is there between sexual frustration and romantic love?

VIDAL: Romantic love is an invention of the Middle Ages. The Greeks dealt in lust, which they understood very well, and friendship.

AUCHINCLOSS & LYNCH: Haven't there always been poignant relationships between individuals, though?

VIDAL: Of course, but the idea of love as we know it, as Madame Bovary knew it, is a complete invention. I don't know what future generations will think when they look back at our popular culture—[but I suspect that] they will think we were absolutely out of our minds. Everything was love, love, love, and you have all these people who don't know quite what they're doing or talking about, but everything is going to be all right, they feel, when they have achieved this one more perfect union. As though it were an *answer!* Of course it isn't. It's only a very small part of life and it may be unachievable or undesirable. Love is like anything else, some people have more talent for it than others. Would we know what love was unless we'd been told?

OUI, 1975:   In *Two Sisters,* you wrote: "Love affairs can only take place after the act, in memory, at a decent remove from urgent flesh, and that colliding of masks that seldom does more than ameliorate the fact that two hostile and alien yet so similar wills. . . . " Aren't you saying that a love affair must be free of intimacy and quite narcissistic?

VIDAL: What is intimacy and what is narcissism? The passage you quote simply acknowledges that every love affair is doomed the moment it begins, since it is based on a series of misapprehensions.

OUI: What are those misapprehensions?

VIDAL: That the other person is the dream complement of oneself. The other person is not; the other person is himself. Few people can deal with this reality. The ancients were more sensible. Since no one had told them about romantic love—that was a medieval concept made sickly by the 19th century—the Greeks and the Romans acknowledged only the force of lust. They thought exaggerated lust unseemly—an illness to be treated comically, like Aristophanes, or, like Euripides, tragically. Romantic love is a recent aberration of the comfortable middle class. Marvin and Madge forever and ever loving, warm, mature . . .

OUI: Is sex, then, an attempt to overpower the other person?

VIDAL: There's that aspect of it—particularly male with female. Some psychologists are beginning to note that aggressivity on the part of the liberated woman today is making the male impotent. If this is true, then male aggressivity is either something innate or learned, a part of the male-centered and male-dominated society.

OUI: Which do you think it is?

VIDAL: I don't know. Probably a bit of both. It's a fact that males are larger than females. This means they can subdue smaller, unwilling creatures and do—male as well as female.

OUI: Do males enjoy dominating one another?

VIDAL: Sometimes. Although sex between two males of—shall we say, in the old-fashioned sense of the word—equal masculinity is of enormous kinetic intensity—like a lightning storm—and since the act is not procreative, it is exciting for its own self, or, to use that word Norman Mailer always misuses, existential. The dictatorship worries a good deal about all this, and to discourage homo or bisexual activity, it has put it about that a man who wants sex with another man is really a woman, and to the red-blooded American hetero, it is almost worse to be a woman than to be a fag. Certainly, in his eyes, any man who wants to behave like a woman is betraying the dictatorship. This is all nonsense, of course, because men who like men never think of themselves as women. There is no activity more classically masculine than sex with your own kind. Those men who change their sex through surgery or like to live *en travestie* are something else again. A small category of misplaced identities.

MICHAEL DEAN, 1974:   . . . Gore Vidal is not a puritan. He has written that sex of any sort is neither good nor bad—it merely is. . . . When you say that sex of any kind is neither good nor bad, I presume you exclude rape and child molesting?

VIDAL: Oh yes. I should have said "consenting," but it would have made the sentence too bulky.

DEAN: What private moral standards would you demand, then, of a political leader?

VIDAL: I suppose the going one which is popular in ... [England], and also in my country, is that you don't get caught. I think that is the most important. I deal at considerable length in *Burr* with Thomas Jefferson, and I find it interesting that his mistress was his slave-girl, who was also the half-sister of his wife by whom he had five children. This is fascinating for the character of the man, but I don't think it has anything either good or bad to do with his Presidency or his Administration.

DEAN: Would you go so far to say that a man who was, in your view, unnaturally sexually restrained might make a bad politician?

VIDAL: It has been my experience—and I've been a politician-watcher for about forty years, and I've been a politician—that there isn't a lot of sex going on. I mean those poor, sad, little wives you see at constituency meetings. Politics—power—is a lot more exciting than sex. I think there is an awful lot of ... [well,] caponism in political life. I can certainly think of a lot of American political figures—some in high places now—that would so qualify. I don't think it's really a matter of enormous relevance. There have been many adulterers who have been distinguished and noble politicians.

DEAN: Lord Longford, I take it you would demand rather different standards of a politician?

THE EARL OF LONGFORD, 1974:   Yes, indeed. I have read *Burr,* and one or two of Gore Vidal's other books, and of course he is an absolutely brilliant writer of fiction. But Jefferson, who used to be one of my heroes, is my hero no longer after reading Gore Vidal's account of him. I don't think he would deny that Jefferson appears as a very dishonest figure in the book. And I think a man who behaves badly in the world of sex will behave badly in other worlds as well. You can find exceptions—perhaps Wellington was an exception—

but, by and large, if a man is very self-indulgent and betrays his wife, he will betray his friends and everybody.

DEAN: How high on your own list of sins would you place sexual promiscuity: Higher than average?

LORD LONGFORD: Let me put it this way: the older you get, the higher it comes. Bertrand Russell was a genius in his way, but he behaved abominably to a whole series of women by any ordinary standards—the standards of John Stuart Mill, or any liberal.

DEAN: But isn't sin a departure from a standard which the sinner himself accepts?

LORD LONGFORD: Bertrand Russell was such an egotist that I don't know what standards he could accept which could possibly put him in a bad light. But the fact is that he not only left a whole string of women in a very unhappy condition but gloried in it. He was a tremendously idealistic man, but in that field he was utterly selfish, and I think if you behave very badly in the world of sex you can reveal yourself as totally selfish. And, in the last resort, leaving out religion altogether, just taking any sort of morals, selfishness is the supreme sin.

VIDAL: Well, I don't really accept any of that. I too have read Russell's autobiography. I've also read him on mathematics, I've certainly read him on philosophy. He was a master of the English language and I don't think adultery made him split infinitives. I don't think his life with women in any way affects his findings in mathematics, nor the nobility of many of the political causes which he espoused in later life, and which I'm sure Lord Longford also espoused. He was a virtuous figure. Putting the two things together is a kind of madness. One has nothing to do with the other. As a matter of fact, I have often found that people who are not particularly well fulfilled with their wives or their women or their boyfriends are sometimes infinitely more virtuous in their public lives or in their art. Also, I don't find Russell in the least selfish sexually: he was a great romantic. If anything, he was rather silly, the way he was falling in love with people.

LORD LONGFORD: He kept leaving these women, and in that autobiography he describes how he ruined some woman whom he didn't marry in the end. I should think, in that field, he was totally selfish. Gladstone said that he had known eleven Prime Ministers, seven of whom had committed adultery. If you take the last eleven Prime Ministers in this country—apart from Lloyd George, who appears to have committed adultery in a very big way—there's no clear evidence anybody did. This is rather interesting, because one assumes that we live in a permissive age, yet the Prime Ministers in the 19th century committed adultery helter-skelter, and now they don't.

VIDAL: But, Lord Longford, the reason we know about them is that the laws of libel no longer apply to them. You cannot say such things about living Prime Ministers, whereas for the 19th century we begin to find out. I'm quite sure that if there is a 21st century, which seems unlikely at the moment, and anybody looks back at the gorgeous pageant of your Prime Ministers of this century, they will find quite a few adulterers, since I assume that they are fairly normal men. By and large, none of the three of us has the slightest notion of what these men are up to privately.

LORD LONGFORD: But the press is not suppressed, you know. If you get into trouble now, you're spotted very quickly and you come to an end. The private life of a man, people say, does not necessarily indicate the public capacity: well, I think it does. I admit one exception, Wellington, about whom my wife has written so truthfully. But Lloyd George was such a wretched figure, and I think he has been finally exposed. And Mr. Asquith—there's a lot coming out about him now. There he was, in the Cabinet, sitting writing these letters to lady friends: that was clearly impairing his performance, I think.

VIDAL: I think it was rather marvelous. I've read those letters [to Venetia Stanley] and I thought they were probably in the long run more important than his Prime Ministership—but now I'm speaking as an artist. You make an exception of the Anglo-Irish Wellington—once you start making exceptions in the Kingdom of Heaven you've no idea what terrible company you're going to get there amongst the angels. But, on my side of the water, take Franklin Roosevelt, who was probably the best American President of this century. Franklin Roosevelt was early on an adulterer—probably encouraged by the fact that his wife turned down sex. His wife did not like sex, that was certainly part of it, and he was obviously a very normal man. He became interested in his wife's secretary—somebody called Lucy Mercer—and Eleanor found out about it in the corniest way, going through the mail, opening a letter by mistake and finding it was a love letter. So they made a truce between them, and he carried on with Lucy Mercer. He also carried on with his secretary, Marguerite—Missy Le Hand, as she was known. And then we don't know if he had an affair, but he was fascinated by a visitor during the war—Princess Martha of Norway. It was said in Washington that they were having an affair—Mrs. Roosevelt was very grim on the subject. I remember talking to her about it once and her attitude was: My lips are sealed. But the great joke in Washington during the war (and this might support Lord Longford) was that Roosevelt gave Norway a submarine-chaser, which he presented to Princess Martha on the White House lawn. Any other man would have given her a ring or a bracelet. He gives her a submarine-chaser—from our money.

LORD LONGFORD: I never heard of Lloyd George doing anything as bad as that, or Asquith either. We don't rise to those heights.

VIDAL: Your Prime Ministers are not also Chiefs of State.

LORD LONGFORD: I defer to Gore Vidal about his own President, but I would imagine that same weakness—that dishonesty—which comes out in an adulterer would reveal itself in these top-level people in their political lives. If a man is very unhappily married, he may be consoled in some sophisticated way. But, by and large, if a man is married and is carrying on with some other woman, he is deceiving his wife and he is therefore a dishonest man. He is living a life of deceit: it's like Philby.

VIDAL: Lord Longford is making categorical statements so I'll make one: a man who is not so sexually geared that he does not want to have affairs with other than the official mate seems to me an unnatural monster. I'll take the point even further. The man who goes into politics is, by definition, obsessed with people. He has to be. Sometimes he wants to master them—sometimes he really gets a feeling of excitement from the crowd. But he is always with people. Something fascinating happened just a day or two ago. Somebody asked Mrs. Lyndon Johnson about her husband's sexual peccadilloes and she said: "Well, you know, Lyndon was a people lover and he was not going to exempt half the population of the world which is female from his love." Good answer. Then she said, "I think that I was wise enough to know that whatever it was that he loved in these other women, I could learn something from it, and our relationship continued to be strong." That to me is a mature relationship between a man and a woman, and an amazingly good one between a President and a First Lady. To me, if you do not love people sexually, you can't love them at all.

LORD LONGFORD: Oh no, no. I can't swallow that. In this country—and I'm sure the same is true of America, which is I think rather more puritanical, in this sense particularly—the vast majority of people never go to bed with anybody but their own wife. That is simply a fact about the vast majority now. You, Mr. [Dean], . . . are a neutral observer of this scene and I think you'll hardly deny that's true.

DEAN: I can't speak for all those people.

LORD LONGFORD: But you're married, aren't you? I mean, you're a respectably married man. You look like it.

VIDAL: I wouldn't take that for anything—I would say: "I'm *not* a respectably married man."

LORD LONGFORD: In this country it would lose him his job if he didn't take it from me.

VIDAL: Come now, we know about the BBC [for whom Mr. Dean works]. They're not that bad.

LORD LONGFORD: The vast majority of married people are what is called respectably married. They don't sleep with other people. A few very brilliant people do—and sometimes they sleep around a lot. But by and large that is the norm.

DEAN: Where do you get your information from?

VIDAL: In America we have statistics on this, and something like seventy per cent of married men commit adultery. It's a smaller figure for women. I highly doubt that our English cousins are so very, very different from us.

LORD LONGFORD: Well, find me the man standing for Parliament who if he were asked if he had ever committed adultery would say "Yes." Find me the man who will say that and you'll find me an exception.

DEAN: Oh, indeed, he might well find himself being sued for divorce very shortly. But I want to put this question to Gore Vidal: if one accepts your position, for the sake of the argument, and the moral climate permits the kind of behavior you recommend, would you say that a politician ought never to take into account—or, conversely, ought always to take into account—the prevailing moral climate? For example, was Lloyd George, at a time when sexual restraint was widely recommended, if not practiced, putting himself and his Government at risk?

VIDAL: I don't think so. Indeed, he proved that he didn't put them at risk. He was obviously a very good operator in that way, but I can't see that it makes the slightest bit of difference. Now that scandal that you had here recently with the Lords Lambton and Jellicoe: I read about it in Italy, and the Italians said it was amazing for an English scandal [in which] boys [weren't] involved. They said that really shows the British are shaping up now that they are getting into the Common Market. That [the scandal] was heterosexual was very thrilling to the Italians. But it occurred to me that if I was in, say, Jellicoe's situation I would have refused to resign. I'd say: "You may remove me if you like, but what I've done is my business. It has nothing to do with how I conduct my office. I haven't given away any secrets and if you think I have you must certainly prosecute me."

LORD LONGFORD: Well, I must say, without being unduly pompous, that Lord Jellicoe was Leader of the House of Lords, which I was at a slightly earlier moment, and he is someone I have great regard for; and I think that, from the point of view of people like myself, he behaved in the honorable way. Whatever we may say ought to be the case, at the present time the fact is that if you are found in that sort of situation you have to go.

VIDAL: Well, you're quite right. But what you're also saying is that moral consensus is really all you need. Well, if you want a moral consensus, you'll bring back hanging, you'll bring back the birch and you'll put homosexuals in jail. That's what the majority in England would want. Since we don't allow the majority to have their way with that, I don't think we should allow the majority to have their way with the private lives of politicians. Obviously, there's a certain front kept up and certain things are considered undesirable to do, and I think politicians must be more careful than other people.

DEAN: You would concede that politicians should set themselves higher standards?

VIDAL: Well, they're obliged to by the hypocrisies of their constituents, who are no better than they are—but this is an agreed-upon game. You do not appear with your mistress and your wife on the hustings. It makes for a bad impression. They must not know she is your mistress if she is there.

LORD LONGFORD: You call it hypocrisy. But the vast majority of people in this country will agree with me if I say that they are in favor of fidelity in marriage.

VIDAL: But you yourself, in your career, have gone against the moral majority very nobly in the case of homosexuality, and in the case of hanging. I recommend you go against that majority again.

LORD LONGFORD: Yes, but you see here my conscience is on the same side as the majority because it is the Christian conscience. The vast majority of people in this country will say, if asked, that they are Christians, and if you are a Christian—whatever sort of denomination or however woozy—you'll be against sex outside marriage. That's the Christian position here and in America.

VIDAL: It's my impression, getting around England for the last thirty years, that Christianity barely took root here and is certainly dying out—at least the Anglican Church. The churches are empty; people say they are Christians, but they certainly don't act like Christians, and I think we'll all agree that none of us really does.

LORD LONGFORD: Well, none of us do that, no.

VIDAL: I think that they mouth certain platitudes that people expect to hear. But this is a secular nation, like the United States. This is, I trust, a nation of law. This is not a Christian nation, is it? Is this a theocratic state?

LORD LONGFORD: No, no, now you're moving a bit fast. "Is this a Christian state?" I see you're full of forensic genius. No, it's not a theocratic state at all. Not a bit.

DEAN: Would you like it to be one?

LORD LONGFORD: No, not at all. I don't know what a theocratic state means, but I suppose it means the Archbishop of Canterbury pronounces and imposes his rules on everybody. But it's a Christian country in the sense that if you ask most people in this country, "Are you a Christian?" they will say "yes."

VIDAL: And the majority of the people will say: "I have not committed adultery, I have not robbed the poor box on [the] one trip I made to church in twenty years." I mean, they'll *say* all kinds of things—but don't you believe it.

LORD LONGFORD: But do you not think that the preservation of the family is essential? I mean, looking to the future, don't you think that a good family life and the upbringing of children in an atmosphere of love and security are essential if we're going to have a good society here?

VIDAL: My answer is this: that I do not believe in the family. In an over-populated world I do not think that people should be allowed to breed incontinently. I think that they should be allowed to do it by the state, just as you have an immigration act. Those who are good at it should be encouraged.

LORD LONGFORD: This is a whole new argument.

DEAN: Would you like a last brief word, Lord Longford?

LORD LONGFORD: Not really, except that I am a Christian, and I think my message—the message which I've very feebly tried to present before the world—will last long after the arguments which Gore Vidal has so brilliantly explained to us.

OUI, 1975: Why do you despise the heterosexual dictatorship?

VIDAL: Because it's [a dictatorship]. To hear two American men congratulating each other on being heterosexual is one of the most chilling experiences—and unique to the United States. You don't hear two Italians sitting around complimenting each other because they actually like to go to bed with women. The American is hysterical about his manhood.

OUI: Why is that?

VIDAL: A lot of it is bullshit from the old frontier, where the only way you could judge a man was if he could knock somebody down—and of course the heterosexual male's obsession with cock is far beyond that of any fag. I remember recently reading about a college where the black boys and the white boys were living in the same dormitory. The black boys asked to move out. When the whites asked why, the blacks said, "Because these white cats are always looking at our cocks. That's all they think about is cock. We're not into that."

OUI: You have written, both in essays and in fiction, about the warrior as a homosexual. Do soldiers indulge in homosexual acts simply because of physical proximity, or is there a connection between the warrior spirit and the homosexual act?

VIDAL: It's probably just proximity. Bisexual highjinks. Sexual relief. I do think that anybody who voluntarily becomes a professional soldier or sailor or baseball player obviously prefers men to women. I've been told of a new book by a baseball player that reads, apparently, like Clare Boothe Luce in a jockstrap. Contrary to the popular myth, full-time homosexuals tend to be more masculine than their hetero brothers. For an obvious reason: To like women, you must have some likeness, some resemblance. Certain men are so entirely absorbed by the idea, the essence of masculinity, that women don't appeal to them—too unlike. I've noticed that the really devoted womanizers often have rather feminine traits and responses. Mick Jagger delights in coming on as a far-out fag, as did my old friend the late Laurence Harvey, in order to resemble what most turns him on, the opposite sex. Not that there wasn't a bit of bi going on in Larry's case, but only because he had an adventurous nature.

OUI: If the natural state for all of us is bisexuality, isn't homosexuality just as unnatural as heterosexuality?

VIDAL: They're both natural. Why is either unnatural?

OUI: And to be one or the other exclusively?

VIDAL: That's simply to be limited. Most of us *are* limited, however—usually due to circumstances.

MONIQUE VAN VOOREN, 1976: It's so funny—I always thought of Nixon sleeping in a double bed yet you see him in twin beds.

VIDAL: Schizophrenics need two beds.

VAN VOOREN: Don't you think that some people can be completely asexual?

VIDAL: I met one once but it's very rare.

VAN VOOREN: I really don't know if what you say that everyone is bisexual [is true].

VIDAL: I am quoting from Freud. It's not a theory, it's a fact. It's not a theory that everybody has two legs, two lobes to the brain which is why we tend to be interested in symmetry, always balancing things. To have an interest in both sexes is equally normal. Whether it's practiced or not is something else again. Some do. Some don't.

PLAYBOY, 1969: In Oscar Wilde's day, homosexuality was known as "the love that dare not speak its name," but today it has become, in Mike Nichols' words, "the vice that won't shut up." Do you consider the growing candor of homosexual spokesmen and homophile organizations a healthy sign, or the price one pays for social progress?

VIDAL: I'm in favor of any form of sexual relationship that gives pleasure to those involved. And I have never heard a convincing argument to the contrary. Our problem is semantic. Tribalists have taught us to view male and female homosexuality as a form of disease, instead of what it is: a term used to describe not personality but a specific sexual act. . . . Since there is no such thing as a heterosexual personality, there can be no such thing as a homosexual personality—though it's certainly true that homosexualists often develop a rich variety of neuroses as a result of persecution; but then, so do Negroes, Jews and—in some cultures—women. In any case, to try to alter the sexual nature of an adult is a lunatic—and hopeless—business. Unfortunately, it is also a very profitable one for quacks like the late Dr. Bergler.

FAG RAG, 1974: One thing you've said is that you didn't think that anyone was a homosexual.

VIDAL: I've always said it was just an adjective. It's not a noun, though it's always used as a noun. Put it the other way. What is a heterosexual *person?* I've never met one. When you say Lyndon Johnson and Adlai Stevenson behaved like two typical heterosexuals over the weekend, in their response, well, I don't know what they had in common [other than liking women]. To me, it's just descriptive of an act.

FAG RAG: What about faggot or fag, the way we use it today?

VIDAL: I prefer the word faggot which I tend to use myself. I have never allowed, actively, in my life the word "gay" to pass my lips. I don't know why I hate that word. . . . Historically it meant a girl of easy virtue in the 17th century. They'd say: "Is she gay?" Which meant: "Is she available?" And this, I don't think, is highly descriptive of anybody. It's just a bad word. You see, I don't think you need a word for it. This is what you have to evolve. These words have got to wither away in a true Hegelian cycle.

FAG RAG: A lot of homosexuals seem to be very concerned about whether they are called gays, faggots, fairies, or homosexuals.

VIDAL: ... I'm a generalist, and I'm interested in a great many other things. Knowing the mania of The Media, they want everybody to be in a pigeonhole. Oh, yes. He's the Official Fag. Oh, yes. He's the Official Marxist. [Well,] I have never allowed myself to be pigeonholed like that. Also I don't regard myself as one thing or another. The point is, why not discard all the words. Say that all sexual acts have parity. Which is my line.

FAG RAG: If they're not forced.

VIDAL: Well, obviously. A voluntary act, voluntarily received, is equal to any other. And why make a fuss about what it is?

DENNIS ALTMAN, 1977:   But the ADL or NAACP were basically organized by those who identified as Jews or blacks, and it was this identification that gave them the incentive to organize. If you deny that there are such people as homosexuals, who is going to organize such a movement?

VIDAL: I'm thinking of something larger and more important than just trying to change laws and attitudes which make life difficult for full-time homosexualists—there's a noun, at last. But a clumsy one. How, by the way, is one to make a noun out of that idiotic adjective, "gay"? A "gayist"? A "sprite"? "Pollyanna"? Anyway, I'd include other "criminals"—gamblers, prostitutes of both sexes, etc. ... In other words, I'm for a much larger coalition ... one that could affect almost everybody. The late Dr. Kinsey said that if all the sex laws in the U.S. were put into effect, something like ninety per cent of the male population would be in prison. The repeal of all these laws is most important. Obviously, full-time practicing homosexualists have the greater motive to join. But don't be exclusive.

ALTMAN: The basic problem is that homosexuals are either too scared to do anything—and this sort of activity means that, to some extent at least, you have to come out—or they believe things are pretty good anyway, so why rock the boat. How are you going to get enough to involve themselves in this sort of movement? Surely the success of . . . [the Anti-Defamation League and the NAACP] was due to the willingness of blacks and Jews to participate.

VIDAL: I'm not so sure—for instance the NAACP had many white members. I used to belong to it. I can remember a good deal of complaint from black leaders about apathy among those they worked to serve and defend. The point is, you must get together as many people as you can whose attitudes toward sex are post-Mosaic, post-Pauline. Then, go to the courts, the legislators, and go to the polls. From the beginning, both blacks and Jews tried to get allies from both whites and Gentiles. Once you start sounding exclusive or superior then you are ringing a change on that "black is beautiful" line of the sixties, which no one really bought, including the blacks . . . after all, if blacks are beautiful, then whites are ugly, and though this may or may not be true in individual cases, you can't generalize. In a way, the Anita Bryant thing has been useful. This essentially Fascist caper convinced a lot of homosexualists (who thought they were having a pretty good time since no one was hassling them at the moment) that they should act. But how? That's when organization is needed. Bryant and the Far Right are organized and rich. They are touching what is known in politics as the "hot buttons"—fags, drugs, Panama Canal—well, let us do likewise. Let's press the cool buttons of the Golden Rule. . . . Of course, the current Nixon Supreme Court is hostile to personal freedom—as opposed to granting any corporation or police department any license it wants to rip off consumers or to terrorize citizens. Even so, I would keep on in the courts. There must be enough homosexualist lawyers willing to give a little free time to this.

ALTMAN: You're talking along the lines used in Britain in the sixties when there were very respectable people pushing for reform. The Law Reform Society . . .

VIDAL: Including my cousin, Lord Arran, many times removed from me by blood but close in spirit.

ALTMAN: . . . was not basically homosexual, and lots of its members who were, went to great lengths to hide it. It's debatable, I think, whether changing the law made any real difference for most homosexuals in Britain, and also whether this sort of strategy does anything about the enormous feelings of guilt and self-hatred and self-loathing most homosexuals still feel.

VIDAL: Now you're moving into something else. You have to go step by step. Whether each step is as broad as you might like is something else again. The Wolfenden Report was necessary, the laws that went through Parliament were necessary. The fact that [to this day,] British police are occasionally inclined to persecute is a fact. After all, the average male in the Anglo-American world is hysterical on the subject of homosexuality. It is in the culture, a vestige of Judeo-Christianity, now in its terminal stage. Everyone knows he has homosexual instincts and since everyone had been told from birth that if he gives way to such instincts, he is sick and evil, and, in most American states, a criminal, fag-bashing is bound to be popular for a long time. Religio-social attitudes change slowly. That's why I'm interested in what the TV commercials call "faster action." Change the laws. Scare the police. Take California. They have got fairly liberal laws on victimless crimes, but the Los Angeles police are still busy entrapping homosexualists because the police chief in Los Angeles is very anti-fag. He is a member of the Far Right and homophobia is the hottest button he's got to push. So he uses police as decoys—[which is] illegal. Now there's a very easy way of stopping this and I may devote some time to it this [1978] winter. Operation: Set Up the Police. Wire someone for sound; put him on Selma Avenue. From a distance train a camera on him. Plainclothesman approaches our decoy. Plainclothesman makes the first move, does the soliciting. Then, as is the merry custom in those parts, a second plainclothesman helps the first to make the arrest, often indulging in a little nonconsenting S/M. Now on tape and film we have the evidence that the police entrapped our decoy, preferably a man: a man with two children and a membership in the Rotary Club. When the plainclothesmen lie in court, as they always do, produce the film and send them to jail. As Thomas Jefferson would say, arrests of this kind would have "a very wholesome effect" on police departments everywhere.

JUDY HALFPENNY, 1977:   You haven't shown your characters suffering in the cause of sexual freedom. I don't recall that even Jim Willard was ever picked up by the police.

VIDAL: . . . Naturally, I hear and read a lot about police brutality (and witnessed one incident in Washington) and entrapment. Recently I proposed in Los Angeles that police entrappers be themselves entrapped. . . .

STANTON, 1979:   Did you set-up the Los Angeles police this past winter?

VIDAL: I didn't have the time. But I did propose the caper at the Arlington Street Church. Perhaps that is why the Chief Justice is now suspended . . . it is a crime in Massachusetts to catch a thief if he happens to be a policeman on duty. This is very sound.

STANTON: Do you have any reaction to the dumping on and of Massachusetts Superior Court Chief Justice Bonin?

VIDAL: When I said in *The Real Paper* [Febraury 24, 1979] that one of the [charges] brought against Bonin was that he had gone backstage to greet me and that this, as much as anything else, brought to an end his career as Chief Justice, Bonin wrote me a nice letter, saying "I was doomed from the beginning."

DENNIS ALTMAN, 1977:   A number of people have argued that what really changed in the homosexual world in the
past ten years in countries like the U.S. is that the ghetto has
come out; most homosexuals still live the sort of life they've
always lived but the ghetto is much larger, much more commercial than it ever was. Would you agree?

VIDAL: I think that's probably true in the major cities.
I certainly noticed it in Los Angeles when I was living there
last winter. Since I have never lived in a ghetto of any kind,
I'm fairly sensitive to in-bred groups: New York literary life,
Bel Air movie makers, homosexual enclaves anywhere. I think
it stunting to live only one kind of life with like-minded people. But then, heteros are as likely to cling to their own kind—
I mean socially, economically, ethnically, rather than sexually—as homos. Anyway, at worst, homosexualists tend to mirror heterosexual society and that the heterosexual society is
deeply ill is of more concern to me than that god-awful
phrase "life-style." The women's role has changed and with it
the role of the family. This is a phenomenon of greater cultural interest than the problems of the homosexualist ... it is
also related. Between the collapse of Judeo-Christianity and
overpopulation-cum-insufficient energy, there is no great
premium on having children—rather, the reverse. Yet everyone's brought up to behave as if the U.S. were a sparsely populated agrarian society that needs lots more babies. These
attitudes are not easily changed.

ALTMAN: Isn't there a contradiction between traditional legalistic procedures on the one hand and arguing on
the other that homosexuals—which I agree with—should become part of a much broader political movement concerned
with the great questions?

VIDAL: I think you have to operate on three, four,
five different levels at once. When I'm out speaking to a
women's group in Parkersburg, West Virginia, I'm going to
speak in certain terms that I wouldn't use, say, when I'm writing for the *New York Review of Books.* You have to get through as

best you can. Means differ. Ends are fairly constant. You must also be prepared to learn from others. Few public figures have this gift. I think that I do—the result of not being a specialist but a generalist. You point to the fact that once the law is changed, you still haven't altered attitudes. Of course you haven't. But one step at a time. Do what you can do. In a country created by lawyers, that means using the law to good ends. Don't worry about being loved or respected or that "gay sensibility" is not recorded as the highest state man has yet achieved.

OUI, 1975:   If gay is now fashionable—not only fashionable but marketable—how do you feel about such people as Dotson Rader and Mart Crowley, who are exploiting homosexuality?

VIDAL: Well, Dotson Rader must eventually learn that it's not enough to be homosexual, you must also have talent. But these are all fashions and they'll be onto something else soon. Just yesterday, it was fashionable to be black. Remember? Any black writer could get away with murder, just as any Jewish-American writer can get away with murder. Women writers are also doing pretty well in their fear of flying.

JUDY HALFPENNY, 1979:   Why must writers tackle people they detest and therefore can't do justice to? Not content with editing it down to size, Peter Green wrote a novel about Alcibiades and it's awful!

VIDAL: It is curious how "hetero" writers (alleged, that is) are drawn to "homo" figures (equally, alleged) in order to diminish them. It is also curious that a scholar as good as Peter Green is not aware that everyone in his chosen epoch took for granted bisexuality . . . with the usual variations in courtship from time to time, place to place. The warm wonderful entirely *dans le vrai* nuclear family was something that if anyone could ever have explained it to Alexander would have evoked Homeric laughter. But then it is the tendency of mass societies to level . . . classes (to me, a good thing), and the sexes (seldom a good thing) . . . The levelers want consumers and obedient workers: the human spirit does not much take to either function much less the deadly tandem.

PLAYBOY, 1969: The charge was recently made by *Ramparts* magazine and critic Stanley Kauffman, among others, that a homosexual coterie—the "Homintern," as some melodramatically term it—has a stranglehold on American culture and advances its own values, and the fortunes of its fellows, at the expense of the heterosexual artist. Do you believe there's any substance to these claims?

VIDAL: No. As far as I know, there exist no protocols of Sodom. All that matters in the arts is excellence; and though the sex life of the artist no doubt affects to some degree his moral tone, the final work must be judged as a thing in itself. Do Saul Bellow's heterosexual preoccupations undermine his considerable art? The question sounds silly, because it is silly. True art is rooted in the common human condition.

6

Politics

FAG RAG, 1974: Politically, do you see any opportunity for using the whole remembrance of the origins of the country in a political way?

VIDAL: One tactic which is useful: you can always promote radical causes under the guise of Going Back to the Constitution. And sometimes quite legitimately. The Bill of Rights is still a radical document. I find sometimes when I'm trying to be an advocate, trying to convince a really difficult audience, I can always refer back to the origins and tell them that this is the way it was meant to be.

FAG RAG: When you've got Daniel Shays, Tom Paine, and all the rest of them, you've got some rich potential.

VIDAL: Yes.

FAG RAG: Is the Constitution pretty much a dead letter except for two or three amendments in the Bill of Rights?

VIDAL: I would just throw the whole goddamn thing out except the Bill of Rights, and start all over again. The system does not work. . . .

EVE AUCHINCLOSS & NANCY LYNCH, 1961: You've said that your only serious interest is in the subversion of a society that bores and appalls you. How do you go about it?

VIDAL: I was talking about the theatre and my role as a playwright, but I would stick by it in the sense that to subvert a society means that you disapprove of it and that is why you write, or run for office, or propose legislation. I've criticized everything from advertising to the method of selecting delegates to Presidential conventions—you name it. I'm very specific-minded, unlike some of my fellow breakers of idols.

AUCHINCLOSS & LYNCH: Will we ever get a real party of opposition, like the European Socialists?

VIDAL: Barring economic disaster or military misadventure, I think it's unlikely. Of course, neither of our parties means anything; but if great pressure is brought to bear on us in the world, I think we might see our party system cracking up, and then all the real interests—this uneasy coalition of Negroes here, Jews there, Middle Western farmers who detest the slick Easterners, and Easterners who look down on the nuts of Southern California—all these groups could go flying off in a thousand different directions, each with its own hierarchy and mystique, which would be horrifying.

NEWSWEEK, 1974:   You sound pessimistic. Is there anything we can do?

VIDAL: We need a whole new constitution. I'd also like to see a movement in the country to stop paying the income tax—for the excellent reason that we get nothing back. We're the only country in the West without a health service; there is no mass transit; the educational system is a scandal. What do we get? This vast amount of armaments which enriches a very small group of bankers, manufacturers, and politicians. So let's not pay any taxes until we get something back. The true end of a democratic society is economic equality; that's an idea whose time has not come. But it's implicit in the idea of democracy, and when our system collapses and gas and food and everything has to be rationed we'll realize that was our goal anyway. Then there will be no rich Rockefellers and there will be no grape pickers without enough money to eat anything but dog food. But we are not going to get this from a Charles Percy or a Walter Mondale; they're part of the system. By the time a man gets to be Presidential material, he's been bought ten times over. He's of no use to the country.

JACOB EPSTEIN, 1976: What must happen before levels of political sophistication in America are raised?

VIDAL: Fifty per cent unemployment. That would do it.

EPSTEIN: Does the rest of the world have anything to do with it?

VIDAL: I suppose if somebody wanted a war with us, bigger than Vietnam. If somebody invaded, maybe. That isn't apt to happen. Nor is atomic war. So—real economic catastrophe.

FAG RAG, 1974: . . . The thing that bothers me is that every other elite—you come out of the liberal elite—in Germany, France, etc., produce leaders, phenomenal people.

VIDAL: No revolution ever came from the bottom.

FAG RAG: Exactly. But the United States, just in the last ten years, has had an attempt on the part of many people who come out of the elite . . .

VIDAL: An attempt to do what? Change things?

FAG RAG: Yes. From the Left. We have no leadership. The media have taken every figure in the "movement" . . .

VIDAL: And used them up. I watched Abbie Hoffman from the beginning. I predicted the first time he appeared on the scene—at a debate between Tom Hayden and me. Abbie was in the audience. He got up and harangued. I could see they loved him on television. "Freako! Wildman!" I said to myself: If that man is around in three years I'll be surprised. They'll use him up. And then there will be another wild man, and he will be on a different kick.

FAG RAG: David Bowie now.

VIDAL: Yeah. Survival in the United States is not easy whether it is for a writer or a singer or anyone else. . . . It's not easy at all.

FAG RAG: The point that continues to plague me is the lack of leadership. I do not see any positive political strategy.

VIDAL: You need a new party. You come back to it again. I made my effort along with those others in '68 and again in '72.

FAG RAG: But what is the base?

VIDAL: If you saw the manifesto I did ["A Dialogue with Myself," in *Esquire* (October 1968)], you have got to have a party of human survival. When they get through freezing this winter, and the factories shut down, and the stock market collapses, and the currency goes down, and you can't buy food, they are going to be ready next spring to look for . . .

FAG RAG: That's not a crisis of Nixon; that's a crisis of capitalism.

VIDAL: Thank God! *That's* what we've been waiting for. I think it's upon us.

FAG RAG: Do you have a conscious feeling about your writing and politics? Do you feel you've got a political role?

VIDAL: No.

PARIS REVIEW, 1974:   What do you think generally about the writer *engagé?* Should a writer be involved in politics, as you are?

VIDAL: It depends on the writer. Most American writers are not much involved, beyond signing petitions. They are usually academics—and cautious. Or full-time *literary* politicians. Or both. The main line of our literature is quotidianal with a vengeance. Yes, many great novels have been written about the everyday—Jane Austen and so on. But you need a superb art to make that sort of thing interesting. So, failing superb art, you'd better have a good mind and you'd better be interested in the world outside yourself. D. H. Lawrence wrote something very interesting about the young Hemingway. Called him a brilliant writer. But he added: he's essentially a photographer and it will be interesting to see how he ages because the photographer can only keep on taking pictures from the outside. One of the reasons that the gifted Hemingway never wrote a good novel was that nothing interested him except a few sensuous experiences like killing things and fucking—interesting things to do but not all that interesting to write about. This sort of artist runs into trouble very early on because all he can really write about is himself and after youth that self—unengaged in the world—is of declining interest. Admittedly Hemingway chased after wars but he never had much of anything to say *about* war, unlike Tolstoy or even Malraux. I think that the more you know the world and the wider the net you cast in your society, the more interesting your books will be, certainly the more interesting you will be.

AMERICAN FILM, 1977:   In writing your historical novels, are you consciously attempting to throw light on today through the use of the past?

VIDAL: I think there's not a great deal of difference from one period to another but, yes, I think re-creating the past illuminates the present. We're a strange society in that we have no [sense of the] past. That's why I wrote my American trilogy: *Burr, 1876, Washington, D.C.* Partly, I wanted to tell myself the story of the history of the country because I found history as boring in school as everybody else did, and I knew the national story could not have been that dull, and it wasn't. But we're a society forever trying to erase yesterday. Because of this we got the Nixons. We live in a world where nobody is accountable for anything. It's quite astonishing. We Nixon-viewers knew he was a criminal years ago, but we couldn't tell anybody. They wouldn't listen, they weren't interested. A society without a recollected history is also peculiarly vulnerable to any one who wants to take it over. I do see Caesars moving in upon the forum, and when they arrive there will not be much resistance. After all, the average person watches six hours of television a day. How can they defend their liberties when they're busy watching "The Gong Show"?

MICHAEL DEAN, 1968: If you had the choice of being a politician who made his mark in the society of which he was part, or a writer who changed the current of thought in his time, which would you choose?

VIDAL: The operative word in what you said is the verb—"to change." And I don't care how I do it. You might call me an old-fashioned social meliorist. If I didn't want to make changes I don't think I would write and I certainly would not be politically active. Particularly in a country like the United States where 25 per cent of the people are madly disturbed and all have guns. It is not a safe thing to be in politics there. You should read my mail.

FAG RAG, 1974: You didn't make [Nixon's] "Enemies List" . . .

VIDAL: [That] was one of their ways of destroying me.

FAG RAG: Have you ever had IRS, passport, or FBI trouble?

VIDAL: I've been broken into twice by the FBI when I was with the People's Party. As was [Benjamin] Spock. You can always tell [it's the FBI] because they never take anything. They should at least take the TV set, but they're so damn lazy and it's heavy.

FAG RAG: These are agents?

VIDAL: Yeah. Then they would go through papers, papers, papers.

FAG RAG: Was this under Johnson or Nixon?

VIDAL: Nixon.

FAG RAG: Have they ever tried to talk with you?

VIDAL: No. I am on the FBI list of people never to talk to about anything, because I went after Hoover about twelve years ago . . .

FAG RAG: Before it was fashionable.

VIDAL: Yeah. And really let him have it.

FAG RAG: Did you ever meet the man?

VIDAL: Yes.

FAG RAG: Did he look you in the eye? My brother always told me you can tell a queer because he'll never look you in the eye.

VIDAL: Somebody was asking me. Said he thought Richard Nixon was obviously homosexual. I said: "Why do you think that?" He said: "You know, that funny, uncoordinated way he moves." I said: "Yeah. Like Nureyev."

PLAYBOY, 1969:   As one who was intimately involved in last year's electoral process—first as an early supporter of Senator Eugene McCarthy's candidacy, then as a political commentator for ABC at the Republican and Democratic Conventions—what do you see as the probable impact of the Nixon Administration on this country and on the world?

VIDAL: "People are what they are," as Eleanor Roosevelt used to say, more in sorrow than in triumph. Nixon is what he is and—again, Mrs. Roosevelt—"You can't change people." There is, of course, a popular myth that people do change: but in real life, they don't. With age and experience, they simply become more adroit at selling themselves. Nixon has never been interested in issues or ideas, only in self-promotion. His Congressional career was a perfect blank—nothing accomplished, no one represented except an occasional favor for those who contributed to his famous slush fund. He did fight the Commies, however, and so became known. Reports on his Vice-Presidential years show that at Cabinet meetings, he seldom had anything to say about issues but a good deal to say about promoting the party.

PLAYBOY: Soon after the election, *Newsweek* suggested that Nixon's qualifications as a complete political technician are among his redeeming Presidential assets. Do you feel there's any truth to that?

VIDAL: If the technician were interested in solving real problems, we would all be in his debt. But if Nixon has ever had any ideas about the American empire or the situation of the blacks, he has been careful not to confide them to us. More to the point, since he is interested only in self-promotion, he is not about to jeopardize The Career by taking a strong position on any issue. The ghettos will be "solved," he tells us, by giving tax cuts to private industry for doing business with the blacks. Well, it doesn't take a profound student of the human heart to know that the tax cuts will be accepted gladly and that the ghettos will be no better off. It is a proof of his banality not only that he thinks we don't know how inadequate what he proposes is but that the very way he puts his "solution" shows that to him the ghetto is something incurable—to be improved, not eliminated. But then, of course, he is a conservative as well as an opportunist, and conservatives believe that the poor are always with us, that the human heart is unchanging—"Basically, we're all rascals," as Barry Goldwater used to say—and, finally, that slaves should obey their masters. It is the liberal disposition that things can be made better than they are. I am a liberal, and so unfashionable at present.

PLAYBOY: Why? Because the conservatives are in power?

VIDAL: Yes, and because they mean to do nothing, while the lively new radicals of the left have given up. The only thing left and right have in common is a disdain for the liberals. The conservatives are now tending toward fascism—crack down on dissent, support your local police, disobey the Supreme Court—while the New Left wants to destroy the entire system. Emotionally, I'm drawn to the New Left. I would certainly go to the barricades for any movement that wants to sweep away the Pentagon, *Time* magazine, and frozen French fried potatoes. But what is to take its place? The New Left not only have no blueprint, they don't *want* a blueprint. Let's just see what happens, they say. Well, I can tell them what will happen: first anarchy, then dictatorship. They are rich in Tom Paines, but they have no Thomas Jefferson.

PLAYBOY: Nixon has announced that after an era of confrontation, we must now begin an era of negotiation. Do you see this as a hopeful sign?

VIDAL: He enjoys taking trips abroad and thinks himself an international expert because, over the years, he has met a great many heads of state with whom he has spoken through an interpreter for as long as thirty minutes. I think he'll do a lot of traveling, but nothing much will change. You know, empires have their own dynamic, and individuals don't much affect their progress. Take the American empire. Up until the end of the 19th century, we were confined to our continent, seizing land from Mexico, trying to invade Canada, and, of course, breaking every treaty we ever made with the indigenous population, the Indians, as an excuse for slaughtering them as well as expropriating their land. By 1899, the continent was full up. We were at the edge of the Pacific Ocean, dressed to kill, with no place to go. The result was a serious national depression—emotional as well as economic. Fortunately, that master therapist, Teddy Roosevelt, was able to contrive a war with Spain that put us into the empire business in a big way: Not only did we "free" Cuba but we took on Puerto Rico and, most significant, the Philippines. Westward the course of empire flowed and still flows. When Teddy's cousin Franklin maneuvered the Japanese into attacking us at Pearl Harbor—so that he'd have an excuse to go to England's aid against Hitler—we became the greatest power in the Pacific. Now America's white hordes are on the mainland of Asia sustaining a much-deserved defeat.

MONIQUE VAN VOOREN, 1976: In your far-fetched imagination do you think that Nixon has a chance to ever again enter politics in any way, shape, or form in America?

VIDAL: No, but I think he thinks he has. The only solution to the Nixon problem is to go there to San Clemente in the daytime, find the box of earth where he lies, and drive a stake through his heart. Otherwise we're all going to have to go around with garlic and silver crucifixes just in case we come across him. The smell would be terrible.

VAN VOOREN: Do you think the Watergate scandal has hurt the Republicans for good, temporarily, or not at all?

VIDAL: No, not at all. Heaven's sakes, there's only one party which I call the Property Party. It's got two wings. One is called the "Republican" and one is called "Democratic." It is the same party so it makes no difference whether a Democrat's elected or a Republican's elected. The ownership remains the same. Those who financed Humphrey in '68 financed Nixon. All this has come to light during Watergate and since. It may well be they don't want to call the party Republican anymore so they'll call it the "True-Blue American Party" or something like that and we'll still have paid lawyers on the make running for office, doing what the people who give them the money ask them to do.

PLAYBOY, 1969: What might a radical politician accomplish?

VIDAL: The word "radical" comes from the Latin word meaning "root." A radical politician could go to the root of things—something no conventional politician dares do, for fear of what he'll find. But, of course, there *are* no radical politicians close to the top of our system, nor are there apt to be until—a paradox—it's changed. Our politicians—like our people—are about equally divided between conservatives and reactionaries, with very few radicals of any kind.

PLAYBOY: Would the leadership of your Party for Human Survival be radical?

VIDAL: By definition, yes. After all, they would be creating a new social order to save our old race.

PLAYBOY: Since the idea for such a party is yours, do you see yourself as a radical?

VIDAL: In thought, certainly. I'm not so sure in deed. Given the power, would I also have the faith in my own rightness to pull down the house and then the energy, as well as the wisdom, to build another? Tall order. But then, Voltaire, safe among his Swiss lakes, made possible the French Revolution—and Bonaparte—just as Bernard Shaw prepared the way for Harold Wilson. Analogies are pointless, thank God. Each case is different. Each life is different. All that can be said of this time is that radical action is necessary if we are to survive.

JUDY HALFPENNY 1977:   Any chance of John Stuart Mill being rediscovered by a world that badly needs him? He explained quite clearly that you can't—in reason—excuse restrictions and prohibitions by claiming that these are for the good of the victims; and if this was accepted we would all become about twice as free overnight.

VIDAL: I often quote John Stuart Mill on that *sine qua non* of a true civilization minding one's own business. Currently an effort is being made to prove him not Serious in his love of liberty, due to Sexual Immaturity. A shrink (female) has tried to shrink him to familiar size, and failed.

OUI, 1975:   You would've liked to have been President?

VIDAL: Oh, yes! The Presidency is the only thing I ever wanted that I didn't get.

OUI: Why would you want it?

VIDAL: Because there are a thousand things I'd like to do. And the Presidency is the place to do them.

OUI: But you need sincerity, which you hate.

VIDAL: I hate hypocrisy, not sincerity.

OUI: You like the power?

VIDAL: Obviously. To change things.

OUI: But you're not a do-gooder. Or *are* you?

VIDAL: If you don't see that I am, you've missed the point of my career and it's too late for me to advertise. I write essays, lecture, go on television in order to change the society.

OUI: Do you really believe in the possibility of change?

VIDAL: Change occurs all the time. Nothing ever remains the same, with the possible exception, as someone said, of the avant-garde theatre.

MONIQUE VAN VOOREN, 1976:   Do you still have political ambitions?

VIDAL: I'd still like to be the President, of course, and I think the best way to do that would be to raise an army and seize the Capitol. This strikes me as true democracy.

VAN VOOREN: In all truthfulness, would you consider entering politics?

VIDAL: No. The game is shut. It's a game for cheerful, opportunistic lawyers who are hired by great corporations to become senators, governors, and presidents. If you're not part of that club, as I certainly am not, you are not presidential.

PLAYBOY, 1969:   Do you believe it matters much who the President is? You seem at times to take the Spenglerian view that individual men don't really affect history.

VIDAL: A good ruler in a falling time falls, too, while a bad ruler at a time of national ascendancy rises. That is the long view. But, men certainly affect events. In physics, there is no action without reaction. Therefore, *any* action matters. And that is why the only moral life is to act as if whatever one does is of great moment. Though the American empire may be collapsing and none can stop its fall, I would still rather have seen McCarthy as President than Nixon or Humphrey. Yet even in McCarthy's case, one cannot be certain how effective he might've been. I suppose the most we can demand of a conventional President is that he have some understanding of what is going on and a willingness to confide in us. Johnson was a compulsive liar, rather like Roosevelt, but without that master's High Episcopal charm. Worse, Johnson did not, does not and never will understand the nature of the American empire and its consequences to us and to the world.

JACOB EPSTEIN, 1976:   If you were . . . running [as a 1976 Presidential candidate], what would you be saying?

VIDAL: I'd be talking about the state of the economy, things that ought to be done. I think the budget should be cut without throwing a lot of people out of work. Which would mean cutting defense spending. And I'd be having a lot of fun with all the candidates running against Washington. I'd be working the negative side of that street. I'd show what idiots they were to be saying this. . . .

STANTON, 1978:   Would you be willing to become active in leading a new political party, one you might base on the issues of survival—the Survival Party?

VIDAL: I could see myself triggering a revolution; I don't see any hope for a political party under the present system. The owners have it all locked up.

STANTON, 1978:   Obviously, America's most recent Presidents have failed America. Why? Is it mainly their fault? Or Congress? Or the lack of vision in the people as a whole? Or a lack of moral character in our leaders?

VIDAL: Individuals don't much matter in politics. The power centers dictate policies. *They* can be changed by, let us say, imposing 99 per cent death duties. No more David Rockefellers, no Nelsons.

STANTON, 1978:   I know you have been asked this question numerous times, but as of today, a hot one in June of 1978, do you desire to be President? What can you offer that has not been done before? How far are you daring to go to see that your ideas are made into acts?

VIDAL: I'm afraid that if I became President by any known route I would be no different from anyone else who had made the trip, and so of no use. I have some advice that might help the country and save Carter (as if that mattered) but he would not be able to get the point. . . . Announce that one is President for a single term. Energy, let us say, will be the four-year task: its conservation, development, etc. Meanwhile, don't bother the President. He's not running again. He doesn't want to be bothered by this pork barrel or that. Then try to create alternatives to fossil fuels. If we could land the Rotary Club on the moon, we are certainly capable of making solar energy cheaply. Any president who followed this sort of scenario might be killed; but that's not as important as actually having done something that the Owners did not want done but once done even they would be happy. In principle, the system is unworkable and probably not even worth tinkering with.

STANTON, 1978:   Lately, you have been calling yourself a socialist. Can you define what you mean by that?

VIDAL: I seem to have evolved into a socialist on the ground that the best countries to live in are those of the northern European tie. This is not opinion but fact; unfortunately, Americans are trained from birth to think Sweden equals socialism equals suicide. The Owners know what they're doing.

FAG RAG, 1974:   ... When it comes to personality and style and reason and argument against the 4.4 per cent [Owners of America] and their money, you're going to lose.

VIDAL: Well, I don't know. I have seen attitudes change a good deal since I began. This magazine of yours would not have existed twenty-five years ago. I think the 4.4 per cent changes in its own inscrutable way, but I do not think it will be done by intelligent advocacy. I have said, if it is going to change, it is going to collapse. The system will collapse. It does not work now. The government does not work. And the economic system is not working. Something will crash. Who picks up the pieces? I would want a social democracy as my replacement. I just want to get the goddamn population down by about two-thirds. Then there's plenty of room for everybody and plenty of wealth for everybody.

FAG RAG: You have been a big advocate for a long time of population control. You've been years ahead of Planned Parenthood, even, much less Norman Mailer ...

VIDAL: He does not believe in contraception or masturbation. An incredible man.

FAG RAG: I think ecology, women's liberation and gay liberation have little future except to the extent that they can all control population.

VIDAL: The 4.4 per cent will agree with you, by the way. They are also the ones who passed the abortion laws.

FAG RAG: On the other hand there's Margaret Mead's position that you can't talk population control to the Third World.

VIDAL: I don't think you bother. They're going to die. They will die. There is nothing to be done about it.

FAG RAG: China's not dying.

VIDAL: No. But Latin America, most of Asia, Africa.

※

JACOB EPSTEIN, 1976:   You went to Phillips Exeter Academy in New Hampshire. Do you remember being there during an election year? Exeter was always one of the candidates' prime stops. The candidates would just stream on stage, mud on their boots, aides in neckties standing in the corners, secret service men all around.

VIDAL: Yes, I remember them coming through. The candidates were nowhere near as good as the Golden Branch (the Phillips Exeter Academy's Debating Society). Our debaters were much better than they were, I thought rather condescendingly.

OUI, 1975:   You've written that believing in *a leader* and taking him seriously is to "enjoy the security of childhood come a second time." Is this peculiar to America? After all, the British have their kings and queens.

VIDAL: They don't take them seriously. We believe in *a man* because we're incapable of facing facts. Everything is euphemized. The country would fall apart if the people knew exactly who got their tax money and why. So, unable to go in for real politics, we address ourselves to personalities. Has the candidate got a nice smile? Is he a good person? Does he like his wife? Is he modest and humble in our presence? All great men are simple, you know. How many times have you read that Nelson Rockefeller had only one Dubonnet on the rocks before a meal? We know very little about his connection with the Chase Manhattan Bank, or what he thinks about the banking system or how much [money] he would like to see given to the Pentagon. Those questions are in bad taste. But we know an awful lot about Happy and the Dubonnet and modern art and the poor boy who got killed and the first wife who got dumped. We know a lot about nothing. It's even worse at election time, when they show spot ads on television—with some cretin disguised to look like Mount Rushmore come to life. All this personality mongering has created a great sense of unreality—to say the least. We are just not a political nation at all. Now, you don't find that in France or England. Those are real countries with real problems and real politics. The trade unions say, "This is what we want." And the people who own the factories say, "You're not going to get it, because we own this and we're not going to let you have it." That's what the fight's about. Who is going to get the money. And is the society to be leveled or not. As you know, I'm a leveler.

PLAYBOY, 1969:   Despite your cynicism—

VIDAL: Realism is always called cynicism. I am a pessimist—who tries to act like an optimist.

PLAYBOY: All right—despite your pessimism about the future of America and the world, and your disenchantment with the democratic process, you campaigned actively last year on behalf of Senator McCarthy's nomination and were subsequently active in the movement to launch a fourth party, the New Party. If everything is so bleak and hopeless . . . why do you bother?

VIDAL: It's better to be futile than passive. I supported McCarthy because he mobilized the youth of the country and acted as if the national institutions might still be made to work. But he failed; *they* failed. The next move, to my mind, was the New Party, which came into being at Chicago. It is a place for the activist young, an alternative to the system that has made Richard Nixon emperor of the West.

FAG RAG, 1974:   What was your motivation behind the People's Party with Spock?

VIDAL: I didn't have any. I was just sort of riding along with it. We started the New Party in '68. That was simply to try and make a representative party. It wasn't worth doing. It was nothing but young group-therapists who didn't believe in "elitism" or "structure." It was pointless.

JACOB EPSTEIN, 1976:   While we're sitting here, it's the eve [February 24th] of the New Hampshire primary. And everybody seems to think the two tough boys who will emerge from that will be Jimmy Carter and Ronald Reagan, two former State Governors whose strongest assets seem to be that they've never worked in Washington, D.C. It seems that what they're capitalizing on is running against Washington.

VIDAL: That's ludicrous to say the least, considering that's where they want to go. That's this year's rhetoric. It changes. First, it was law and order. Then in '68 it was 'end the war,' and 'peace with honor.'

Every time I'm appalled all over again and then I forget about it until the next time. . . . Nobody [ever] talks about anything that you want to listen to. Imagine Reagan running against the government! It's the government that supports him. They support Northrop and Boeing and all the rich people who give him the money. "We have socialism for the rich," [I once wrote,] "and free enterprise for the poor." . . .

EPSTEIN: I cannot understand it when, on the stat sheet at least, this 1976 election should be such an important election: it's the Bicentennial year. For the first time in twenty years Vietnam is no longer an issue. It's the first time people have had the chance to pick a man in the hope that he can reverse the economic disaster that began in earnest four years ago, to pick a man in the hope that he can put things back together again. It's incredible to me that no one's saying anything about all this. The candidates are just flapping their arms.

VIDAL: . . . Politicians are not necessarily wicked and stupid (although sometimes they're both). They know [that] they get boxed in when they get specific. Reagan was pressed to come up with something to support his rhetoric, which is, we're going to cut taxes, we're going to give power to tax back to the states, we're going to get rid of a lot of people on the federal payroll (whom you'll have to pay for later on the welfare payroll). So somebody asked him for specifics. Well, he came up with his ninety billion dollar scheme, and he has to

live with it. He might very well be right. I think you could cut
ninety billion dollars from the federal budget—I'd do it from
the Pentagon—you could do that. And you might be able to
let all those people go and then find other jobs for them. But
you'd have to work out a plan. And the second you do that
you're absolutely [vulnerable to attack]. Because, let's say,
you have a marvelous plan. Well, . . . by the time your enemies get through with it, it'll look like you want to give a
thousand dollars to every member of the Rockefeller family,
which is the way poor McGovern ended up. So just to keep
the flack away, [politicians] never become specific. I mean has
anyone said anything about the unemployment question,
which I should think would be the decisive issue. There'll be
about nine million angry adults, or whatever it is, voting
against the Party in power. Nobody's paying the slightest attention to the unemployed. I suppose Fred Harris is, but then
they don't record his speeches. You don't hear anything about
them. The so-called front runners keep to a very small set of
clichés. Furio Columbo, an Italian journalist, covers America
occasionally. He interviewed all the candidates and he said to
me, "I couldn't tell which one I was with unless I looked at
my notebook. I remember Fred Harris, because he's the fat
one. I remember Udall because he's the tall one with one eye."
He went down . . . the . . . list for me. [Then] he said, "Here
are the things they said . . . " and they were all saying the
same kind of generalities. Since the Federalist Papers our
country has never been a great one for wise political debate. . . .

EPSTEIN: Reagan's angle that you were just talking
about, about chopping up the centralized government in
Washington, and giving authority and power back to the
states, isn't it the same debate Americans have been engaged
in since Thomas Jefferson versus Alexander Hamilton? And
wasn't that question more or less settled, or buried, by the
Civil War?

VIDAL: Well, since the Civil War, we've decided for
better or worse to centralize our government, it's true, so as to

become a great military power. That's actually the residue of the Civil War, I think. I do believe societies are like the old pendulum cliché, like a kind of bellows: it goes in, [then] it goes out. Once you compress it [too] much, it's sort of like the theory of the universe, the big bang. It all falls in, then it explodes and goes out again. Remember that these cycles come and go. Until lately there's been a push to centralize for a number of reasons, some of which are too many people, too little food, too little energy to go around without some federal agency making the distribution. You can't get away from that. That's what the old People's Party was all about. But now . . . particularly the environmentalists, whom I'm all in favor of, are simultaneously talking about decentralizing, turning everything over to the communities, the smaller the better. But when you turn the power over to the communities, you're never going to clean up the water and the air. If you . . . build a factory [in a small town], the factory hires everyone in the town including the mayor. [Then] the factory poisons the river. Finally the people who live in town, the wives of the men who work in the factory, say "Look here, we're all getting cancer of the bladder from the water." The owner of the factory will slyly say, working in concert with the [mayor], "Well, I guess there's nothing we can do but shut down. That's the end of [all your jobs]." The factory won't shut down and that town isn't going to change [and the communities downriver will be poisoned, too, because, in the eyes of the de-centralizers, each community can do as it pleases.] . . . Nothing Carter says . . . makes any sense. [He's] running against the government, therefore: "You're not going to have a government, therefore I'm going to be the government . . ." "And what are you going to do with the government?" "I'm going to give it back to the states . . ." "And why and how are you going to give it back to the states?" "I can't tell you that." It goes round and round.

NEWSWEEK, 1974: What do you think about the new era of total media security?

VIDAL: It's very sick, very sick. The problem with our journalism, in fact our whole life, is that we never talk about anything very important because if we did everything would come unstuck. We don't say that 4 per cent of the people own the country, that the owners of the country are ruthless and predatory. The people are getting sullen; instinctively, they know they are being ripped off but they don't know how. And since nobody will talk about the issues, the press has to talk about something; so they focus on the personality of Nelson Rockefeller without really studying the character of the man. Look at Rockefeller's career up in Albany and you have an idea of the kind of egomaniac, megalomaniac [man he is. A] sinister arrogant man who adores the Pentagon, adores war, adores a sort of regulated society with himself as chief regulator. Now that's the thing to write about instead of the one Dubonnet on the rocks he's always drinking.

MONIQUE VAN VOOREN, 1976: What is your opinion of American newspapers?

VIDAL: They're all pretty bad. *The Washington Post* disturbs me the least because it knows what it's doing and it's well edited. Of the rich papers *The New York Times* is the worst in that hardly anybody can write English over there. Most of it reads like sight-translations from the German. I wish they would let Canby write the whole paper. Politically, of course, it's to the Right but then the whole country is to the Right. The *Times* represents the country's [eastern] ownership as best it can and is rather horrified of the Southern Rim politicians like Nixon.

PLAYBOY, 1969: What about Eisenhower? He certainly indicated in his farewell speech that he understood the military-industrial complex, which many people now think dominates our foreign policy.

VIDAL: Eisenhower understood the military-industrial complex better than any other man for the simple reason that he was its chairman of the board for eight years and a loyal branch manager before that. What is puzzling is that he decided to bring up the subject just as he was retiring. Bad conscience? Who will ever know? All in all, a fascinating man, and a master politician. I've heard a good deal about him over the years: My late father was at West Point a few years after Eisenhower and they shared many friends. In fact, Eisenhower's doctor, General Snyder, delivered me some forty-three years ago in the cadet hospital at West Point, when a star shone over the Hudson Palisades, and shepherds quaked.

Eisenhower's career demonstrated how it is possible to fool all the people all the time. He was a highly intelligent, cold-blooded careerist who was determined—much like a Stendhal hero—to rise to the top, and did. "I may be stupid," he once said at a press conference, "but at least I'm sincere!" Actually, he was neither, but it suited his purpose to play the part of the bumbling man of goodwill who was "not an expert in these matters" but somehow would do his best. The people loved the performance and, of course, The Smile. Intimates report that until the great promotion, he was a gloomy, scowling officer who was miraculously transformed when he arrived in England where, said an admiring general, "he learned to smile."

The proof of his political genius is that he left the White House almost as popular as when he entered it. His secret? He never committed himself to any cause or to any person. All that mattered was the single-minded conserving of his own popularity. I once asked General Snyder if he thought Eisenhower would campaign actively for Nixon in 1960. He shook his head—and discussed at some length the care with which Eisenhower separated himself from others. Loyalty to others was never his weakness.

Nor is this kind of selfishness a bad quality in a politician. That other General, De Gaulle, has flourished in a similar way. But then, army staffs are the same everywhere, and those who rise to the top, particularly in peacetime, are usually master politicians of Byzantine cunning. It is true that a lifetime spent in the military hierarchy makes one totally un-fit to respond to the needs of a civilian population, but that is another problem. Even so, had Eisenhower been less lazy and self-loving, he might have done some good. But, unfortunate-ly for us, he regarded the Presidency as a kind of brevet-rank, a sign of the nation's gratitude, involving no fixed duties to disturb his golf game.

PLAYBOY: Yet, in foreign affairs, Eisenhower managed to keep the peace more effectively than his two Democratic predecessors.

VIDAL: Political generals hate real wars. That is an axiom. Or, as the laundry-minded General Powers says in *Visit to a Small Planet*, "If there is one thing that destroys an army's morale and discipline, it is a major war. Everything goes to hell. Lose more damned sheets and pillowcases." Although John Foster Dulles pursued what seemed to be a militant for-eign policy, full of massive retaliations, agonizing reappraisals and calls for captive nations to throw off the Red yoke, in ac-tual fact, Dulles was just another "good American": that's to say, a spontaneous hypocrite who was able to say one thing, mean another and do a third, yet genuinely be indignant if he was thought inconsistent or insincere. While Dulles spouted Scripture to the heathens, Eisenhower resolved to do noth-ing—and I must say, those years look positively golden in ret-rospect. A State Department friend of mine once gave a briefing to Johnson. The subject was a Latin-American coun-try where it looked as if one of our military juntas was about to be replaced by a liberal non-Communist regime. Johnson was distraught. "What, *what,*" he cried, "can we *do?*" To which one of his advisors—whose name must be suppressed, though his wisdom ought to be carved over the White House door—replied, "Mr. President, why not do nothing?" That was the Eisenhower genius. When come such another? Or has one come already?

PLAYBOY: You feel it better for our Presidents to do nothing. . . .

VIDAL: Let us say that, ideally, it is probably better for conventional politicians to do as little as possible, since their actions tend to make worse whatever it is they're dealing with. Even Eisenhower managed to begin the Vietnam war by not following his normal instinct of staying out of mischief. In his memoirs, he tells us why we didn't honor the Geneva accords and hold elections in Vietnam: because some eighty per cent of the country would have voted for Ho Chi Minh. This is very candid. The sort of thing one might have found in Stalin's memoirs, had he not made ghosts even of ghosts. But at least Eisenhower did not commit the troops. That was for Kennedy to do, acting on the best military advice. Eisenhower at least knew that our generals are not warriors but bureaucrats, dreaming of expanded T.O.s, promotions, graft—all things that *small* wars make possible. . . .

RICHARD GRENIER, 1975:   Tell me about the Kennedys.

VIDAL: Oh, dear, are people still interested in them? . . . Yes, Jackie and Lee are the two most successful adventuresses of our time. . . . Jackie knows who she is. She wanted a lot of money. She got it. Jack Kennedy, Aristotle Onassis . . . she hasn't changed. She certainly profited more from our relationship than I did. The first time I ever heard of her, they told me this girl had come backstage at the ballet saying she was my sister, asking for interviews. At that point I'd never . . . met her. She got all kinds of interviews with people by claiming to be my sister. . . . Nina [Vidal's sister] has had the heaviest burden to bear, not only being associated with me and that never-ending Kennedy soap opera but cast in a perverse revision of the Cinderella story: The two stepsisters move in and take over Cinderella's house, then one marries Prince Charming and the other marries a second Prince Charming, leaving Cinderella to settle down to a quiet life with a good citizen.

. . . I liked Jack [Kennedy] personally to the end. The search for attractive women always came first with him. He was a wonderful gossip, great fun. But . . . to say [that] he was a great President . . . !

Sometimes, I think my disenchantment [with the holy family] started as far back as Halloween 1960, when I was campaigning for Congress. . . . Bobby came up to hear my speech and said to me afterward: . . . "Why is it that you never mention the [Kennedy/Johnson] ticket?" [I told him that] the reason I didn't "mention the ticket" was that I was running in a strong Republican district and it would have hurt my chances. [As it turned out,] I not only ran ahead of Jack [meaning he polled more votes for congressman in the district than Kennedy polled for President] but doubled the usual Democratic vote. I can still see the scene now: night time, the kids dressed up in their Halloween costumes, and beside me that snarling little terrier: *"Why is it that you never mention the ticket?"* . . . You were always expected to do things *for* the Kennedys; they never did anything for you. [One] day Jack telephoned me: . . . "I hear Rovere is writing about my health. I do not have Addison's disease." He was lying. Of course he had it. That's why they were giving him cortisone. [Anyway, I did my best to convince Rovere that Jack was in splendid shape.]

PLAYBOY, 1969: Despite your long-standing animosity toward the late Senator Kennedy, you were ready to support him for the Presidency before McCarthy announced his nomination. Supporters of Kennedy still argue that, despite the tardiness of his entry into the race after McCarthy's New Hampshire primary victory, Kennedy was the only peace candidate with a real chance of victory, and that McCarthy's failure to withdraw in his favor—allegedly prompted by personal pique—merely played into the hands of Hubert Humphrey and made his nomination inevitable. If Kennedy had lived, do you believe that McCarthy's role would have been that of a spoiler?

VIDAL: I believe just the opposite. I think Kennedy was the spoiler and that *he* should have withdrawn in favor of McCarthy. After all, it was McCarthy who went into New Hampshire and destroyed L.B.J., something Bobby did not have the courage to do. For all of Bobby's renowned toughness and abrasiveness, he was politically conventional and timid. He wanted to be President in the "normal" way. He wanted "to put it together." Well, it isn't together anymore. It was his bad luck to be caught in a revolution he didn't understand, though he did like its rhetoric. Yet the conservative majority of the country hated him and thought him a revolutionary. I wonder what will happen when the *real* thing comes along. The two Kennedys were charming, conservative politicians, nicely suited for the traditional game but hardly revolutionaries or innovators.

PLAYBOY: Would you have preferred Kennedy to Johnson?

VIDAL: Certainly. Although Bobby had been very much involved in getting us into Vietnam—he once said we had "every moral right" to be there—toward the end, he saw the light, or the votes, and became a peace candidate. Also, though I don't believe in character changes, I do have a theory that if you keep giving a conservative politician liberal speeches to read, he will eventually become a liberal, and vice versa. Friends of mine who were close to Kennedy tell me that in the last months of his life, he really *seemed* to believe his own rhetoric, had come to identify with the poor and the dispossessed. If so, good. Strangely enough, I always found him a touching figure under the bad manners. He was obsessed by his relative inferiority to his older brothers. As a result, he had to be twice as tough as everyone else, have twice as many children. What a tense life if must have been—and, finally, sad.

PLAYBOY: How did you feel when you learned of his assassination?

VIDAL: Depressed. In a strange way, you come to like your enemies rather better than your friends. I will say I wasn't surprised. It seemed inevitable. Not long ago, something like thirty per cent of those living in one Manhattan neighborhood were found to be in need of psychiatric help. At the same time, there are 200,000,000 guns in private hands in the United States; that's one for every citizen. Were it not for fear of J. Edgar Hoover, we would all be dead.

PLAYBOY: In this kind of society—with that many guns—do you think that public men can effectively be protected from assassination?

VIDAL: No. Anybody can murder a President. Once, sitting next to Jack Kennedy at a horse show, I remarked how easy it would be for someone to shoot him. "Only," I said, "they'd probably miss and hit me." "No great loss," he observed cheerfully and then, beaming at the crowd and trying to appear interested in the horses for Jackie's sake, he told me the plot of an Edgar Wallace thriller called *Twenty-Four Hours,* in which a British Prime Minister is informed that at midnight he will be assassinated. Scotland Yard takes every precaution: 10 Downing Street is ringed by guards; midnight comes and goes. Then, the telephone rings. Relieved, the Prime Minister picks up the receiver—and is electrocuted. The President chuckled. He often spoke of the risk of assassination, but I doubt if he thought it would ever happen to him. His virtue—and weakness—was his rationality. He had no sense of the irrational in human affairs.

PLAYBOY: Do you?

VIDAL: I think so. But then, the artist is always more concerned with the moon's dark side than the man of action is. However, I am not prone to mysticism or Yeatsian magic. Only once have I ever had a—what's the word?—presentiment. In 1961 I dreamed, in full color, that I was in the White House with Jackie. Dress soaked with blood, she was sobbing, "What will become of me now?" Yet I don't "believe in" dreams, and I certainly would not believe this dream if someone else told it to me.

PLAYBOY: Do you believe that the assassinations of John and Robert Kennedy were the work of lone lunatics—or of a well-organized conspiracy?

VIDAL: I tend to the lone-lunatic theory.* Oswald. Sirhan. They are so typical, as anyone who ever served in the Army knows. We are a violent country with a high rate of mental illness, much of it the result of overcrowding in the cities, where—like rats under similar conditions in a laboratory experiment—we go insane. To allow any nut to buy a gun is a folly no other country in the world permits. During last year's French revolution, involving millions of people, there were fewer casualties in two weeks than there were in the first hour of Newark's ghetto riot.

PLAYBOY: To return to the Kennedy assassinations, don't you feel there may be some evidence to support the conspiracy theory, particularly in the Oswald case?

VIDAL: Like everyone else, I believe the last book I read: "Zapruder Frame 313, J.F.K. pitches backward, not forward." It does seem as if Oswald might have had help; and if he did, then there was, indeed, a conspiracy. I realize that a generation brought up on horror comics and *Gunsmoke* is convinced that the MacBirds did in our Prince, just so they could make the White House their aviary; but I think it not very likely. The villains, if they exist, are probably Texas oilmen, fearing a Kennedy repeal of the oil-depletion allowance: in other words, a conspiracy as unserious politically as the John Wilkes Booth caper. Nevertheless, just as a phenomenon, it is curious that a nation that has never experienced a *coup d'état* should be so obsessed by conspiracy—but then, a fear of "them" is a symptom of paranoia. Look at Joe McCarthy's great success. Look at Mr. Garrison in New Orleans. Incidentally, I used to know Clay Shaw; and if there is anyone less likely to have been involved in a political murder, it is that charming apolitical man. As I predicted, Mr. Garrison's case against Shaw was nonsense.

PLAYBOY: Whoever assassinated John Kennedy, and for whatever reasons, do you believe that if Kennedy had

---

* I don't anymore. I saw a pattern to these murders when Governor George Wallace was shot. [G.V., 1979]

lived, he could have reversed, or at least arrested, the social decay you decry?

VIDAL: No. But then, no one could—or can. These things are cyclic. By and large, Kennedy drifted. When he did act, the results were disastrous. Consider the Bay of Pigs, which took for granted that the United States has the right to intervene militarily in the affairs of other nations; and Vietnam, in which he—not Eisenhower—committed us to active military support of a corrupt regime. There are those who believe that had he lived, he would have got us out of Asia. But I doubt it. The week before his assassination, he told an associate, "I have to go all the way with this one"—and left it at that. Domestically, he was simply carrying forward the program of the New Deal. It was left to Johnson to complete the New Deal. He rounded out not only Kennedy's interrupted first term but Roosevelt's fourth.

PLAYBOY: In the foreign-policy area, many political historians cite Kennedy's handling of the Cuban missile crisis as an undeniable and major accomplishment—perhaps the greatest of his career. They point out that it set the stage for a subsequent thaw in U.S.-Soviet relations and thus substantially reduced the danger of nuclear war. Do you agree?

VIDAL: In 1963, when asked whether or not Soviet missiles in Cuba really jeopardized the security of the United States, Kennedy said, "Not really. But it would have changed the balance of political power. Or it would have *appeared* to, and appearances contribute to reality." Kennedy's handling of the crisis was a public-relations masterpiece, which changed nothing at all except his own image; he had made himself seem forceful. Yet when the matter ended, the Soviets were still in Cuba, ninety miles away, and we were neither stronger nor weaker, despite all the theatre.

PLAYBOY: Is your hostility to the Kennedy family prompted exclusively by political considerations, or is there an element of personal animus in your opposition?

VIDAL: Personally, I didn't like Bobby but I did like Jack. The others don't interest me. As for my opposition—is it likely that, with my views of what needs doing in this country, I would ever be much pleased with the works of such conservative and conventional politicians?

PLAYBOY: What was it you liked personally about President Kennedy?

VIDAL: He had a fine dry kind of humor, not very American, coupled with a sort of preppish toughness that was engaging. I remember once giving to a particularly bright magazine writer a very guarded report about my childhood, which was much the same as Jackie's. We were both brought up in Hugh Auchincloss's—our stepfather's—house in Virginia. I lived there from ten to sixteen. Then Jackie's mother married Mr. Auchincloss and Jackie moved into my room, inheriting several shirts of mine, which she used to wear riding. I don't remember her in those days . . . but our lives overlapped: We have a half brother and a half sister in common. I was unaware of her, however, until the forties, when I began to get reports from friends visiting Washington that she had introduced herself to them as my sister; I was, pre-Kennedy, the family notable. In 1949, we finally met and I allowed her claim to be my sister to stand. Anyway, I certainly know what her childhood was like, since it was pretty much the one I had endured. So I told the interviewer something about life in that world, described how sequestered it was, how remote from any reality: Great money is the most opaque of screens.

During the Depression, which was unknown to us, the Roosevelts seemed Lucifer's own family loose among us; the American gentry liked to call them the Rosenfelds, on the fragile ground that they were really Dutch Jews and, therefore, Communist, since all Jews were Communists except the Rothschilds, who didn't look Jewish. You have no idea what a muddled view of things the American aristocracy had in those days, with their ferocious anti-Semitism, hatred of the lower orders and fierce will to protect their property from any encroachment. Liberal hagiographers will always have a difficult

time recording the *actual* background of our Republic's Grac-
chian princes.

Anyway, not wanting to give the game away, I made a
vague reference in that interview to what I thought was an
unreal "golden season" and let it go at that. One night while
playing backgammon at Hyannis Port, Jack Kennedy said,
"Gore, what's all this golden season shit you've been peddling
about life at Merrywood?" I thought him ungrateful. "You
hardly expect me to tell the truth, do you?" He ignored that
and chose instead to mount, as Jackie listened, a fine tirade
against our family, how each of us was a disaster, ending
with, "Merrywood wasn't golden at all. It was . . . it was . . ."
he searched for a simile, found one and said triumphantly, "It
was the little foxes!"* But, of course, he was a cheerful snob
who took a delight in having married into what he regarded as
the American old guard—another badge for the Kennedys,
those very *big* foxes who have done their share of spoiling in
the vineyard. But the Kennedy story is finished. . . .

PLAYBOY: Edward Kennedy might not agree that the
Kennedy era is over.

VIDAL: When Teddy Kennedy first ran for the Senate, there was a great cackling from even the most devoted of
the Kennedy capons: He was too young, too dumb—in fact,
they were so upset that a number of them openly supported
his opponent in the primary, Speaker McCormack's nephew.
At about that time, I asked a member of the Holy Family why
the President had allowed his brother to run. The member of
the H.F. admitted that it was embarrassing for the President,
even admitted that Teddy was not exactly brilliant, but added, "He'll have wonderful advisors and that's all that matters."

Politics today is big money. X can be stupid or a drunk or a
religious maniac, but if he has the money for a major political
career and enough political flair to make a good public impression, he will automatically attract to himself quite a num-

---

* Someday I will publish my response to what he said. [G.V., 1979]

ber of political adventurers, some talented. With luck, he will become the nucleus of a political team that then creates his speeches, his positions, his deeds, if any—Presidential hopefuls seldom *do* anything—until, finally, X is entirely the team's creation, manipulated rather than manipulating, in much the same way that the queen bee is powerless in relation to the drones and workers.

At the moment, the Teddy Kennedy hive is buzzing happily. There's honey in the comb and perhaps one day the swarm will move down Pennsylvania Avenue to occupy the White House. But, once again, I doubt it. . . . The future is obscure. But one thing is certain: The magic of the Kennedy name will have faded in four years, be gone in eight years. By 1972, E.M.K., as he's now being touted, will no longer be a Kennedy as we have come to think of that splendid band of brothers. Rather, he will be just another politician whom we have seen too much of, no doubt useful in the Senate but nothing more—and so, familiar, stodgy, cautious, trying to evoke memories that have faded, he will have to yield to new stars, to a politically-minded astronaut or to some bright television personality like Trudeau. By 1976, Camelot will be not only forgot but unrestorable, if for no other reason than that Arthur's heir will by then be—cruelest fate of all—unmistakably fat.*

OUI, 1975:   Feeling as you do about the Kennedys, why do you have in your study a photograph of you and Tennessee Williams with President Kennedy?

VIDAL: Feeling *what* about the Kennedys? I . . . said I liked Jack. It is actually possible to like someone you regard as a bad President. What has one to do with the other?

OUI: Had Kennedy ever met Williams before?

VIDAL: No. Both he and Jackie were looking forward to meeting Tennessee, so I took him up to Palm Beach, where

---

*Like the electorate's collective brain! [G. V., 1979]

they were staying—this must've been 1958. Tennessee, of course, didn't know who they were, even though Jack was already running for President. "You a guvnuh or a Senatuh?," Tennessee kept asking.

OUI: What did Kennedy do?

VIDAL: He was very sweet about it. He also knew that if you want to flatter a writer—and God knows, *that's* not difficult—you say how much you like one of his failures. So Jack said how much he had liked *Summer and Smoke*. And Tennessee was duly beguiled. As we drove away, I said, "You know, that's going to be our next President." Tennessee said, "Not a chance. They're much too attractive."

OUI: Are writers particularly envious people? Can you, for instance, forgive the success of others, people such as the Kennedys?

VIDAL: Successful people tend not to envy other successful people. Why should they? Why should I? If I *had* envied anybody, it would have been Jack Kennedy. Not Jack himself—just his fate. I find that the envious direct their attention to those whom the gods favor instead of the gods, to the throw of the dice that gave Jack, say, a rich father intent on making him President. It wasn't Jack's doing. It was chance.

NEWSWEEK, 1974: Should people as rich and powerful as Rockefeller hold public office?

VIDAL: As they say, it's a free country, laughingly. But you have to watch them like hawks. They do buy everything. The Kennedys thought it was *cute* the way they bought West Virginia; all the Kennedys would giggle about how Steve Smith left a case of $20 bills to be handed out to voters, how he left it in the barbershop and didn't remember it until he was halfway to the airport. We've got to get used to the idea, as un-American as it may be, that the man who corrupts, who gives the money, is as guilty as the man who takes the money. A Rockefeller is as guilty as an Agnew. Americans are very, very cringing before authority as represented by the President on the one hand and big money on the other.

PLAYBOY, 1969: How do you feel about the Age of Johnson?

VIDAL: Sad. He did so much in his first eighteen months. He was able to force through the Congress all sorts of constructive legislation, ranging from public health to civil rights. He was something of a wonder, in marked contrast to his predecessor, who treated him with contempt; the Kennedy courtiers, in fact, fled at his approach. He had every reason to dislike them. It's been argued that Johnson's programs were inadequate, but then, what is adequate in times like these? At least he did what he could do, given the kind of Government we have, and that is the most any conventional party politician can be expected to do.

PLAYBOY: In your opinion, did L.B.J.—though by your definition a conventional politician—have any sense of what the times required? Or was he merely shoring up what you consider the old, outmoded social and political institutions?

VIDAL: Like Kennedy, he simply continued the New Deal—which, in his youth, had all the glamor of radicalism, without its substance. Roosevelt saved capitalism by accepting a degree of welfarism. Johnson applied the same formulas, with less dramatic results. When Roosevelt's experiments began to go sour, the Second World War disguised their inadequacy. I've often wondered if Johnson instinctively hoped to repeat the Roosevelt career: domestic reform, followed by the triumphant prosecution of a war. Poor man! He was doomed from the beginning. After Kennedy, he was the wrong age, the wrong class, from the wrong region. I always thought the fact that he wasn't a bogus Whig nobleman was a point in his favor—but his public manner gave offense, and I could never understand why, since his sort of folksy hypocrisy is the national style. But perhaps that *was* why: The people recognized themselves in him and recoiled. He was the snake-oil salesman, just as Nixon is the Midwestern realtor, gravely intent upon selling us that nice acre of development land called Shady Elms that turns out to be a swamp. We're used to these types and prefer something grander as our chief of state, a superior con man, preferably of a patrician origin, who can disguise with noble phrases who and what we are; to euphemize, that is, the Presidential task. God knows they all do it. Take Latin America. In that sad continent, we support a wide range of military dictatorships that our Presidents, invariably, refer to as necessary links in the bright chain of freedom with which we are manacling the world. In our way, we are as predatory as the Russians, and every bit as maniacal in our confusing—and debasing—of language: Free means slave, democratic means oligarchic, liberated means slaughtered. A fine pair of superpowers, suitable for history's wastebasket!

NEWSWEEK, 1974: What do you think of President Ford's character?

VIDAL: I should think pretty bad. How did he get there? Nixie picked him, and never underestimate Nixie's sense of fun. Ford is sort of a Halloween pumpkin that's been left on our doorstep, and who knows what horrors are inside of it? Nixon would not have picked anyone who was any good.

STANTON, 1978: What effect will the Carter Administration have on foreign and domestic life? What is Carter's greatest political strength, if any? What is his greatest weakness? What role should America be playing in world affairs? Do you support Carter's defense of human rights policy? How well has he succeeded in defending it himself?

VIDAL: The owners of the country have not decided what is to take the place of the holy wars against monolithic Communism as a means of uniting the country in order to build armaments and maintain their wealth and power. At the moment they are desperately trying to get us involved in an African war. That will rev up the economy (they think) and the people will be obedient, etc. Carter is their man. He is no outsider. But until they decide on a policy he will look to be (and be) incoherent. I don't think the personality of the President is ever very important. He does not rule the country. He executes the will of Chase Manhattan, and others. Obviously, a pair of maniacs like Johnson and Nixon make the Owners appear a bit stupid for having set them up in the White House, but life goes on and the imperium must keep expanding one way or another. The fact that Russia and China represented huge markets meant that Cold Warrior Nixon was obliged to make trips to the devil. The beautiful irony of this performance was lost on our political commentators who are always looking in the wrong direction. Human Rights? Rhetoric. Appealing to the South as well as to Jews and/or liberals. If Carter were serious, he might support human rights here at home. For instance, he could work to release from prison those Americans who are unjustly held and punished . . . such as the hundred men in Massachusetts prisons who are there for life for having had consenting sex with adolescent boys.

7

Survival

Eve Auchincloss & Nancy Lynch, 1961: What part of the range of experience interests you most?

Vidal: How the society works, even on the most pedestrian level—the politics of it. Shaw once said that the only two subjects that need concern grown men are politics and religion. Politics meaning how people make a society work, how we get on with one another; religion in the sense of what is proper preparation for death. I would say those are pretty much my two concerns.

Auchincloss & Lynch: How do you apply them in your writing?

Vidal: My novels depend on a great deal of bravura invention to establish a mood, in which one can then set an argument going.

Auchincloss & Lynch: Is the argument that interests you what people will do for power?

Vidal: No. The argument is, I hope, more interesting than that. It is survival. A double survival: the survival of ourselves, physically, in the world; and second, the survival of an individual in a society so enormous that he tends to be obliterated. Nearly everything one does is influenced by that theme. I think the main problem of living that we are now faced with is how to maintain an identity in a super state. A vast agoraphobia may be one of the neuroses of the next century—too many people. A feeling of, "My God, I'm getting lost, I'm going to drown in them. Stop, stop, no more!"

AUCHINCLOSS & LYNCH: How have you personally experienced this sense of obliteration in society?

VIDAL: I've been very lucky. I was able in many ways to get outside of organized society at an early age and I never joined it again, which put me in the position of being able to watch it and observe it, and from my place outside it I'm able to enter it from time to time, either politically or as a writer. I have had, I would say, almost the luckiest time of it of any writer I know. Things seemed to work out so that I could do what I felt I had to do, to watch and judge and then try to act. I like action. The operative word, though, is "judge." There are the judges and the judged. It has never occurred to me at any moment of my life that my function was not to judge others and to judge the world I was in. I'm perfectly aware that judgments may be delivered upon *me* daily, and unpleasant ones, but they hardly disturb what I think my . . . vocation.

MONIQUE VAN VOOREN, 1976:   What is it about Italy or Europe that you find enjoyable?

VIDAL: That it's not America.

VAN VOOREN: But since you do make most of your money here in the United States, do you still enjoy the vitality and the tensions of the States?

VIDAL: Yes. After all, the United States is my subject and that's all that really interests me. If I write about Europe it's always as an American in Europe. The United States is my subject, but as Hawthorne once wrote, "the United States are suited for many admirable purposes, but not to live in." So I like the distance that Europe gives me. . . . I'd never had written *Julian* [for example] if it hadn't been for the sequestered life that I led in Rome and the classical library at the American Academy.

AMERICAN FILM, 1977: You're a frank critic of this country. . . .

VIDAL: . . . I come back [from Italy] every six months or so, and sometimes I see things other people don't see because they're living here day after day. For instance, everything in New York is bent. I don't know who does it. But somebody gets up in the morning and goes out and twists every piece of metal until he's bent it. But nobody in New York seems aware that everything is bent. I keep pointing it out. I say, "Who's doing the bending?" They don't know. All the cars coming in from the airport are dented.

AMERICAN FILM: That's because you spend your time in taxicabs.

VIDAL: No, actually, I make it a point to walk in from the airport. That's how I get to know the northern reaches of Manhattan. The cars are too big—that strikes you right off—these huge tanks moving along with the drivers all talking to themselves.

AMERICAN FILM: Is there a country that you think has a healthy society?

VIDAL: I did a play called *An Evening with Richard Nixon,* which was ahead of its time. It was done in 1972, just when all the newspapers were getting ready to come out for him, so you can see my sense of timing was excellent. We had a marvelous actor, George Irving, and he now has a marvelous Nixon number, which he does on television: "I see a nation without poverty, a nation without violence, a nation that is clean, a nation that is prosperous. I see Switzerland." That's your answer—Switzerland. But I wouldn't live there.

OUI, 1975: Do you think we fantasize more [than other people]?

VIDAL: Much more. And there's more bitterness. In the cities, Americans' faces look pretty sullen, discontented.

OUI: And you don't see that in Paris or Rome?

VIDAL: Until the recent depression, no. You never saw that look of disappointment, bewilderment. What have they done to me? I was meant to be this or that. This is the theme of *Myra,* by the way. Buck Loner's Academy of Drama and Modeling was filled with young people who didn't know who they were. Like those people who [are "into"] astrology on the ground that although you may not have a personality, at least you've got an astrological sign, which can take the place of a personality.

OUI: Do you think that man is evil by nature?

VIDAL: No, man is compulsive by nature. And a civilized society is one that holds the various compulsions in a certain kind of balance. I always liked the way the English arranged matters. They made their brightest people prefer honor to money. Service to the society as opposed to ripping it off. In America, the brightest people have always gone into business. I need not describe the sort of people we get in politics. But then, the national motto is: If you can't be good, be careful. It's no accident Nixon was elected President. The people are not stupid. They knew he was a crook, but they thought he was a crook in the same way most of them were. Most important, they thought he wouldn't get caught, and that has been a humiliating experience for those who elected him. They're used-car dealers, too. Fortunately, they will have forgotten he ever existed in a year or two.

EVE AUCHINCLOSS & NANCY LYNCH, 1961:   What kind of relationship can exist between individuals?

VIDAL: Well, it depends. A relationship (a word I particularly hate from the 1940s, which is now much misused) is simply moment to moment. One moment may be sex, another may be agreement or disagreement—or simply nothing.

AUCHINCLOSS & LYNCH: Nothing?

VIDAL: Yes, I think much of the time we're quite un-plugged and not responding to one another at all. Something is usually going on unconsciously, but I think the conscious mind certainly does not dwell on another person at every waking moment.

AUCHINCLOSS & LYNCH: And yet you hear so much talk about loneliness.

VIDAL: It's probably because people aren't much in-terested in anything other than pondering their own fate. Like that wonderful line from [Jules Renard's] journals: "I find that when I do not think about myself I don't think at all." It's fas-cinating to examine your own mind from moment to moment and see, now just what is going on? Personally, I get bored thinking about myself, yet I have great difficulty getting away from it. I'll think, "Well, now I'm really going to try to understand economics." And I begin to go over the theorems of Lord Keynes. A few minutes later I'm right back thinking about myself again: "What am I going to do?" Sometimes I put it in the third person. "What is *he* going to do?"—just to vary it, you know! Its fascinating to brood on your own mind and what it's up to.

AUCHINCLOSS & LYNCH: Do you think as the human race evolves we will become more self-conscious?

VIDAL: Yes, and I think we're going to lose the novel as a result. It already shows signs of going, and as it goes, autobiography takes over. Almost all the interesting prose of our time has had a narrative "I." People want a direct shortcut to experience as it actually happened to a man; they don't want invention.

NEWSWEEK, 1974:   What else depresses you?

VIDAL: The use of language really offends me deeply and terrifies me. The language has absolutely been so euphe-mized, so corrupted, so *burgered* that it just doesn't mean any-thing any more. It isn't just the politicians; it's any American with the "likes," the "ahhs," the "you knows," the inability to say *anything*. I noticed this particularly going around the colleges—that the kids can't talk, they cannot arrange sentences in their heads, maybe because of . . . television, God knows what the reasons are. They can't ask a question. Well, language is what defines intelligence. Language is what civilization is all about.

JACOB EPSTEIN, 1976:   What happened to all the hope and energy and sweat and money that went into the universities in the last fifty years? How did it get so fouled up?

VIDAL: They learned the wrong things, as it turned out. The world did not go in the direction it had gone in before the war. That's nobody's fault. It's just [that] there are times when education becomes irrelevant. Suddenly everybody realizes that the way to run the British Empire is not to teach everybody Latin and Greek for eighteen years, that there must be something else you might learn, like adding and subtracting. [At the moment, if I were young, I'd stay away from what is known as higher education.]

EPSTEIN: That's your advice to young America?

VIDAL: Yeah. . . . Everything is now irrelevant, really. And you just have to work out your own way of survival. It's very interesting in my generation, the ones who really made it, by and large, regardless of whether they're good or bad, from Capote to myself to Hemingway and Faulkner, none of us went to college. Which is quite interesting because we all came from families that would ordinarily have sent us to college. Tennessee only went to [college so that the] drama department [would put] his plays on. . . .

MICHAEL DEAN, 1968:   One got the feeling in *Myra* that you were having a go at the sort of reverence for youth we encounter now.

VIDAL: I don't revere youth and nobody I know does. No, I think youth is nothing but younger versions of ourselves: they are no wiser, no brighter. They are more hopeful at a certain point, but I suspect that's glandular. They think that the great changes will be made in their lifetime, and in old age you know they weren't made. That's why old people are rather somber.

MONIQUE VAN VOOREN, 1976:   What do you think of children?

VIDAL: What children?

VAN VOOREN: Any children . . .

VIDAL: I keep as far from them as possible. I don't like the size of them; the scale is all wrong. The heads tend to be too big for the bodies and the hands and feet are a disaster and they keep falling into things, and the nakedness of their bad character. . . . You see, we adults have learned how to disguise our terrible characters but a child . . . well, it's like a grotesque drawing of *us.* They should be neither seen nor heard. And no one must make another one.

JUDY HALFPENNY, 1977:   We [in Canada] can't match the U.S.A. for real grotesques like Anita Bryant.

VIDAL: I followed Anita Bryant last March in the ABC morning show. I was more sad than angry. I wondered if she was truly evil or truly stupid. I decided, generously, that she was probably a mixture of both. I also warned the Floridians who might be watching that although she and her twice-born brethren were out of the closet as anti-fag, they were also anti-nigger, anti-kike, and anti-spick (I used more decorous phrases).

MICHAEL DEAN, 1974:   Malcolm Muggeridge, you have often said of our century, indeed of the decade just past, that it reminded you of the Gadarene Swine on their headlong rush to the precipice. So, clearly, you think the liberal society, the permissive society, for the last ten years has, in fact, ushered in a degenerate age?

MALCOLM MUGGERIDGE, 1974:   I think it is an age bent on self-destruction. By the way, I don't criticize it as a traditionalist or as a Puritan, but as a Christian—the basis of my criticism is Christian. No, Christianity's not in the least a Puritan religion, but as a Christian I criticize it. And, of course, in a word, what is wrong with it from the Christian point of view is not really how people behave, because they always behave fairly badly, but because it is, in fact, an amoral society. It has no sense of good and evil, and having no such sense it's a society in a kind of moral vacuum.

DEAN: Gore Vidal, what do you think? Clearly, you don't share Malcolm Muggeridge's views, but what exactly is it about these views that you find repugnant?

VIDAL: Well, I've been reading with great fascination the two volumes of his memoirs, and a thrilling experience it has been for me, if not precisely a religious one. But I take great exception to the notion that you can't have ideas of good or evil without a religion, because there is something called ethics—which Mr. Muggeridge repeatedly makes fun of, often quite correctly—or the liberal temperament. But I notice there's a liberal position which he seems to disagree with.

On the subject of the Indians in India, you say that they believe in fecundity as against contraception. Then you quote yourself, years ago in India, writing about family-planners bringing the precious gift of fornication without tears. That, I should have thought, is rather a nice thing. You think there is something fatuous about a liberal dispostion to encourage, let us say, contraception and abortion and reduce population in order to reduce human misery. This strikes me as a good thing, and you reversed it to a bad thing.

MUGGERIDGE: Well, on this question, first of all let me say I think the whole notion of the population explosion is a piece of sharp practice. I don't think there are too many people in the world, nor do I think there's too little food in the world. What is the matter is simply that the distribution of what is available is run on a completely egotistic and selfish basis. The amount of food we can produce, thanks to modern technology, is almost unlimited. The world is nowhere near being overcrowded or populated beyond its resources. What's happened is simply a shuffling out of this responsibility to make available to everybody the plenty that exists. You say there are too many of those people, they must become fewer.

When I was young, which was a long time ago, the British middle classes all used to say that the reason the poor were in such a bad way was that they *would* have too many children. This let them off beautifully, because instead of having to re-arrange things they just said: "Everything will be all right." I think, in all seriousness, that this is the most fraudulent prop-osition. But there's a built-in fallacy, because if you go to the Indians and say: "You must be fewer," and you take them the blessed gift of contraception, what happens is the Indian mid-dle classes use these contraceptives and reduce their numbers: the doctors and engineers and so on. The poor people natural-ly find this particular practice abhorrent, and I entirely agree with them. I have not practiced it at all. So the situation is far worse than it was before. In fact, the Indian Government re-cently dropped the whole plan in despair.

DEAN: That's a very unfashionable view of the popu-lation explosion. Gore Vidal, would you like to answer that?

VIDAL: If all the food in the world was evenly distrib-uted, everybody would have just enough calories but insuffi-cient protein; and the population would double again in about thirty years. So, it isn't a case of better distribution—and I'm charmed by Muggeridge's idea that contraception in India was a class thing, that in India the professional classes use contra-ception and do not make replicas of their precious selves, whereas the ordinary people make altogether too many ba-bies. Numbers is the most terrible thing facing the world to-day. Contraceptions are perfectly normal [not to mention necessary].

But to go back to these eternal truths and verities: you con-tinually refer to Eleanor Roosevelt as being the wickedest of creatures because she's trying to do good! Eleanor Roosevelt did not believe in perfectibility. She had a sense of responsi-bility for others. She did not say: "The kingdom of this world is not for me," and she did not try to make a deal, as it were, with God for her own salvation. Her idea was that we have responsibility towards other people to be social ameliorists, which is not quite the same thing as saying people are "progressive." In other words, if a road is broken up you have somebody to repair it; you don't sit back and say: "That is God's will." That is the difference between what I would regard as a social ameliorist, somebody who believes in good and evil in terms of doing something good for the majority, or those who need help. I would think that those who were making too many babies—I'm sorry, I seem to be hooked on this—need some help.

MUGGERIDGE: Well now, first of all, you said some very nice things about my autobiography, and I will say that your account of Mrs. Roosevelt's funeral ["Eleanor," in the *New York Review of Books,* 18 November 1971; reprinted in *Homage to Daniel Shays,* pp. 410–424] is one of the most delightful things of its kind that I've ever read. I also met her and had a slight acquaintance with her. Have you read Solzhenitsyn's account of her visit to the prison camp? From my point of view, this is absolutely perfect. It's a very humorous account, too. The prisoners were cleaned up and they were given extra food, and in came this lady. The point is, she was totally taken in.

DEAN: So were many others.

MUGGERIDGE: Yes, they were—but this illustrates the essential weakness of the idea of doing good without reference to people *being* good, you see. She didn't see through this ludicrous charade.

VIDAL: I would rather suspect that she did. She saw through the Soviets very, very early. She had a terrific row with Franklin Roosevelt after Yalta on how he could have made the agreement to sell the Baltic States, Latvia, Lithuania and Estonia, down the river. She saw through all these things. Obviously, she could be tricked at times, but that wasn't the point. Solzhenitsyn didn't know what was in her mind—he was just saying what was in *his* mind because he was being put on view.

OUI, 1975:   Do you think the time will come when the American people will know they're being had?

VIDAL: How could they find out? Television and the newspapers are all a part of the con game. Revolution will begin when people find they haven't got the money to buy what they need, and when this happens, they'll get angry, and since a fair percentage own Saturday-night specials, the consumer society will fall apart.

OUI: When and if it happens, will its replacement come from the right or the left—or don't these terms mean anything anymore?

VIDAL: *I* don't know what they mean. I do think there will be an authoritarian future. We have too many people, not enough resources—we must ration, control, preserve the environment. It's inevitable. But everything depends on the spirit of the dictatorship. The wise dictator or oligarchist remains in power by allowing the people perfect liberty in their private lives while controlling their economic lives. American society has always been just the opposite. Here private lives are vigorously controlled by the state—sex, gambling, number of wives or husbands, pot, alcohol [but only in a paper bag] . . . We have always taken it for granted that the state has the right to regulate our private lives but that it is deeply un-American to interfere with our public lives—that is, how we exploit our neighbors, the environment. Well, I would reverse this. I'm for strict control in the public sector and total freedom in the private.

PLAYBOY, 1969:   Do you think Americans, at this point in time, are more susceptible to fascism than other people?

VIDAL: Traditionally, we are less susceptible. But we are not what we were in the 18th century. The 19th century waves of immigration from slave societies like Ireland, Poland, and Sicily have not yet been absorbed, and these new Americans, by and large, do not take easily to the old American values. It is unkind to mention this, but nonetheless true. Look at the success of George Wallace in the Irish and Polish communities of the North. Our new Americans are profoundly illiberal. They hate the poor, the black, the strange. To them, life's purpose is to conform to rigid tribal law. A conception like the Bill of Rights is alien to them. Until they've been here a while longer, they will always be susceptible to Wallace-style demagogues—unless, of course, *they* change *us,* which is always a possibility.

PLAYBOY: If you really believe a fascist takeover is in the works, what do you propose to do about it . . . ?

VIDAL: I am of two minds—my usual fate. . . . Dissent? But I'm losing heart. For one thing, I'm convinced that man is biologically programmed for war; and now that we have the means to end human life on the planet, is there anything in our past record to give one cause for optimism? But assuming I'm wrong and we avoid what editorial writers refer to as "nuclear holocaust," how are we to survive on an overpopulated planet? Even if we fully exploit our food resources—including sea farming—and develop effective and equitable international systems of distribution, it still won't be possible to feed the coming generations. So there will be famine and disorder. Meanwhile, we are destroying our environment. Water, earth, and air are being poisoned. Climate is being altered. Yet we go on breeding, creating an economy that demands more and more consumers to buy its products— an endless, self-destructive cycle. But though most thoughtful people are aware of what we are doing to ourselves, nothing is being done to restore the planet's ecological balance, to limit human population, to create social and political and economic institutions capable of coping with—let alone solving—such relatively manageable problems as poverty and racial injustice. Who will tell Detroit that they must abandon the fossil fuel-burning combustion engine? No one. And so the air goes bad, cancers proliferate, climate changes.

STANTON, 1978: Are intellectuals doing anything to guide and educate the people to help them come to terms with our social and political problems? Is there any intellectual force in America which you would support?

VIDAL: Our intellectuals are generally hopeless. They are paid for by universities, foundations, magazines that are supported by the Owners and they conform to the will of those who pay them. I don't know whether or not there is much likeness between Edmund Wilson and me (we are often compared but I don't think we have much in common aesthetically or politically) but we did have in common one important thing: we stayed out of the university-foundation-publishing world. Freer lancers than most.

STANTON: Do you think that America might become an openly fascist regime in the near future?

VIDAL: Fascist? We'd call it something else. We do have more secret police, etc., than any other society. Yes, I could see an openly authoritarian state in order to . . . *Preserve the Environment.*

MICHAEL DEAN, 1968: Are you the kind of man who believes that we're born with a rope around our neck and that the best we can do is to wear it like a cravat?

VIDAL: Very nicely put. I see we are all under sentence of death and to the extent that one's aware of it, life is much pleasanter.

STANTON, 1978: Are you pessimistic about America's chances to survive in the modern world? As a nation, what is America's greatest weakness?

VIDAL: I don't think that the world as we know it (good and bad) is going to survive the approaching crisis. Familiar forms of energy will vanish; new forms will be invented . . . but not in time. There will be a bad century. After that . . . ?

STANTON, 1977:   In your own mind, is America as she is worth saving? What would you save for yourself, given the chance?

VIDAL: Well, the U.S.A. is probably more worth saving than the U.S.S.R.; but the whole thing is pretty academic. People-plus; energy-minus—equals The End of The World as We Now Know It. *Tant pis.* At my age there is relatively little to save; also, I'm not very personal, as you may have noticed (isn't that the opposite of narcissism? The state of the union does concern me as opposed to me in a state about the union). I expect, if spared, to spend the next year or two recreating (while learning) the 5th century B.C.

OUI, 1975:   Do you see America as a particularly unjust society?

VIDAL: I would say paradigmatic! The United States was built on injustice. The country was invented to protect the property of the few. The Constitution was designed to preserve property. It's highly class-conscious, always has been. From the peculiar institution of slavery to the peculiar penchant for murdering Indians, we have been a predatory and wicked country from the beginning. In this century, we have been imperial, defeating Spain and Mexico, acquiring Cuba, the Philippines—and killing three million Filipinos—conquering or subverting the governments of Cambodia, Laos, Chile, Turkey, Guatemala, the Dominican Republic, Greece and Cyprus.

OUI: And you do not think other societies are unjust?

VIDAL: In my lifetime, no, with the obvious exceptions of Stalin's Russia and Hitler's Germany. But the mysterious thing about the American society is the total hypocrisy of everybody. As soon as you get anywhere near the truth about anything with an American, he becomes a . . . squid:

Black ink begins to fill the atmosphere as he tries to disguise what he's up to, which is usually stealing your watch. Ditto the politicians—in spades.

OUI: Why are Italians so aware of themselves?

VIDAL: I suppose because they've lived in a more traditional society, with less moving about. When you fuck up in America, you just move on. You rip off a forest and make a desert, then move on and rip off another forest. It's our flush-toilet mentality. After all, most of the people who started America were on the lam—either criminals or people who had somehow screwed up in the old country. I suspect that one of the reasons Americans are so long-winded is that, from the beginning, they were always lying about where they came from and what they were up to. Out on the frontier, you could never say, "Who are you?" or "Where are you from?" That was considered very bad form. For conversation, they substituted anecdote: "Hey, did you hear the story about the two Irishmen?"

OUI: But at least they were on the move.

VIDAL: But no longer. The great American notion that we are a mobile people moving upward no longer applies. Most people now stay at the same level at which they were born, and there's less and less [social] mobility and more and more bitterness, because they've been taught to believe that they, too, can be President or be rich or be a movie star.

PLAYBOY, 1969:   Is there such a great difference between the values of the "educated few" and the "kulaks" of this country?

VIDAL: The difference between civilization and the Dark Ages. One Chicago cabdriver told me: "You know what those hippies want? They want to show people *fucking*. They want everybody to do it all over the place." After some probing, I discovered that he'd heard one of the dissenters say in an interview that there was something sick about a society that preferred its children to watch people being murdered on

TV instead of making love. I said I thought this a reasonable point of view. Sex is good. Murder is bad. Wouldn't he prefer his kids to watch love being made to violence and killing? Voice shaking with rage, he said, "I'd rather have them watch Custer's last stand than some degenerates fucking! The cops should kill them all!" It was as if Max Lerner and Dr. Rose Franzblau had never lived.

PLAYBOY: Though it's certainly repugnant, there's little really new about the violence and intolerance you abhor, and the nation has survived periods of even more intense right-wing hysteria in the past; the Joe McCarthy era is a case in point. Is there any cause for more than the usual degree of pessimism about our current prospects?

VIDAL: Yes. The strain of violence that has always run deep in our society has been exacerbated by two race wars: the one at home against the blacks and the one abroad against the yellows. It is not a sign of pessimism to suspect that a series of showdowns is at hand. The tensions have been building up, of course, ever since the Puritans arrived on these shores. Incidentally, it is part of our tribal lore that the Puritans came here to escape persecution. In actual fact, they were driven first out of England, then out of Holland, because of their persecution of others. We had a bad start as a country. But then things improved in the 18th century, and we had a good beginning as a nation, with a rich continent to sustain us. Unfortunately, our puritan intolerance of other races and cultures, combined with a national ethos based entirely upon human greed, has produced an American who is not only "ugly" but, worse, unable to understand why he is so hated in the world. The social fabric is disintegrating. We face the prospect of racial guerrilla warfare in the cities, institutionalized assassinations in our politics, suppression of dissent in our Chicagos and a war in Asia that can at any moment turn nuclear—and terminal. Yet the white majority is blind to all that is happening. Violence is still our greatest pleasure, whether on television or in the barroom.

EVE AUCHINCLOSS & NANCY LYNCH, 1961:   What useful outlets for violence could you suggest?

VIDAL: Well, sex is one. Juvenile delinquency has been the obvious . . . one for kids, and I think it comes out of the paralyzing boredom with the society around them. They are sexually operative long before they are allowed—morally, legally, economically—to do anything about it. And when one is blocked and bored, one erupts. I would suspect that the whole attitude toward marriage and sexual relations is going to have to undergo extensive alterations. Marriage, after all (apart from religious grounds), is an economic state, not a biological one. Once a woman can look after herself economically and raise her own children, the reason for marriage is gone. I know very few people who have any talent for it. But the sad thing about the human race is that when something doesn't work we never think to ask if the institution is at fault; we assume instead there's something wrong with us, with men and women. So we try to alter ourselves at enormous expense—through psychiatry, prayer, popular writing—when the fault isn't in us but a custom no longer useful. Our appetites are what they are, and as long as they are not destructive of others—physically, even perhaps morally—they are not the concern of the state. I should be very much surprised if the institution of marriage as we have known it will exist in a hundred years' time.

AUCHINCLOSS & LYNCH: Probably most men would agree with you. But how about women? They seem to want just one husband for life.

VIDAL: They've been propagandized. Women who've moved into the urban, mechanistic world tend to be very like men in their attitudes toward what they want and how they mean to go about it.

STANTON, 1978:   Can you see any way where America's violent forces might be used in creative rather than destructive ways?

VIDAL: The Owners are hipped on armaments and war. If Boeing were to reconvert to mass transit and a part of the Pentagon budget would go to reviving what was once the best railroad system in the world we would be better off, but . . .

DENNIS ALTMAN, 1977:   I sometimes think the gay movement would be much better off if it said, "Yes, we do harm society and it's a good thing."

VIDAL: Well, it's a society that should be harmed— that is, altered. Certainly, Judeo-Christianity should be smashed to bits. Except for Christianity, there is no religion more deeply depressing and anti-life than the Jewish. But then, Christianity is a Jewish heresy. The hatred of women in the Old Testament is pathological. St. Paul is no improvement. Worse, Christianity is based on murder and torture . . . study the lives of our blessed saints and martyrs . . . that one result of all this emphasis on blood and pain should be S and M is hardly surprising. Which other major religion is based on the Godhead incarnate being whipped, tacked to a cross, stabbed? Only the Marquis de Sade could have made up a sicker religion. It's no wonder that those brought up in such a culture hate life and enjoy inflicting pain. All societies are sick but some are sicker than others. Christian societies are certainly among the sickest. As for the Eastern European paradises . . . well, an Archbishop of Canterbury once called Communism a Christian heresy. We mirror each other.

ALTMAN: Which puts you in conflict with the fastest growing section of the gay movement, the gay churches.

VIDAL: I'm perfectly willing to accept the gay churches as a tactic. It may be a good idea to get in with the Jesus Christers. When you run with the wolves, said St. Lenin (Eastern rite orthodox), you must howl with the wolves.

ALTMAN: I don't think gay Christians are any less earnest about their Christianity than anyone else.

VIDAL: If so, they're in trouble, for their religion does not smile upon their practices. But then there were Nazis who were Jews and in the early days of the movement they would not believe that Hitler really planned to put good National Socialists into concentration camps.

ALTMAN: I suspect the gay churches will be successful in legitimizing homosexual marriages just when heterosexual marriage ceases to exist as a major institution.

VIDAL: My impression is that the only people interested in marriage are Catholic priests and homosexualists. Most enlightened heterosexuals now avoid marriage in much the same way as Count Dracula steers clear of garlic.

ALTMAN: Is that a form of homosexual self-hatred— it's all right to be homosexual provided you live according to the most rigid tenets of heterosexual society?

VIDAL: I think society is essentially a whole with many fractured elements within it. Years ago I noticed in so-called enlightened Amsterdam that the faggot arrangements were exactly like the heterosexual arrangements. Everybody was solemn and solid and married—exactly like mummy and daddy, or brother and sister-in-law. Nothing wrong with that, of course. But it is not the world of Plato's *Symposium* where my imagination has its being.

ALTMAN: You're . . . regarded as very cynical about romantic love, and since the gay movement is, by and large, a great believer in romantic love you've come in for a certain amount of criticism on that.

VIDAL: I should hope so. But my lips are sealed on that subject. Since those who believe in romantic love suffer so much anyway, I would not dream of adding to their sufferings.

MONIQUE VAN VOOREN, 1976:   . . .You do have as friends an awful lot of very important clergy in Italy. How do you explain that?

VIDAL: I believe it's my pastoral duty to convert them to atheism.

VAN VOOREN: Are you successful?

VIDAL: I believe that, one by one, they do drop from the Church.

PLAYBOY, 1969:   Do you think drastic reform is likely to be effected by our present system of government?

VIDAL: No. And I find that hard to admit, because for all of my adult life I've generally accepted what we call the democratic process. But it no longer works. Look at Congress. Last year, 81 per cent of the people wanted strong gun-control legislation. But 70 per cent of the Congress did not, in instructions from the National Rifle Association. Congress, President, courts are not able to keep industry from poisoning Lake Erie, or Detroit from making cars that, aside from the carbon monoxide they create, are murderous weapons. To this degree, at least, the New Left is right: The system cannot be reformed. I part company with them on *how* it's to be replaced. They are vague. I would like to be specific—"programmatic," to use a word they like even less than "liberal."

PLAYBOY: And what is your program?

VIDAL: I would like to replace our present system with an Authority—with a capital A—that would have total control over environment. And environment means not only air, earth and water but the distribution of services and products, and the limitation of births. Where the Authority would have no jurisdiction would be over the private lives of the citizens. Whatever people said, wrote, ate, drank, made love to—as long as it did no harm to others—would be allowed. This, of course, is the direct reverse of our present system. Traditionally, we have always interfered in the private lives of our citizens while allowing any entrepreneur the right to poison a river in order to make money.

PLAYBOY: Isn't what you're proposing—a dictatorship demanding absolute control over the most vital areas of our lives and yet granting absolute social and political freedom—a contradiction in terms? Isn't it inevitable that the power of your Authority would sooner or later circumscribe the private life of every citizen?

VIDAL: Though the Authority would, in its own sphere, be absolute, it would never be the instrument of any one man. There would be no dictator. The thing should be run like a Swiss hotel, with anonymous specialists going about their business under constant review by a council of scientists, poets, butchers, politicians, teachers—the best group one could assemble. No doubt my Venetian ancestry makes me prone to this sort of government, because the Most Serene Republic was run rather like that and no cult of personality ever disturbed those committees that managed the state with great success. It can be done.

PLAYBOY: Would you explain what you mean when you say the Authority would be able to limit births?

VIDAL: I mean just that. Only certain people would be allowed to have children. Nor is this the hardship that it might at first appear. Most people have no talent for bringing up children and they usually admit it—once the damage is done. Unfortunately, our tribal propaganda makes every woman think her life incomplete unless she has made a replica of herself and her loved one. But tribal propaganda can be changed. One can just as easily convince people that to bring an unwanted child into the world is a social crime as grave as murder. Through propaganda, the Japanese made it unfashionable to have big families after the War and so—alone of the Asian countries—kept their population viable.

PLAYBOY: Your ends may be commendable, but let's discuss the means. What would happen to the citizen who didn't wish to live in your brave new world—to the devout Roman Catholic, for example, who refused to accept your population-control measures?

VIDAL: If he didn't want to emigrate, he'd simply have to accept the Authority's restrictions. The right to unlimited breeding is not a constitutional guarantee. If education and propaganda failed, those who violated the birth-control restrictions would have to pay for their act as for any other criminal offense.

PLAYBOY: With imprisonment?

VIDAL: I don't believe in prisons, but there would have to be some sort of punishment. Incontinent breeding endangers the human race. That is a fact with which we now live. If we don't limit our numbers through planned breeding, they will be limited for us in the natural way: famine and war. I think it more civilized to be *un*natural and voluntarily limit population.

PLAYBOY: What would become of the family if only a few people were allowed to have children?

VIDAL: . . . In today's cities, it is not possible to maintain the old American idea of the family—which was, essentially, peasant; a tribal group working together to create food. For better or worse, we are now on our own, and attempts to revive the ancient family ideal—like Daniel Moynihan's proposal for the blacks; apparently he wants to make Irish villagers of them—will fail. As for the children that we do want, I'd like to see them brought up communally, the way they are in certain of the Israeli kibbutzim. I suspect that, eventually, the whole idea of parenthood will vanish, when children are made impersonally by laboratory insemination of ova. To forestall the usual outraged letters declaring that I am against the "normal" sexual act, consider what I'm talking about: the creation of citizens, *not* sexual pleasure, which will continue, as always. Further, I would favor an intelligent program of eugenics that would decide which genetic types should be continued and which allowed to die off. It's within the range of our science to create, very simply, new people physically healthier and intellectually more competent than ourselves.

After all, we do it regularly in agriculture and in the breeding of livestock, so why not with the human race? According to the somber Dr. William Shockley—the Nobel Prize-winning physicist who once contravened liberal doctrine by suggesting that we *should* look for genetic differences among the races— our preservation, through advanced medicine, of physically and mentally weak strains is now making the race *less* fit with each generation.

PLAYBOY: Your critics would charge that the utopia you propose is actually a nightmarish world reminiscent of Nazi Germany and of George Orwell's *1984.* How would you answer them?

VIDAL: Most things human go wrong. The Authority would probably be no exception. But consider the alternatives. Nuclear war to reduce population. World famine. The coming to power of military dictatorships. The crushing of individual freedom. At least the Authority would guarantee more private freedom to its citizens than they now enjoy.

PLAYBOY: Realistically, do you see any chance of such an "enlightened" dictatorship coming to power?

VIDAL: Dictatorship, no; enlightened, yes. Could it happen? Probably not. It takes too long to change tribal thinking. The majority will always prefer a fiery death, howling tribal slogans. A pity—but then, it is not written in the stars that this peculiar race endure forever. Now may be a good time for us to stop. However, since I believe that one must always act as though our affairs were manageable, I should like to see a Party for Human Survival started on an international scale, to try to persuade people to vote willingly for a life-enhancing as well as life-preserving system.

PLAYBOY: Your detractors, on both right and left, would argue that the proposals you've just made reflect a characteristic Vidal trait: intellectual arrogance and a basic elitist contempt for the people and their ability to govern themselves. Do you think they have a point?

VIDAL: I do not admire "the people," as such. No one really does. Their folk wisdom is usually false, their instincts predatory. Even their sense of survival—so highly developed in the individual—goes berserk in the mass. A crowd is a fool. But then, crowds don't govern. In fact, only in America do we pretend to worship the majority, reverently listening to the herd as it Gallups this way and that. A socialist friend of mine in England, a Labor M.P., once said, "You Americans are mad on the subject of democracy. But we aren't, because we know if the people were given their head, they would bring back hanging, the birch and, of course, they'd kick the niggers out of the country. Fortunately, the Labor Party has no traffic with democracy." I want the people to be happy, but more than that, I want them to be *humane*—something they are not, as everyone from Jesus to Karl Marx has had occasion to notice.

PLAYBOY: Do you think that under your Authority, the average citizen would find himself more or less happy?

VIDAL: More. After all, he would be denied only one "pleasure"—the unauthorized bringing into society of a new citizen. Otherwise, he would be freer in his private life than he is now. At present, nearly every form of sexual activity outside marriage is forbidden him, as that legendary cunnilinguist in California discovered when he was sent to Alcatraz for an act of extreme—indeed, positively Christian—unselfishness performed upon his legal mate. Of the countries of the West, the United States is the only one to have laws against fornication as such. Though these laws are spottily enforced, they still exist—a joy for blackmailers, particularly those who are entrusted with the power to enforce them: the police.

One of the reasons for the great rise in crime in recent years is that most police departments are more concerned with cracking down on prostitutes, gamblers and homosexualists than they are with what should be their proper function: the protection of life and property. The Authority would make it very clear that morals are not the business of the state. If a woman can get $100 from a man for giving him an hour's pleasure, more power to them both. She is a free agent under the Authority and so is he. In any case, she is no worse than the childless wife who insists upon alimony once a marriage ends.

That various religious establishments might find certain kinds of behavior sinful is their business, not the state's. Nor will that Baptist minister or Christian brother be allowed to impose his primitive superstitions upon a secular society, unlike the past—and even the present—when whatever the churches thought to be sin was promptly made illegal by state legislatures: whiskey, gambling, sex. The result has been a society of peculiar corruption in which the police, more than any other group, have been literally demoralized. The Authority would guarantee everyone the right to do as he pleases, as long as his activities are not harmful to the general welfare.

PLAYBOY: And who will interpret "the general welfare?"

VIDAL: The Authority. I don't think it will be a particularly difficult task. Take cigarette smoking. Cigarettes kill and cripple many of those who smoke them. That is a fact. Yet cigarette advertisers are allowed to spend millions of dollars a year to convince young people that cigarette smoking is a glamorous, status-enhancing thing to do—and so the young are hooked early and made addicts. I think this sort of advertising is against the general welfare and should be forbidden. After all, the survival of the race is slightly more important than the market listing of the American Tobacco Company. . . . I suspect we are in for a drastic upheaval—a long overdue revision of the nation's ethical standards, and that would be the Authority's work.

PLAYBOY: Could it succeed?

VIDAL: Why not? The worst of dictatorships now have the means to maintain themselves in power as a result of advanced communications. So why not those same means toward good ends? The preserving of the human race, the hammering out of a new code of ethics.

PLAYBOY: Would your Authority legalize pot?

VIDAL: Certainly. In the private sphere, everyone has a perfect right to kill himself in any way he chooses—gin, cigarettes, heroin, a bullet through the head. As I said before, it is not for the state to decide whether or not he is to live or die, what he is to eat, drink, smoke, make love to. Obviously, it would be inconvenient if everyone decided to stay drunk or stoned; but the point is, everyone won't. I remember when the Wolfenden Report first came out in England and proposed that homosexuality between consenting adults be made legal. There was an enormous outcry. The baby supply would be endangered, the fabric of society disrupted, the streets crowded with young men selling their bodies. There was a marvellously insane premise at work here: If homosexuality were legal, heterosexuality would wither away! A state of affairs that not even the most militant pederast has ever dreamed of. Since England finally made legal whatever consenting adults choose to do, not only has the oversupply of babies continued, as usual, but there has been no noticeable decline in heterosexual relationships.

In the debate before the laws were changed, however, one heard the tribal voices loud and clear, calling to us from the Stone Age, when our lives where short and our natural enemies many and, to protect the tribe, it was a duty to breed. Now, 50,000 years later, the tribal mind is still programmed in the same way: Make as many babies as possible and try to discourage any sort of behavior that might curtail the supply. Yet we live with daily evidence that the human race is committing suicide through overpopulation. This sort of doublethink is usual with us. A perfect example was the astronaut who saw fit to read to us from the moon a barbarous religious text, disproved by the very fact it was being read from the moon.

PLAYBOY: Do you foresee a drug culture if everyone is free to turn on in any way he pleases?

VIDAL: We are a drug culture already. Sleeping pills, aspirins, the nightcap that too often becomes an Indian war bonnet. Ideally, reality should be so interesting that we don't need tranquilizers and stimulants. But since there are too many people in the world and not enough for them to do—certainly very little that is interesting—the American majority serve their forty hours a week in order to stun themselves with beer, television, whatever, come the weekend. Fewer people with more interesting things to do is as good an aim as any for a society.

PLAYBOY: Do you speak from experience with drugs?

VIDAL: Yes, and mostly from an unpleasant experience. Marijuana has no effect on me, possibly because I've never smoked cigarettes. But I've tried hashish and mescaline and found the results physically depressing. One attempt to smoke opium made me ill. But I'm fortunate; my life is sufficiently interesting to make me want to keep alert what senses I have. That's why I gave up whiskey two years ago and now drink only wine, a slower and more graceful way of heightening and then pleasantly losing reality. But if I had to choose between the aggressive drunk who smashes up a car and the passive marijuana smoker who bores me to death at a party, I'd take the pothead any day. Incidentally, those who oppose drugs because they breed crime should realize that if all drugs were made legal and sold at cost—as would be done under the Authority—there would be no criminal trafficking in drugs and, hence, no desperate hopheads committing murders in order to get money for the next fix. Unfortunately, this solution is much too intelligent for our people ever to accept. Punishing others is one of the great pleasures of the tribe, not easily relinquished.

STANTON, 1978:   Do you still advocate the creation of an Authority to be in control of our public activities? Do you think the people are now ready for it, given the vast problems we face for even basic physical survival?

VIDAL: I never favored the Authority. I threw it out as a possible notion. The nation-state is dying. Who knows what will take its place? My Authority is, probably, too rational. Besides, the name is ominous. Let's call it "America is Beautiful." In "The State of the Union" [in *Esquire,* May, 1975; reprinted in *Matters of Fact and of Fiction,* pp. 265–285], I came back to the subject: Proposed nationalizing all energy, then forming an authority to administer and allocate energy beyond the reach of our corrupt Congress—but not the courts. I suspect that what I'm doing is trying to humanize the dictatorship that I see on the horizon, as plain as the date 1984.

PLAYBOY, 1969:   You wrote once that "In a sense, I'm not an 'American' writer. My whole attack—my wit and irony—is distasteful to Americans." Would you elaborate?

VIDAL: Wit and irony are distasteful to Americans, who believe that to be serious is to be solemn. This is not only a hangover from our Puritan beginnings but also a stage through which second- and sometimes third-generation Americans go as they try to make their own the language and the customs of a country still somewhat alien to them but to whose flag and prejudices they feel they owe a passionate commitment. In absorbing a new culture, the ironies are the last thing to be noted, and those who indulge in them are the first to be condemned.

PLAYBOY: You have written, "That wide graveyard of stillborn talents which contains so much of the brief ignoble history of American letters is a tribute to the power of democracy to destroy its critics, brave fools and passionate men." How is this done?

VIDAL: De Tocqueville predicted that a society organized like ours would prove to be hostile to the original man. He believed that a terror of public opinion was an essential characteristic of democracy—nor have we entirely fulfilled De Tocqueville's grim prognosis—but no one can say that we are not resourceful in our ways of dealing with dissidents. We turn them into show-business characters, not to be taken seriously. The clumsy exhortations of Paul Goodman, the shrill dialectic of Dwight MacDonald, the visceral rhetoric of Norman Mailer are all rendered small by television, by magazine profiles and—yes!—by interviews. But that is no reason to stop. Something is bound to break eventually—other than one's self or art.

PLAYBOY: You've used the words "tribal" and "civilized" a number of times. What do you mean by them?

VIDAL: Tribal is what we were and to a degree—vestigially—still are. By tribal, I mean relationships anthropologists have noted: among gibbons, among aborigines, among Stone Age tribes still surviving, hidden away in various parts of the earth. The Old Testament is a genuine tribal document; the New Testament, an abortive attempt to civilize the Old. To civilize means, literally, to citify. Put another way: Tribal versus civilized is the village versus the city. To this day, the village is a reactionary and non-creative unit. Only in the city, where men and ideas are thrown together, do we get that interplay of ideas that makes it possible to write *King Lear* or to put a man on the moon. Naturally, the village has its virtues— good manners, a degree of kindness—and the city its demerits, too easily named: but man's great advance in the past 2,000 years has been the work of those in cities; after all, Shakespeare left the village of Stratford to be great in the city of London. Or, to put the matter in a large frame, it was the city of Rome that, for all its horrors, represented man's best, — and the marauding tribes from north and east, who destroyed it, man's worst. The irony, of course, is that culturally, in America, we are descended from the tribesmen, not the city men, and so it is hard for us to make a civilization—but we are beginning to.

PLAYBOY: Could this be an optimistic note about America?

VIDAL: If I dwell on our imperfections, it is to see them changed. As one who lives in Europe as well as America,

I can say with some confidence that only the Americans can save the world from America; only our dissidents can curb the Pentagon, restore the planet's ecological balance. Oh, I'm very American in my ambitions for our second-rate culture. If we survive, we may yet be civilized, and that is something to work for.

Index